JUN     2012

D0025303

# THE
# HISTORY OF
# GREECE

ADVISORY BOARD

# THE HISTORY OF GREECE

Elaine Thomopoulos

The Greenwood Histories of the Modern Nations
*Frank W. Thackeray and John E. Findling, Series Editors*

GREENWOOD

AN IMPRINT OF ABC-CLIO, LLC
Santa Barbara, California • Denver, Colorado • Oxford, England

**Library of Congress Cataloging-in-Publication Data**

Thomopoulos, Elaine.
    The history of Greece / Elaine Thomopoulos.
        p. cm. — (The Greenwood histories of the modern nations)
    Includes bibliographical references and index.
    ISBN 978-0-313-37511-8 (alk. paper) — ISBN 978-0-313-37512-5 (ebook)
1. Greece—History.   I. Title.
    DF214.T46   2011
    949.5—dc23        2011020939

ISBN: 978-0-313-37511-8
EISBN: 978-0-313-37512-5

16   15   14   13   12   11      1   2   3   4   5

This book is also available on the World Wide Web as an eBook.
Visit www.abc-clio.com for details.

Greenwood
An Imprint of ABC-CLIO, LLC

ABC-CLIO, LLC
130 Cremona Drive, P.O. Box 1911
Santa Barbara, California 93116-1911

This book is printed on acid-free paper ∞

Manufactured in the United States of America

BULGARIA

FORMER YUGOSLAV
REPUBLIC OF
MACEDONIA

TURKEY

ALBANIA

Alexandroupolis

Sea of
Marmara

Kavala

Thessaloniki

Mount
Olympus +

Ioannina

Limnos

Larisa

Corfu

Volos

Lesbos

TURKEY

Igoumenitsa

Aegean
Sea

Lefkada

Chalkis

Kefalonia

Chios

Patras

Elefsina

Zakynthos

Samos

Piraeus  ATHENS

Ionian
Sea

Tripoli

Laurion

Sparta

Naxos

Kos

Sea of
Crete

Rhodes

Mediterranean Sea

Irakleion
Crete

0    75    150 km

0         75         150 mi

# Contents

# Series Foreword

The Greenwood Histories of the Modern Nations series is intended to provide students and interested laypeople with up-to-date, concise, and analytical histories of many of the nations of the contemporary world. Not since the 1960s has there been a systematic attempt to publish a series of national histories, and as series advisors, we believe that this series will prove to be a valuable contribution to our understanding of other countries in our increasingly interdependent world. Some 40 years ago, at the end of the 1960s, the Cold War was an accepted reality of global politics. The process of decolonization was still in progress, the idea of a unified Europe with a single currency was unheard of, the United States was mired in a war in Vietnam, and the economic boom in Asia was still years in the future. Richard Nixon was president of the United States, Mao Tse-tung (not yet Mao Zedong) ruled China, Leonid Brezhnev guided the Soviet Union, and Harold Wilson was prime minister of the United Kingdom. Authoritarian dictators still controlled most of Latin America, the Middle East was reeling in the wake of the Six-Day War, and Shah Mohammad Reza Pahlavi was at the height of his power in Iran. Since then, the Cold War has ended, the Soviet Union has vanished, leaving 16 independent republics in its wake, the advent of the computer age has radically transformed global communications, the rising demand for oil makes the Middle East still a dangerous flashpoint, and the rise of new economic powers like the People's Republic of China and India threatens to bring about a new world order. All of these developments have had a dramatic impact on the recent history of every nation of the world. For this series, which was launched in 1998, we first selected nations whose political, economic, and sociocultural affairs marked them as among the most important of our time. For each nation, we found an author who was recognized as a specialist in the history of that nation. These authors worked cooperatively with us and with Greenwood Press to produce volumes that reflected current research on their nations and that are interesting and informative to their readers. In the first decade of the series, more than 40 volumes were published, and as of 2008, some are moving into second editions. The success of the series has encouraged us to broaden our scope to include additional nations, whose histories have had significant effects on their regions, if not on the entire world. In addition, geopolitical changes have elevated other nations into positions of greater importance in world affairs and, so, we have chosen to include them in this series as well. The importance of a series such as this cannot be underestimated. As a superpower whose influence is felt all over the world, the United States can claim a "special" relationship with almost every other nation. Yet many Americans know very little about the histories of nations with which the United States relates. How did they get to be the way they are? What kinds of political systems have evolved there? What kind of influence do they have on their own regions? What are the dominant political, religious, and cultural forces that move their leaders? These and many other questions are answered in the volumes of this series. The authors who contribute to this series write comprehensive histories of their nations, dating back, in some instances, to prehistoric times. Each of them, however, has devoted a significant portion of their book to events of the past 40 years because the modern era has contributed the most to contemporary issues that have an impact on U.S. policy. Authors make every effort to be as up-to-date as possible so that readers can benefit from discussion and analysis of recent events. In addition to the historical narrative, each volume contains an introductory chapter giving an overview of that country's geography, political institutions, economic structure, and cultural attributes. This is meant to give readers a snapshot of the nation as it exists in the contemporary world. Each history also includes supplementary information following the narrative, which may include a timeline that represents a succinct chronology of the nation's historical evolution, biographical sketches of the nation's most important historical figures, and a glossary of important terms or concepts that are usually expressed in a foreign language. Finally, each author prepares a comprehensive bibliography for readers who wish to pursue the subject further. Readers of these volumes will find them fascinating and well written. More importantly, they will come away with a better understanding of the contemporary world and the nations that comprise it. As series advisors, we hope that this series will contribute to a heightened sense of global understanding as we move through the early years of the twenty-first century.

*Frank W. Thackeray and John E. Findling*
*Indiana University Southeast*

# Acknowledgments

I did not write this book alone. Many assisted me along my odyssey. The first on my list is my husband and best friend, Nick Thomopoulos. I could interrupt him at any time while he was in the middle of his own projects to share a story, ask a question, or ask him to scan photos. Never did he say, "Don't bother me." His interest in Greek history, his suggestions, his support, his confidence in me, and his sense of humor made a difference.

Also many thanks to Andronikos Falangas, whose knowledge of Greek history is phenomenal and whose help was invaluable. He encouraged me throughout the process. Historians dating back to Herodotus have their own accounts of what happened. They disagree about personalities, politics, even dates of important events. By his meticulous editing of the manuscript and his referring me to various resources for further study, Falangas helped me sort out the truth.

Others helping me traverse the path of Greek history include Joachim Billis, Constantinos Blathras, Chrys Chrysanthou, Vassilis Chrysikopoulos, Thanasis Economou, Dan Georgakas, Savvas Koktzoglou, Kostas Kourtikakis, George Mavropoulos, Thomas Mantzakides, Nanno Marinatos, George Papadantonakis, Danae Papaioaonou, Mathilde Pyrli, Anastasia Stefanidou, George Tsonis, and Evaggelos Vallianatos. Some of them read the book cover to cover. Others read specific sections. Each helped me gain valuable insights, at times providing me with their firsthand experiences, explaining, "I was there."

I appreciate George Dervis's selection of books, articles, and maps from his own personal library and his and Ann Dervis's help in doing research about Epirus. Stavros Constantinou, Franklin Hess, Alexandros K. Kyrou, and Jim Stoynoff also provided resources. Vivian Kallen gave me books that I will always treasure. They came from the collection of her mother, Theano Papazoglou Margaris, preeminent chronicler of the Greek immigrant experience in America.

I learned from conferences and lectures these past couple of years. They include the Modern Greek Studies Conference in Vancouver, the Pontian Society Academic Conferences, and the conference "Foreigners in Greece: Then and Now" organized by the Modern Greek Studies Department at my alma mater, the University of Illinois at Urbana-Champaign. The excellent lectures presented by Hellenic Link Midwest and the National Hellenic Museum have also been important resources.

The writer's groups I attended helped me write better, but, more important, they gave me the push and encouragement I needed to keep trudging on. They include the Day Writers' Group at the Box Factory in St. Joseph, Michigan, led by Isabel Jackson; Writers' Bloc Group at St. Paul's Episcopal Church in St. Joseph, Michigan led by Marnie Heyn; the Writers' Group at the Lincoln Township Library in Stevensville, Michigan; and Westmont Public Library Writers' Group in Westmont, Illinois, led by Kate Buckson.

Thanks to those who have helped me edit the manuscript. John Rassogianis and Kenneth Wood meticulously red-penned the entire manuscript, pointing out overlooked errors of grammar or spelling. Others offering their assistance included Michael Cortson, Alexander Fatouros, Sue Goens, Marnie Heyn, Isabel Jackson, Bob Jones, Philip J. Magnan, April Satanek, Toni Schalon, Suzanne Sherif, Jackie Taglia, Lois Jean Thomas, and Ann Vandermolen. Their helpful suggestions on making the book more readable are appreciated. Also thanks to Sarantis Alexopoulos who helped me with translating.

Writing is a solitary sport, and thank goodness I had cafés and libraries to hang out in. The cafés included Caribou Coffee in Willowbrook, Illinois, as well as McDonald's in Bridgman, Michigan, and Darien, Illinois. Sophe Fatouros's Greek coffee and spicy soups at 105 East Internet Café and Gallery in New Buffalo, Michigan, gave me stamina to keep on trekking.

The libraries included Elmhurst Public Library in Illinois as well as the New Buffalo, Benton Harbor, and Bridgman libraries in Michigan. A special thanks is due to Denise Malevitis and Kay O'Brien from Bridgman Library, who have ordered countless books for me through MeLCat.

The National Hellenic Museum in Chicago gave me access not only to their library, but has done so much more. Staff member Allison Heller alerted me to the exciting opportunity of writing this book. Athanasios Tzouras helped me by providing transcripts of oral histories collected through the Frank S. Kamberos Oral History Center.

My trips to Greece in 2010 and 2011 yielded great results. I am especially appreciative of Marinos Argyriades of the National Historical Museum in Athens, who introduced me to the museum and acted as my tour guide. The vintage photos, dating to the 19th century, added a valuable dimension to the book. Other staff members who helped me included Niki Markasioti, Natassa Kastriti, and Dimitra Koukiou.

Mathilde Pyrli of the Hellenic Literary and Historical Archive patiently guided me through the amazing photographic collection of the archive—an enjoyable way to spend an afternoon in Athens. The photos regarding World War II and the civil war packed a punch that could not be conveyed by words alone.

Steve Frangos has offered his guidance and expertise for the past 25 years and got me started on my present path of research regarding Greece and Greek Americans. Thanks also to Faye Peponis, who years ago helped me become more adept with the computer and thus gave me the wings to soar on my book-writing adventures. More recently members of the Indian Prairie Computer Club and the Computer Users Group, which meet at the Community House in Hinsdale, Illinois, have helped me with any questions I have about my trusty companion, my laptop computer.

I am also indebted to my children, Marie, Melina, Diana, and Christopher, and grandchildren, Lauren, Daniel, Jillian, Grace, Michael, and Christopher. Time spent with them fills me with joy and recharges my battery.

Not to be forgotten is my editor, Kaitlin Ciarmiello, who gave me valuable support along my journey and guided me with patience and perseverance. Thanks also to Nicole Azze who coordinated the production of the book. I much appreciate Rajalakshmi Madhavan and the team at Apex who helped me fine-tune the book on the final stretch.

Finally, I would like to acknowledge the contribution made by my mother, Emily Cotsirilos. Although she passed away more than a year ago, I continue to feel her love and encouragement. Her smile lives in my heart. I dedicate the book to her.

# Timeline of Historical Events

| | |
|---|---|
| 30,000–3000 BC | Early settlements. |
| c. 3000–1100 | Cycladic civilization. |
| c. 2500–1150 | Minoans on Crete and nearby islands. They use writing system called Linear A. |
| 1700 | Palaces on Crete destroyed. |
| 1600 (+/−50 years) | Eruption of volcano on Thera (Santorini). |
| c. 1600–1100 | Mycenaeans become a major power in Peloponnese, Athens, Thebes, Tiryns, and Crete. Their writing system is called Linear B. |
| c. 1200–900 | Mycenaean civilization declines. Evidence of writing disappears. |
| 900–800 | City-states develop. Writing used again, although in different form. |
| c. 750–500 | Mainland Greeks migrate and establish colonies in Italy, eastern Mediterranean Sea, and Black Sea. |

| 776 | Olympic Games held in honor of god Zeus. |
| 566 | Panatheniac games held in honor of goddess Athena. |
| 546 | Persians extend their domination over Greek territories throughout Asia Minor. |
| 507 | Cleisthenes's constitution grants equal rights to all male citizens of Athens. |
| 490 | Greeks defeat Persians at Battle of Marathon. |
| 480 | Persians defeat Spartans at Thermopylae and occupy Athens. Greeks defeat Persians at Salamis. |
| 479 | Persians defeated at Plataea. |
| 477 | Delian League, alliance of city-states, founded to ward off Persians. |
| 461–430 | Pericles establishes democracy. There is blossoming of philosophy, sciences, and the arts. |
| 438 | Parthenon completed. |
| 431–404 | Peloponnesian War between Sparta and its allies and Athens and its allies. |
| 430–429 | Plague in Athens leads to death of Pericles and weakening of the city-state. |
| 404 | Athens surrenders to Sparta. Thirty tyrants rule Athens. |
| 403 | Democracy restored to Athens. |
| 399 | Socrates condemned to death for impiety and destroying the morals of minors. |
| 387 | Plato founds the Academy in Athens. |
| 371 | Thebes defeats Sparta at Leuctra and becomes leading power. |
| 338 | Philip of Macedon defeats Athens and its allies at Battle of Chaeronea. |
| 336–323 | Alexander the Great's reign begins after the assassination of his father, Philip of Macedon. Establishes an empire |

|          | reaching to North Africa, India, and Afghanistan. He died at the age of 33. |
|----------|-----------------------------------------------------------------------------|
| 335      | Aristotle establishes Lyceum in Athens. |
| 281–275  | Pyrrhus of Epirus leads the Greeks in a series of battles against the Romans. |
| 146      | Macedonia becomes Roman province. |
| 86       | Roman general and statesman Sulla sacks Athens. |
| 31       | After Battle of Actium, Ptolemaic dynasty of Empress Cleopatra of Egypt ends. |
| AD 49–51 | Saint Paul introduces Christianity to Greece. |
| 49–128   | Romans construct buildings and monuments in Athens, which becomes a center of education. |
| 313      | Edict of Toleration of Christianity put into effect by Roman emperors Constantine and Licinius. |
| 330      | Constantine assumes sole rule of Roman Empire and establishes capital in Byzantium (renamed Constantinople). |
| 380      | Theodosius establishes Christianity as the official religion of the Roman Empire. |
| 395      | Roman Empire permanently divided into Eastern and Western Empires. |
| 476      | Western Empire collapses. Eastern Empire (Byzantine Empire) continues. |
| 537      | Hagia Sophia Church in Constantinople rebuilt after the Nika riots. |
| 533–554  | Byzantine Empire extends to North Africa, Italy, and Southern Spain. |
| c. 650   | Slavs invade Greece. |
| 1054     | Schism between Roman Catholic and Eastern Orthodox churches. |
| 1204     | Fourth Crusade sacks Constantinople. Venetians take possession of Corfu. |

| | |
|---|---|
| 1210–1669 | Venetians occupy Crete until the Ottomans take possession. |
| 1259–1261 | Michael VIII Paleologos becomes emperor of Nicaea. He captures Constantinople and resurrects Byzantine Empire, although it is smaller. |
| 1393 | Venetians take possession of Kythira. Ottomans take possession of Thessaly. |
| 1430 | Ottomans take possession of Thessaloniki. |
| 1453 | Ottomans take possession of Constantinople. |
| 1456 | Ottomans take possession of Peloponnese. |
| 1479–1684 | Ottomans rule Lefkada. |
| 1482–1483 | Venetians take possession of Zakynthos, Kefalonia, and Ithaka. |
| 1798 | Rigas Feraios, advocate of revolution, executed by the Ottomans. |
| 1814 | Secret society, Philiki Etairia, plans overthrow of Ottoman rule. |
| 1815 | United States of the Ionian Islands established under British protectorate. |
| 1821–1828 | War of Independence from Ottoman rule. |
| 1821 February | Alexander Ypsilantis and his army unsuccessfully combat the Ottomans in Moldavia and Wallachia. |
| 1821 | Greeks defeat Ottomans in Battles of Gravia and Tripolitsa (Tripoli). |
| 1825 | Egyptians land 10,000 troops in the Peloponnese, followed by Ottoman-Egyptian victories. |
| 1827 | French-British-Russian fleet defeats Ottoman-Egyptian fleet in Bay of Navarino. |
| 1827 | Ioannis Kapodistrias becomes first president. |
| 1831 | Kapodistrias assassinated. |
| 1832 | Treaty of Constantinople places new nation-state of Greece under the Great Powers (Britain, France, and Russia). |

| | |
|---|---|
| 1833 | Prince Otto of Bavaria, 17, becomes king. Greece governed by three Bavarian regents until he turns 20. The Orthodox Church of Greece declares itself autocephalous, no longer controlled by the Patriarchate in Constantinople. |
| 1834 | Capital transferred from Nafplion to Athens. |
| 1843 | Military coup forces king to grant constitution. |
| 1844 | Constitution sets up democratic parliament, reducing king's power. |
| 1863 | Prince George of Denmark becomes king after King Otto is forced out. |
| 1864 | Ionian Islands annexed. |
| 1881 | At Congress of Berlin, Ottoman Empire cedes Thessaly and part of Epirus to Greece. |
| 1893 | Prime Minister Charilaos Trikoupis declares Greece bankrupt. |
| 1896 | First modern Olympics held. |
| 1897 | Thirty-Day War, with Turkey victorious. Crete proclaimed autonomous Cretan State. |
| 1897–1924 | 500,000 emigrate to America. |
| 1901, 1903 | Use of demotic (vernacular) Greek in Bible and in performance of Aeschylus's trilogy, the *Oresteia*, causes riots. |
| 1905 | Prime Minister Theodoros Deliyiannis assassinated. |
| 1909 | Military coup at Goudi, Athens. Eleftherios Venizelos leads new government. |
| 1912 | Greece, Serbia, Bulgaria, and Montenegro fight the Ottomans and win First Balkan War. |
| 1913 March | King Constantine becomes king after his father, King George, is assassinated. |
| 1913 June/July | Greece, Serbia, Montenegro, Romania, and Ottoman Empire fight Bulgaria in Second Balkan War. Greece adds Epirus, Macedonia, Crete, and some of the other Aegean islands to her territory. |

| | |
|---|---|
| 1915 | Venizelos resigns twice as prime minister over disagreement with King Constantine's refusal to support the Entente forces in World War I. |
| 1916 | Venizelos becomes president of rival government governing northern Greece and Crete. |
| 1917 | King Constantine passes crown to his son Alexander and leaves the country. Venizelos assumes leadership of reunited Greece. Thessaloniki burns. |
| 1918 | Greece assists Entente in defeating Central Powers in World War I. |
| 1919–1920 | Treaty of Neuilly awards Western Thrace to Greece. Voluntary exchange of populations takes place between Greeks living in Bulgaria and Bulgarians living in Greece. |
| 1919–1922 | Greece goes to war with Turkey to redeem lands in Asia Minor but is defeated. |
| 1920 August | Treaty of Sevres provides for a Greek presence in eastern Thrace and on the Anatolian west coast, as well as islands of Imbros and Tenedos. |
| 1920 October | King Alexander dies of infection from a monkey bite. December plebiscite results in the return of King Constantine. |
| 1922 August/ September | Greece loses war with Turkey. About 30,000 Greeks and Armenians perish in the burning of Smyrna. About 200,000 refugees evacuated from Turkey to Greece. Greece loses claim to territory gained in Treaty of Sevres. |
| 1922 September | Colonel Nikolaos Plastiras launches coup, and the Revolutionary Committee forces King Constantine to abdicate. His son, George II, succeeds him. |
| 1922 November | Nine brought to trial for their role in the military disaster, with six executed. |
| 1923 | Convention of Lausanne mandates the relocation of Greeks from Turkey to Greece and Muslims from Greece to Turkey. Treaty of Lausanne reverses territorial claims gained in Treaty of Sevres. |
| 1922–1928 | About 1.2 million Greeks relocated from Turkey to Greece, and about 450,000 Muslims leave Greece for Turkey. |

| | |
|---|---|
| 1924 | Plebiscite abolishes monarchy. |
| 1928 | Venizelos resumes leadership of Greece. |
| 1932 | Greece declares bankruptcy. Venizelos resigns. |
| 1935 | Plebiscite restores monarchy. King George II returns as king. |
| 1936–1941 | Ioannis Metaxas appointed prime minister of Greece and assumes dictatorial powers. |
| 1940 August | Greek warship *Elli* torpedoed by Italian submarine. |
| 1940 October– December | Metaxas says no to Italy's demand to enter Greece. Italy invades Greece. Greek forces defeat the Italians in the Pindos Mountains of Greece and advance into Albania. |
| 1941 April | German forces invade mainland, with Germany victorious. |
| 1941 May–June | German air force and paratroopers invade Crete, with Germany victorious. |
| 1944 March | Communists establish rival government, Political Committee of National Liberation. |
| 1944 November | Liberation from Axis. |
| 1944–1945 | For six weeks in the streets of Athens, the Communist-dominated Greek People's Liberation Army (ELAS) fights British troops and Greek government forces. |
| 1946–1949 | Civil war erupts between government troops and Communist-led Democratic Army, with government troops victorious. |
| 1947 | United States, through the policy of Truman Doctrine, gives aid. King George II dies and his brother Paul becomes king. |
| 1948 | Annexation of Dodecanese Islands. |
| 1948–1949 | About 28,000 Greek children transported by Greek Communists to Communist countries. |
| 1948–1951 | United States, through the Marshall Plan program, gives aid. |
| 1950–1974 | At least a million emigrate, mainly to Germany, Australia, the United States, and Canada. |

| | |
|---|---|
| 1952 | Women's suffrage granted. Greece becomes member of NATO. |
| 1953 | Earthquakes hit islands of Kefalonia and Zakynthos. |
| 1955 September 6 and 7 | Pogrom against Istanbul's Greek and Armenian communities. |
| 1963 | George Seferis wins Nobel Prize for Literature. Prime Minister Konstantinos Karamanlis resigns. |
| 1964 | King Paul dies and his son, Constantine, becomes king. |
| 1965 | King Constantine II and Prime Minister Georgios Papandreou disagree about control of armed forces. Papandreou resigns. |
| 1967–1974 | The Junta, mid-level military officers, governs Greece after bloodless coup. King goes into exile. |
| 1973 | Protest at Athens Polytechnical University against rule of the Junta results in loss of lives. |
| 1974 | Turkey invades Cyprus in response to coup attempt against Cypriot president Archbishop Makarios. In Greece, democracy restored. Communist Party legalized. Monarchy abolished by plebiscite. |
| 1975 | New constitution establishes Republican democracy. Karamanlis of New Democracy (ND) becomes prime minister. |
| 1980 | Odysseus Elytis wins Nobel Prize for Literature. |
| 1981 | Greece joins European Economic Community. Panhellenic Socialist Movement (PASOK) wins election and Andreas Papandreou becomes prime minister. |
| 1982–1983 | Revision of civil code changes family law, including abolition of dowry, reforms regarding women's rights within marriage, and recognition of civil marriages. |
| 1983 | Turkish Federated State of Northern Cyprus established but recognized only by Turkey and the Nakhchivan Autonomous Republic. |
| 1987 | Prime Minister Andreas Papandreou's order that Turkish ship *Sismik-I* be sunk if it enters Greek waters brings Greece and Turkey to brink of war. |

| | |
|---|---|
| 1988 | Greece's and Turkey's leaders meet in Davos, Switzerland, to try to resolve differences. |
| 1990s | Greece expels thousands of illegal Albanian immigrants. |
| 1996 | Territorial dispute between Greece and Turkey over Imia/Kardak in Aegean brings Greece and Turkey to brink of war. U.S. president Bill Clinton intervenes. |
| 1999 February | Rift between Turkey and Greece occurs when Öcalan, leader of Kurdish separatist movement PKK, enters Greece and then is flown to Kenya and housed at the Greek embassy in Nairobi. |
| 1999 August | Earthquake hits first Turkey and then Greece, with outpouring of aid from each country. |
| 2001 | Religious affiliation omitted from mandatory Greek identification card. Greece joins Economic and Monetary Union of the European Union. |
| 2002 | Euro replaces drachma. |
| 2004 | ND wins elections, with Kostas Karamanlis prime minister. Athens hosts Olympics. |
| 2007 | Three thousand forest fires burn in several areas, but mainly the Peloponnese and southern Euboea. |
| 2008–2009 | In December and January, riots follow death of 15-year-old student who was shot by a police officer. |
| 2009 | Forest fires lasting four days affect area northeast of Athens. PASOK wins election, with Georgios Papandreou prime minister. |
| 2009–2011 | Economic crisis, strikes, and demonstrations. |

# 1

# The Land and Its People

The Hellenic Republic, the official name of Greece, is a parliamentary republic. Greece declared its independence from Ottoman rule in 1821 and officially became a nation-state in 1832. Greeks refer to their country as Hellas or Ellada, but Greece is the name that is internationally known and accepted.

Greeks have identified themselves as Hellenes, Romaioi, and Greeks. Greece comes from the Latin *Graeci* and is believed to have originated when colonists called Graeci came to Italy. Before long it was used when referring to all residents of Greece. Romaioi has been used from the fourth century AD until recent times. The people of Turkey continue to refer to Greeks as "Rums." It means the "people of Rome" and was used to denote the Greeks of the Eastern Roman Empire (Byzantine Empire), which continued to flourish after the fall of Rome in 476. The Greeks retained that name for themselves even after the War of Independence from Ottoman rule.

To the Christians, the name "Hellenes," supposedly derived from a mythical ancestor Hellen, denoted paganism and thus fell out of favor in the fourth century AD. It was used again at about the seventh century. Greeks of today take pride in the name since it harkens back to their illustrious ancestors.

## THE CONSTITUTION AND BRANCHES
## OF THE GOVERNMENT

The current constitution of Greece, drawn up and put into force in 1975, was amended in 1986, 2001, and 2008. It provides for three branches of government: executive, legislative, and judicial.

The executive branch includes the president (head of state) and the prime minister (head of government). The president's position is largely ceremonial.

The legislative branch is a unicameral parliament. Every four years, 288 of the seats are elected by the people. The remaining 12 seats are appointed by the parties based on the proportion of the total vote each party receives. The president appoints a prime minister who can command the support of a majority in the parliament.

Ordinary sessions of Parliament are to be held for a period of 3 to 6 months a year. However, normally they are held for a period of 9 to 10 months a year. There are also extraordinary convocations of the Parliament. The Parliament passes laws and can amend or revise the constitution, except for the articles dealing with the form of the state and articles safeguarding rights, obligations, and freedoms.

The judicial branch has both civil courts, which judge civil and penal cases, and administrative courts. Disputes between citizens and the state are adjudicated in the administrative courts.

Greece consists of 13 regions, which include Attica, Central Greece, Central Macedonia, Crete, East Macedonia and Thrace, Epirus, Ionian Islands, North Aegean, Peloponnese, South Aegean, Thessaly, West Greece, and West Macedonia. There is also one autonomous area, Mount Athos, an Eastern Orthodox monastic territory.

Men and women citizens over the age of 18 can vote. Voting is mandatory, except for those ages 70 and older. Greece does recognize dual citizenship but as of 2010 had not yet set up a mechanism for voting at locations outside of Greece.

## NATIONAL ANTHEM

The current national anthem was adopted in 1864 after King George came to power. The first anthem was based on the Bavarian National Anthem, which included praise for the king. The new anthem, with lyrics by Dionysios Solomos of Zakynthos and music by Nicholas Mantzaros of Corfu (in Greek Kerkyra), captured the true character of Greece. Several stanzas of Solomos's 158-stanza poem, "Ode to Freedom," became the national anthem. Solomos penned the poem in 1823, inspired by the Greeks' struggle for independence from the Ottomans. The first two stanzas of the anthem, as translated by Rudyard Kipling, follow:

We knew thee of old,
Oh, divinely restored,
By the light of thine eyes
And the light of thy Sword.
From the graves of our slain
Shall thy valour prevail
As we greet thee again—
Hail, Liberty! Hail!

## GREEK FLAG

On the top left side of the national flag is an equal-armed white cross on a blue background. The rest of the flag features nine alternating stripes of first blue and then white. The blue symbolizes the sea and sky, and the white the waves of the sea. The cross symbolizes the Greek Orthodox faith. There are various explanations as to what the stripes signify. According to one, the stripes represent the number of syllables in the phrase *Eleftheria ee Thanatos* (Freedom or Death), a slogan used in the Revolutionary War fought against the Ottomans. The five blue stripes represent the number of syllables in the phrase *Eleftheria* (Freedom), and the four white stripes the number of syllables in *ee Thanatos* (or Death). A flag like the one that is used at present has been in use since the revolution.

Greece had the largest flag on a flagpole in the world, as recorded in the *2008 Guinness Book of Records.* Located in the town of Keri on the island of Zakynthos, it measures 59.4 feet in height and 121.1 feet in length.

## GEOGRAPHY

### Location

Greece, 51,146 square miles, is just a bit smaller than Alabama. The country consists of a mainland; the Peloponnese, a peninsula off the southern tip that is separated from the mainland by the Isthmus of Corinth; and many islands. The Corinth Canal provides a passageway from the Ionian Sea to the Aegean. Greece, in southeastern Europe, is on the southern end of the Balkan Peninsula. Greece is strategically located at the crossroads of three continents: Europe, Asia (east), and Africa (south across the Mediterranean Sea).

Greece has a land boundary of 721 miles. It is surrounded on the north by Bulgaria, the Former Yugoslav Republic of Macedonia (FYROM), and Albania.

To the west lies the Ionian Sea, to the south the Mediterranean Sea, to the east the Aegean Sea and Turkey.

## Terrain

According to a Greek tale, God created the world by shaking soil through a sieve. Over his shoulder, he tossed the stones and boulders left in the sieve, and that was Greece!

Greece consists of a mountainous interior with coastal plains. Much of the beauty of Greece resides in its mountains and hills, which cover three-quarters of the country. Some, especially in the north, are wrapped with greenery; others, like the volcanic outcrops in Santorini, rise up stark, like a moonscape. One of the mountain ranges, the Pindos, runs from northwest to southeast, dividing the mainland in two. The Rhodope Range lies in northern Greece, in the regions of Macedonia and Thrace. Mount Olympus, in Thessaly in northeast Greece, is the legendary home of the ancient Greek gods. It forms the highest point at 9,577 feet above sea level.

Forests take up about 20 percent of Greece and include the Dadia-Lefkimmi-Soufli Forest, near the Rhodope Mountain Range. Only 20 to 30 percent of Greece is arable.

The sea embraces most of Greece, with the farthest inland point only about 80 miles away. Greece's jagged coastline consists of about 8,498 miles. Statistics on the number of Greek islands range from 2,000 to 3,000, with 170 to 250 inhabited. Crete, the largest island at 3,218 square miles, lies in the Mediterranean, at the entrance to the Aegean Sea.

## FAUNA AND FLORA

### Mammals

There are about 116 species of mammals; 57 belong to the International Union for Conservation of Nature's endangered species list. Wild animals include boar, brown bear, chamois, lynx, wild cat, brown squirrel, jackal, fox, roe deer, and wolf. The rare wild goat makes its home in Crete. Dolphins and seals frolic in the seas around Greece. Many of the world's critically endangered Mediterranean monk seals live in Greece's seas.

### Birds

Northern Greece becomes a bird-watcher's paradise in the spring, when millions of birds migrate north from Africa. Of the approximately 400 species of birds found throughout Greece, two-thirds are migratory. Indigenous birds include the owl, pelican, pheasant, partridge, woodcock, and nightingale. In the Dadia-Lefkimmi-Soufli Forest of northern Greece, near Alexandroupolis,

36 of the 38 predatory birds of Europe have been sighted, including the rare imperial eagle, the lesser spotted eagle, and the black and griffon vultures. At the crossroads of Europe, Asia, and Africa, the forest is one of the two main bird migration routes in Europe.

### Amphibians and Reptiles

Greece has at least 18 species of amphibians and 59 species of reptiles. Turtles include the leatherback and caretta-caretta (loggerhead). The endangered caretta-caretta is found on the beaches of Zakynthos, Kefalonia, Crete, and the Peloponnese. The caretta-carettas hatch at night and usually follow the brightest light to the ocean's edge. Thus, even in tourist areas, there is a lights-out policy. Short plastic fences (posted with "Keep Out" signs) keep humans and predators out yet allow the newly hatched turtles to leave their nests. Other amphibians and reptiles include tree frog, Turkish gecko, wall gecko, fire salamander, viper, sand viper, lizard elapi, lizard snake, ladder snake, and Greek tortoise.

### Marine Life

Some 246 species of marine life have been identified, including squid, octopus, starfish, jellyfish, lobster, sea urchin, shrimp, crab, oyster, mussel, mullet, flying fish, swordfish, tuna, grouper, sardines, smelt, mackerel, and sea bream. Sharks are found in Cretan waters.

### Insects

A variety of insects thrive in Greece, including mosquitoes, bees, flies, butterflies, moths, locusts, spiders, scorpions, ladybugs, dragonflies, grasshoppers, fireflies, and cicadas. The red weevil, noticed in Crete in 2005, has recently decimated many of the palm trees of Greece.

### Flora

Botanists have recorded more than 6,000 plant species in Greece, with about 700–750 found only in Greece. The flora consists of a variety of trees including white poplar, oak, chestnut, spearheaded cypress, pine, fir, olive, palm, laurel, and various fruits. Flowers, which decorate the countryside with brilliant colors, include poppy, anemone, violet, tulip, peony, narcissus, parthenium, and primrose.

## CLIMATE

Travel brochures portray azure skies and sea, with the sun exuding a heavenly luminosity. The brochures do not show the overcast sky that changes the blues to dull grey during the spring and fall rains, or the pure-white blanket of snow that envelops much of the countryside during winter.

The climate varies from season to season, from the north to the south, from coast to interior, and from the plains to the mountains. Even in the summer, on the mountains of the Pindus and Rhodope, occasional thunderstorms echo, and sometimes hail falls with ferocity. In the winter, skiers come to frolic in several ski areas, including one in southern Greece. Temperatures in the mountains can be as low as –18 degrees F during the winter, and mountain roads can become impassable.

Greece's Mediterranean climate generally consists of mainly mild and wet winters and hot, dry summers. The cold and wet season lasts from the middle of October until the end of March, and the warm and dry season lasts from April until September. However, warm weather can span from April to November in the warmer southern islands such as Crete and Rhodes.

## POPULATION

Preliminary results of the 2011 census show that the population totaled 10,787,690 (49.2 percent men and 50.8 percent women). It shrank more than one percent from the previous census. The highest concentration (35.3 percent) was in Attica, where Athens is located, while the second highest concentration (17.4 percent) was in Central Macedonia, where Thessaloniki is located. Tables 1.1 and 1.2 show the population of cities and regions in 2001.

## ETHNIC COMPOSITION

### Foreigners

The 2001 census showed a huge increase in the number of immigrants when compared to the census of 1991. The 1991 census registered 167,000

## Table 1.1  Population of Cities—2001 Census

| | |
|---|---|
| Greater Athens | 3,566,060 |
| Athens | 772,072 |
| Greater Thessaloniki | 1,057,825 |
| Thessaloniki | 824,633 |
| Piraeus | 182,671 |
| Greater Piraeus | 880,529 |
| Patras | 170,452 |
| Iraklion | 132,117 |
| Larissa | 113,090 |

## Table 1.2 Population of Regions—2001 Census

| | |
|---|---|
| Aegean Islands | 508,807 |
| Central Greece | 4,591,568 |
| Crete | 601,131 |
| Epirus | 353,820 |
| Ionian Islands | 212,984 |
| Macedonia | 2,424,765 |
| Peloponnese | 1,155,019 |
| Thessaly | 753,888 |
| Thrace | 362,038 |
| **Total** | **10,964,020** |

"foreigners" in a total population of 10,259,900, or 1.6 percent of the population. In 2001, foreigners living in Greece numbered 762,191 (47,000 of them were EU citizens and 2,927 were registered as refugees). Out of a total population of 10,964,020, they made up approximately 7 percent. Some believe that 10 percent more accurately reflected the number of foreigners in the country. According to the 2001 census, 10.5 percent of the municipality of Athens were foreigners.

Albanians made up 57.5 percent of the total foreigners and Bulgarians 4.6 percent. Other foreigners included those from the former USSR, Bulgaria, Romania, United States, Cyprus, United Kingdom, Germany, Poland, Pakistan, Australia, Turkey, Italy, Egypt, India, Iraq, Canada, Philippines, France, Syria, as well as other countries.

## Citizens

Other ethnic groups who have resided in Greece for centuries include Muslim Turks (who reside in Thrace and the islands of Rhodes and Kos) as well as Muslim Pomaks and Eastern Orthodox Vlachs and Arvanites. Pomaks speak a Slavic dialect, and Vlachs, a Latin language related to Romanian. Christian Arvanites, who immigrated to Greece between the 13th and 16th centuries, speak an Albanian dialect called Arvanitika. However, many of the younger members of these groups no longer speak the language of their parents or grandparents. The Vlachs and Arvanites consider themselves Greek, claiming Greek heritage dating back to antiquity.

There are about 250,000 to 300,000 Roma (gypsies). Many of them are nomadic and speak Romani. The majority are Greek Orthodox, with the others, especially those living in Thrace, professing the Muslim faith. About 5,500 Jews live in Greece, much less than the 76,000 that existed prior to the genocide of World War II.

## RELIGION

The last time the Greeks were asked about their religious affiliation was in the census of 1951. The numbers cited in the following paragraphs are estimates.

### Eastern Orthodox

From 95 to 97 percent of Greek citizens are Eastern Orthodox (also known as Orthodox Christians). About three hundred million throughout the world practice this religion, which traces its roots to the original Christian church. Eastern Orthodox Christians of various ethnicities share the same faith. They agree on matters of doctrine and celebrate the same liturgy and sacraments. In Greece, the church is known as the Church of Greece. It is autocephalous (self-governing), with an archbishop based in Athens at its head. The archbishop has jurisdiction over most of Greece. The Ecumenical Patriarchate, based in Istanbul, has direct jurisdiction over Crete, the Dodecanese Islands, and the monastic communities of Mount Athos.

About 5 percent of Orthodox Christians in Greece are Old Calendar adherents who maintain their own churches separate from the Church of Greece or the Patriarchate. They refused to go along with the government's and the Church of Greece's change from the Julian to the Gregorian calendar in 1923. Also, they object to ecumenicalism, such as participation of the Patriarch of Constantinople in the World Council of Churches and the attempt by the Patriarch of Constantinople to forge closer ties between the Eastern Orthodox Church and the Vatican. Old Calendarists number between 500,000 and 800,000.

### Muslims

The Muslim population is concentrated mainly in Thrace, Athens, and Thessaloniki, with smaller communities in the islands of Rhodes and Kos. Officials estimate the current size of the Thrace Muslim community (which consists of mostly ethnic Turks, with smaller numbers of Pomaks and Roma) at 98,000, although unofficial estimates range up to 140,000. There are approximately 375 mosques in Thrace.

In Athens, the Muslim population is estimated to be more than 200,000, according to a 2009 report released by the U.S. Department of State. It has grown because of new immigrants from Albania, the Middle East, and Southeast Asia. Since there is no official mosque in Athens, Muslim believers meet in over 30 sites in metropolitan Athens. On September 7, 2011, the Greek parliament voted to build a mosque at taxpayer expense. It is expected to seat 500 people and cost about 21 million dollars. Target date for completion is the end of 2012.

## Roman Catholic

Catholics number about 200,000. Catholics have increased with the influx of new immigrants from the Philippines, Poland, and Iraq. Most of the immigrant Catholics and their families reside in Athens and the surrounding area. There are also Catholics on the islands of Syros, Tinos, Naxos, and Corfu, as well as in the cities of Thessaloniki and Patras. Some of the Catholic families on the islands date their heritage back to the occupation of the Venetians and Genovese hundreds of years ago.

## Other Religions

Protestants number about 30,000; Jehovah's Witnesses, 30,000 active members; and the Church of Jesus Christ of Latter-day Saints (Mormons) about 420.

The long-standing Jewish community is estimated at 5,500. Its members mainly reside in the Athens area and Thessaloniki.

Scientologists report about 500 active registered members, and there are approximately 300 members of the Baha'i Faith. Worship of ancient Greek gods recently "came out of the closet." About 200 worshiped at the Temple of Olympian Zeus in Athens in 2007, in defiance of a government ban. Estimates of the number of followers range from 2,000 to 100,000.

## Abolishing Religion from I.D. Card

Greece requires I.D. cards from anyone over the age of 12. The government abolished the category of religion from I.D. cards in 2002. Although the EU had required the abolishment of religion on the I.D., the church and many of the people objected. Three million people (27 percent of the population) signed a petition to submit this provision to a referendum. A rally held in Athens attracted 500,000, while another in Thessaloniki attracted 120,000. At the rally in Thessaloniki, Archbishop Christodoulos, accompanied by 30 bishops, gave a stirring speech, saying, "We are first and foremost Greek and Orthodox, and only secondarily Europeans."[1]

## Constitutional Provisions Regarding Religion

In Greece there is no clear separation of church and state, and it has been this way since the country's beginnings. The constitution says:

> The prevailing religion in Greece is that of the Eastern Orthodox Church of Christ. The Orthodox Church of Greece, acknowledging our Lord

Jesus Christ as its head, is inseparably united in doctrine with the Great Church of Christ in Constantinople and with every other Church of Christ of the same doctrine, observing unwaveringly, as they do, the holy apostolic and synodal canons and sacred traditions. It is autocephalous and is administered by the Holy Synod of serving Bishops and the Permanent Holy Synod originating thereof and assembled as specified by the Statutory Charter of the Church in compliance with the provisions of the Patriarchal Tome of June 29, 1850, and the Synodal Act of September 4, 1928.

The ecclesiastical regime existing in certain districts of the State shall not be deemed contrary to the provisions of the preceding paragraph.

The text of the Holy Scripture shall be maintained unaltered. Official translation of the text into any other form of language, without prior sanction by the Autocephalous Church of Greece and the Great Church of Christ in Constantinople, is prohibited.

Freedom of religious conscience is inviolable. The enjoyment of civil rights and liberties does not depend on the individual's religious beliefs. All known religions shall be free and their rites of worship shall be performed unhindered and under the protection of the law. The practice of rites of worship is not allowed to offend public order or good usages.

Proselytism is prohibited. The ministers of all known religions shall be subject to the same supervision by the State and to the same obligations toward it as those of the prevailing religion.[2]

## Government Support for the Greek Orthodox Church and the Muslim Faith in Thrace

The Greek Orthodox Church receives government support for salaries, religious training of clergy, and upkeep of church buildings. Following the provisions of the 1923 Treaty of Lausanne, Muslim religious leaders of Thrace (muftis and acting muftis) also receive government support in terms of salaries. Imams from Thrace receive a small monthly allowance. Besides the Greek Orthodox and the Muslim religion in Thrace, no other religious groups enjoy governmental financial assistance.

Although the Greek Orthodox religion is taught in the public schools, non-Orthodox children can be excused from attending. Besides observing the national holidays, the schools also observe the following religious holidays: Clean Monday (first day of Lent), Good Friday, Easter Monday, Holy Spirit Day (the Monday after Pentecost), the Assumption of the Virgin Mary, and Christmas Day.

Monastic communities, which are scattered throughout Greece, contain several thousand monks and nuns. A description of a couple of the monastic communities follows:

## Mount Athos

Mount Athos, which contains 20 monastic communities, was established in the fifth century AD. It receives male pilgrims; females have not been allowed since 1045. There are 17 Greek monastic communities, as well as one Serbian, one Russian, and one Bulgarian. There is also a Romanian skete. According to the Greek constitution, Mount Athos is a self-governed part of the Greek state. In spiritual matters it comes under the jurisdiction of the Ecumenical Patriarchate. Prince Charles of the United Kingdom regularly visits the Vatopedi Monastery on Mount Athos. He and his father are supporters of the Friends of Mount Athos organization.

## Meteora

Monks first came to the site of the Meteora monasteries in the ninth century, living in the hollows and fissures of the mountain. Later they built the buildings that housed the monastic orders. Monasteries, some dating to the 14th century, are scattered among the jagged sandstone pinnacles of the mountains. Six small monastic communities, one of them composed of nuns, remain today.

## LITERACY

Greece compares favorably with other developed nations in terms of literacy rate, defined as the percentage of those over age 15 who can read and write. For the total population, according to 2001 census figures, the literacy rate was 96 percent, with 97.8 percent of males and 94.2 percent of females literate.

## FERTILITY RATE

Based on a 2010 estimate, the fertility rate is 1.37 children per woman. At that rate the population will decrease. The new immigrants have larger families than native Greeks.

## HEALTH AND WELFARE

Based on 2009 estimates, life expectancy for males is 77.11 years and for females is 82.37 years. This is higher than 2009 estimates of life expectancy in the United States. Researchers have pointed to the benefits of a Mediterranean diet, which might help explain the Greeks' longevity. The traditional Greek diet consists of little red meat (although this is changing) and many fruits and vegetables. The Greek diet also includes grains, olive oil, nuts, cheese, fish, and red wine.

Greeks take naps. Offices and stores close at midday. The relationship of taking naps to good health has been established. Researchers surmise that it may cut down on stress. Free or low-cost health care is available through national health insurance programs.

Smoking, a health concern, is widespread and frequently starts in the teen years. Although Greece has instituted a ban on smoking in public places, including restaurants and bars, numerous violations occur.

## FOLK MEDICINE

Herbal medicine and *venduzes* (cupping), although not as prevalent as 20 years ago, continue to be used in addition to Western medicine, especially in rural areas. In cupping, an alcohol-soaked cotton ball at the tip of a fork is lit and inserted for a couple of seconds into each of a number of cups. After the cotton is removed, the cups are placed upside down on the affected body part. The vacuum created by the fire sucks up the skin. The heat and relative vacuum causes dilation of vessels and increased blood flow in the area. A common herbal remedy is the use of chamomile tea to cure an upset stomach. "Tea of the Mountain," made with the ironwort plant, is believed to relieve coughs and lung congestion as well as indigestion. Belief in the *mati* (evil eye) still exists. The mati can be given without ill intent but is believed to be conveyed by someone who is jealous. *Xematiasma* (undoing of the mati by the reading of prayers by a trained layperson) is believed to get rid of the ill effects of the evil eye. Some believe that wearing an amulet protects against the evil eye. A popular amulet is colored blue and white and resembles an eye. The movie *My Big Fat Greek Wedding* shows family and guests of the bride pretend to spit at her three times. They say, "ptou, ptou, ptou," as she goes down the aisle, hoping to ward off the evil eye.

## NATIONAL PARK SYSTEM

In 1938, during the dictatorship of Ioannis Metaxas, Greece's first national park, Olympus National Park, was established. Metaxas then created the Parnassos National Park. The national park system now consists of more than 20 parks, including the Zakynthos and Alonissos Marine Park.

## ARMED FORCES

Military service is compulsory for males from ages 19 to 45, usually for a period of nine months, with time following in the reserve. Women can join the armed forces. A citizen abroad is exempt if he has lived abroad for at least

11 consecutive years or worked abroad for at least 7 years and has not remained in Greece for more that 185 days in a year.

## ECONOMY

Greece is a member of the Eurozone, a group of 16 European Union member nations that use a common currency, the euro. Greece started using the euro on New Year's Day, 2002. It replaced the drachma.

Greece is a capitalistic state with socialized medicine and certain government industries. In 2010, there was a push to privatize some of the industries. Greece's deficit was 13.6 percent GDP for 2009. In 2010, Greece faced a serious economic crisis, with a huge deficit and high unemployment.

The public sector accounts for 40 percent of Greece's gross domestic product (GDP), with tourism producing about 15 percent, according to 2009 estimates provided by the CIA Factbook. The number of tourists, according to the Statistical Service of Greece, was 18,754,593 in 2007, with 92.7 percent of the tourists coming from Europe.

According to the U.S. Department of State statistics (2009 estimate), agriculture was 5.4 percent of GDP. The products include sugar beets, wheat, maize, tomatoes, olives, olive oil, grapes, raisins, wine, oranges, peaches, tobacco, cotton, livestock, and dairy products. For manufacturing the GDP was 21.3 percent and for services it was 73.3 percent. Manufacturing included the following industries: processed foods, shoes, textiles, metals, chemicals, electrical equipment, cement, glass, transport equipment, and petroleum products. Services included transportation, tourism, communications, trade, banking, public administration, and defense. Natural resources include bauxite, lignite, magnetite, oil, and marble.

## LABOR FORCE AND UNEMPLOYMENT

Immigrants make up about one-fifth of the work force, mainly in unskilled and agricultural jobs. The labor force participation, according to a 2005 estimate given by the CIA, was agriculture, 12.4 percent; industry, 22.4 percent; and service, 65.1 percent.

According to a press release by the Hellenic Republic Hellenic Statistical Authority: "In the 1st Quarter of 2011 the number of employed amounted to 4,194,429 persons while the number of unemployed amounted to 792,601. The unemployment rate was 15.9% compared with 14.2% in the previous quarter, and 11.7% in the corresponding quarter of 2010. . . . The unemployment rate for females (19.5%) is considerably higher than the unemployment rate for males (13.3%) . . . the highest unemployment rate is recorded among young people in the age group of 15–29 years (30.9%). For young females, the unemployment rate is 35.8%."[3]

## STATUS OF WOMEN

Women first voted in the municipal elections of February 11, 1934. They had to be literate and age 30 or older. In 1949, a law giving women the right to vote in municipal elections was extended to illiterate women. It was ratified by parliament in 1951.

World War II and the civil war that followed had a profound effect on the status of women. They learned to fend for themselves and had even fought as soldiers. During World War II, the Axis occupation authorities set up a puppet government in Athens, and the Greek government was in exile in Egypt and other countries. In 1944, the Communists set up a third government, a provisional rebel government known as the Political Committee of National Liberation (PEEA). The PEEA challenged the deeply engrained patriarchal system of Greece by giving women the right to vote in their elections.

On May 28, 1952, women finally received the right to vote in Greek national elections. However, they did not vote until the next national parliamentary elections, which were held on February 19, 1956.

Today, although much of the Greek patriarchal system remains, especially in the countryside, women have made important gains. In the 1980s, the gap in the educational level between men and women started lessening. Women began attending universities and entering professions. Today, more women than men enter and graduate from the universities. Between 70 and 80 percent of those enrolled in law schools are women, and women doctors and dentists are numerous. More men than women enroll in both secondary and tertiary education.

High profile women have made an impact in the political arena. They include the late Melina Mercouri, minister of culture, Gianna Angelopoulos-Daskalaki, who excelled in her role as head of the Greek Olympic Committee, and Dora Bakoyiannis, who served as mayor of Athens and then as minister for foreign affairs of Greece.

Life for women has improved. However, when comparing the role of women in Greece to that in other countries throughout the world, things don't look as good. According to the *World Gender Gap Report 2009,* Greece ranked 85 out of 134 countries in terms of gender-based inequality. The gender gap was especially noticeable in the categories of "economic participation and opportunity" and "political empowerment."[4]

## EDUCATION

The government operates free coeducational schools from preschool to the university level. Education is compulsory for children ages 6 to 15. Children attend the *dimotiko* (1st to 6th grade), the *gymnasio* (7th, 8th, and 9th grades), and the *lykio* (10th, 11th, and 12th grades). There are two types of lykio, a technical school or a college preparatory school. In the third year of lykio, students take a college admissions exam.

Since 1964, the primary grades have been taught in demotic Greek. Since 1976, instruction in secondary schools has also been in demotic rather than the formal katharevousa. Since 1993, beginning in grammar school, English has been taught in the state schools.

Greece's public tertiary educational institutions include universities that award MD and PhD degrees. Students can also enroll in state-sponsored educational institutions that prepare them for careers in the merchant marine, priesthood, armed forces or as firemen and policemen. The Open University offers distance-learning classes for those 23 or older who wish to continue their studies but can't attend school full-time. A lottery is conducted for those interested in attending. Effective May 2010, degrees from universities in the European Union have been fully recognized. Many Greeks attend universities outside Greece for their higher education. This is especially the case for those who pursue graduate degrees. For many years, Greece has experienced a "brain drain," with some of the brightest graduates lending their talents to countries outside of Greece.

Private schools called *frontisteria* tutor students in foreign languages and in other subjects, so that students can do better in school and obtain better scores in the college admissions examination.

## THE DIASPORA

The diaspora includes about six million people scattered throughout the world. Approximately 500,000 emigrants, mostly young men, left Greece from the 1880s to the 1920s. They left the poverty of Greece behind them and came to the United States to make some money and return home. Between about 30 and 50 percent of them did repatriate. The second wave of emigrants left Greece from 1950 to 1974. They numbered more than a million and included about one-quarter of the labor force. They went primarily to Western Europe, Australia, the United States, and Canada. Both waves of emigrants left because of lack of opportunity in Greece.

However, the second wave also included university students as well as those fleeing from the dictatorial rule of the Junta from 1967 to 1974. In contrast to the first wave, they often emigrated as family units and were better educated. After the restoration of democracy in Greece in 1974 and the improvement of the economy, the emigrants started to return. Between 1974 and 1985, almost half of them had returned. By 2000, about 400,000 had returned from Germany alone. Many of the emigrants had to leave Germany. Their host country, which had welcomed them as guest workers in the 1950s, 1960s, and 1970s, no longer needed them.

Some of the older emigrants returned to retire in Greece. Others, with younger families, often brought money earned in the foreign lands and opened small businesses. Throughout Greece you can meet young people speaking perfect English without an accent. They returned as youngsters from the United States or Canada with their parents. The returning emigrants and their children often retain dual citizenship. Those born in another land but of Greek ethnicity are eligible to apply for Greek citizenship.

Remittances sent by emigrants have been a significant part of Greece's income, helping support family members left behind in Greece. Emigrants have also contributed to building schools and hospitals and the reforestation of the areas hit by forest fires.

For many years the Greek government has encouraged the teaching of Greek to the children of the diaspora and has given support to overseas teachers and schools. In 1983, the government established the General Secretariat

Yannis Tsarouchis, painter and stage designer; Alexis Minotis, director; and opera star Maria Callas take a bow after the August 6, 1961, performance of the opera *Medea* by Luigi Cherubini at the ancient theater of Epidauros. (Photo by Ch. Patsiavos. Hellenic Literary and Historical Archive—National Bank of Greece Cultural Foundation [E.L.I.A.-M.I.E.T.])

for Greeks Abroad, which coordinates and implements policy regarding Hellenes of the diaspora. In 1995, a presidential decree instituted the World Council of Hellenes Abroad (SAE). Through public programs, publications, and conferences, it reaches out to Greeks throughout the world.

The Greeks of the diaspora have achieved prominence in business, science, education, politics, and the arts. They include Georgios Papanicolaou, whose research led to what is known as the Pap smear, a screening test to detect cervical cancer. Born and raised in Greece, he emigrated to the United States, where he had better opportunity to conduct his research.

A darling of the diaspora was the world-famous opera star Maria Callas. She was born in New York but at age 13 moved to Greece, the land of her parents, where she continued her music education.

The esteemed poet Constantine Cavafy was born and died in Alexandria, Egypt. His poetry, written in Greek, has been translated into many languages.

## TRANSPORTATION

Athens benefits from a modern subway system that opened in 2000. The construction unearthed ancient bathhouses, building foundations, roads, city walls, and burial sites, including a mass grave that probably contained plague victims dating back to the fifth or fourth century BC. Unusual artifacts included the tomb of a dog, complete with offerings and the dog's collar. Some of the artifacts, as well as replicas of the friezes found on the Parthenon, turn the sparkling subway stations into mini museums.

Buses and electric-powered trams supplement the subway system. The system transports Athenians and tourists from the airport to the city center or to beaches and suburbs. By 2012, the Thessaloniki subway is expected to be completed.

The Eleftherios Venizelos (Athens International) Airport connects Athens to cities throughout the world, as well as within the nation. Many of the larger cities and islands also have airports that serve international as well as national flights.

Trains and buses connect various areas of the mainland. Ferries transport passengers, autos, and trucks from mainland to islands.

## SPORTS

Throughout the country, on the days one of Greece's soccer teams is playing, Greeks crowd around TV sets in cafés and bars. They are passionate about soccer, and they triumphantly celebrated when Greece won the 2004 European championship. The team bus had the following slogan: "Ancient Greece had 12 gods, modern Greece has 11."

Musicians perform at the Arekia Taverna in Zakynthos in 2009. They sing canta-das, songs of the Ionian islands that celebrate women and love. (Photo by Elaine Thomopoulos)

Basketball is also popular. Greece became the EuroBasket winner in 2005. Greek American Nick Galis, who previously played for the Boston Celtics before coming to Greece, became an icon in Greek basketball, like Michael Jordan in the United States. He played for Greek teams from 1979 to 1995.

Baseball is not popular in Greece, although Greece did compete in baseball at the 2004 Olympics, with the players mostly Greek Americans and Greek Canadians. Peter Angelos, Greek American owner of the Baltimore Orioles, helped fund the team. Currently there are 15 teams, with 400 players who play in tournaments.

## CULTURE AND THE ARTS

Greeks take pride in the priceless relics of Greek antiquity but also appreciate their modern art and culture. The art of Greece takes you on a time-travel tour. The palace of Knossos, with brightly colored frescos, opens a window to life in Minoan Crete. The Acropolis of Athens, as well as Olympia, Epidaurus, Delphi, and Vergina, give evidence of the grandeur of ancient Greece. The somber domed churches built during the days of the Byzantine Empire remind the traveler of the era before the 400-year rule of the Ottomans. The clean architecture of the subway and the Acropolis Museum reflect Greece's emergence as a modern nation.

Modern Greek works of art adorn museums and galleries. Primitive painter Theophilos Hatzimihail (1870–1934) brought attention to larger-than-life heroes such as Alexander the Great and soldiers of the War of Independence through his unique use of color and composition. Theophilos, whose everyday dress was a *foustanella* (kilt), also took pride in dressing himself up during the Mardi Gras Carnival as an ancient Greek warrior, in a makeshift shield and sword. Another celebrated artist was Yannis Tsarouchis (1910–1989), who used an impressionist style to capture the somber moods of everyday people. Nikos Hadjikyriakos-Ghikas (1906–1994) transformed landscapes and people to geometric shapes and abstractions.

Greece developed into a country with distinct regional differences that are evident in food, customs, dress, dialect, dance, music, and songs, even in embroidery. Although Western-style dance is popular, the traditional Greek line dancing is alive and well. Children learn the dances as part of their physical education programs or at after-school programs. Folk songs are still sung, especially in the rural areas, sometimes accompanied by traditional instruments. Depending on region, they include bagpipes made from sheep stomachs; the tambouri (drum); and the lyre, baglama, and bouzouki (stringed instruments).

Youth enjoy pop music and hip-hop. The rebetiko, a blues-type music that became popular in the 1920s, continues to have a following among all ages. Popular icons of contemporary music include Sakis Rouvas, George Dalaras, Yiannis, and Mikis Theodorakis. Theodorakis, because of his leftist political leanings, was jailed by the Junta and lived in exile from 1970 to 1975. On his return to Greece, he received wide acclaim. He composed the movie score for *Zorba the Greek* as well as more than 1,000 songs.

Literature and drama have constituted an important part of the Greek identity since the time of Homer, Sophocles, and Sappho. More recently, two poets won the Nobel Prize: George Seferis in 1963 and Odysseus Elytis in 1979. Others whose literary achievements have gained prominence include Constantine Cavafy (1863—1933), Yiannis Ritsos (1909–1990), and Nikos Katzanzakis (1885–1957). His book *Zorba the Greek* became a popular American movie.

Movies, which in the 1960s and 1970s featured a lot of lighthearted comedies and musicals, have in more recent years become more serious, addressing themes such as the Greek civil war (Pantelis Voulgaris's *With Heart and Soul*) and the nostalgia of a refugee from Istanbul for his home (Tassos Boulmetis's *Taste of Spice*). American movies, as well as popular American TV shows, have continued to be popular throughout the years.

## NOTES

1. "Greek Orthodox Church and Identity Cards," Ontario Consultants on Religious Tolerance, http://www.religioustolerance.org/chr_orthi.htm.

2. "The Constitution of Greece," HR-NET Hellenic Resources Network, http://www.hri.org/docs/syntagma/artc125.html/artc150.html.

3. "Press Release: Labour Force Survey 1st Quarter," Hellenic Republic, Hellenic Statistical Authority, June 16, 2011, http://www.statistics.gr/portal/page/portal/ESYE/BUCKET/A0101/PressReleases/A0101_SJO01_DT_QQ_01_2011_01_F_EN.pdf.

4. Ricardo Hausmann, Laura D. Tyson, and Saadia Zahidi, *World Gender Gap Report 2009* (Geneva, Switzerland: World Economic Forum, 2009).

# 2

# From Prehistoric Man to the Golden Age of Classical Greece

## ARCHANTHROPUS

The 1960 discovery of the Archanthropus, forerunner to *Homo sapiens,* in the Petralona Cave near Thessaloniki created a sensation in the scientific community. The ancient man whose skull was discovered lived about 700,000 years ago, according to archaeologist Aris Poulianos. However, other scientists date it from no earlier than 240,000 years ago. Also discovered in the cave were the remains of early animals such as lions, hyenas, bears, panthers, elephants, rhinos, megacerines, bisons, and various species of deer and equids (horselike animals), as well as 25 species of birds, 16 species of rodents, and 17 species of bats. In the cave are traces of what appeared to be the first known human-generated fire. A local goatherd discovered the cave serendipitously. While in the mountains, he heard what sounded like running water and with the help of others dug a well. He found not water, but a dry cave that stretched about a mile into the hill. The sound was caused by wind rushing through the cave.

## EARLY SETTLEMENTS, 20,000–3000 BC

According to archaeological evidence, early humans lived in Franchthi Cave in the Peloponnese from about 20,000 BC until about 3000 BC. Thus archaeologists could see the development that transpired from a hunting and gathering society to a farming community. Archaeologists discovered tools made of obsidian—evidence of trade—dating to the eighth millennium BC. The obsidian was probably transported by boat from the Aegean island of Melos to the Peloponnese.

Archaeologists discovered another Neolithic settlement in Dispilio, Kastoria Prefecture, dating from 5000 BC. In 1993, they discovered an early form of linear writing inscribed on a wooden tablet.

## THE CYCLADIC CIVILIZATION, C. 3000–1100 BC

Christos Tsountas, a Greek archaeologist who investigated several burial sites in the Cycladic Islands during 1888 and 1889, found evidence of a bronze-age civilization dating back to the third millennium. This prehistoric Cycladic civilization is believed to have predated the Minoan civilization. The Cycladic Islands include Mykonos and Thera (now known by its Venetian name of Santorini), Paros, Naxos, and many more. The Goulandris Cycladic Museum in Athens features marble sculptures uncovered in the excavations of the Cycladic Islands. The primitive depictions of mostly female forms resemble the abstract art of modern artists such as Modigliani, Henry Moore, and Picasso. At first glance, the Cycladic art seems to lack facial features or any decoration. However, closer examination of the white marble figures indicates that the artists had painted on facial features, jewelry, and tattoos.

## MINOAN CIVILIZATION, C. 2500–1100 BC

The palace that British archaeologist Sir Arthur Evans excavated at Knossos, Crete, in 1899 proved to be spectacular. It revealed an intricate maze of buildings, pillars, and frescos that depicted joyful scenes of life and nature. Terracotta pipes brought in water to use in baths and toilets. Archaeologists also discovered the palaces of Phaistos, Malia, and Zakros in eastern Crete. The palaces were the centers for economic production and contained storehouses for grain, oil, wine, and other products. Artisans such as leatherworkers, goldsmiths, and potters produced goods for the local people and for export.

Evans named his find in Knossos the Palace of Minos in honor of legendary King Minos, thus coining the name Minoan. According to an ancient legend, seven young men and seven young women throughout Minos's domain were taken as tribute to the king. They were placed in a labyrinth, to be eaten by the Minotaur, who was half man and half bull. The story, passed down generation to generation by oral tradition, tells of a young man named Theseus, who slew the monster, with the assistance of love-struck Ariadne, King Minos's daughter. She handed him his sword and a ball of yarn she had been spinning. With the sword, he killed the Minotaur; with the yarn, he found his way out.

Whether young men and women were taken as tribute is not known. However, Minoan frescoes and sculptures depict young men and what some archeologists believe to be women performing with bulls. The acrobats do flips on the backs of bulls, a death-defying act.

The Minoans, a seafaring people, traded with people throughout the Middle East and Europe. They learned to fuse copper with about 10 percent of tin to create bronze, a hard metal that could be forged into tools and weapons. The artisans acquired copper from Cyprus and copper and tin from what is now the Czech Republic. Amber was brought in from the Baltic Sea. Gold possibly came from Egypt.

The Minoans had a writing system, not yet deciphered, called Linear A.

They probably established the colony of Akrotiri, in the Cycladic island of Santorini. Archaeologist Spyridon Marinatos began systematic excavations on Akrotiri in 1967. Christos Doumas continued the excavations after the death of Marinatos in 1974. Archaeologists unearthed a settlement dating back to the Bronze Age. They discovered an elaborate plumbing system as well as pottery and colorful frescoes that resembled the art of Knossos, Crete. Akrotiri was abandoned just prior to a massive volcanic explosion c. 1650 BC. No human remains have been discovered.

## MYCENAEANS, C. 1800–1100 BC

The Mycenaeans probably first established their presence in the Peloponnese c. 1800 BC, although they didn't become a major power in Greece until 1600 BC. A warrior society, they exerted their authority in Athens, Thebes, Tiryns, and as far as Crete.

The Mycenaeans borrowed from the Minoan culture, adding their own unique elements. Their frescos show a resemblance to the art of the Minoans. Talented craftsmen produced vases, bronze artifacts, and jewelry as well as glass ornaments. The Mycenaeans, unlike the Minoans, excelled in metalwork, using inlays on daggers and swords. Their vases, which probably held oil and wine, have been found as far away as Spain and the Levant, indicating the extent of their trade. Amber found in Mycenaean tombs hail from the area of the Baltic Sea. Whether the goods came directly from their place of origin is not known for sure.

### Linear B Writing

The Mycenaeans used an early form of Greek writing called Linear B to record economic transactions. About 1,250 tablets of the writing have been discovered. In 1952, Linear B was deciphered by Michael Ventris and John Chadwick from the United Kingdom.

The Mycenaeans may be the Achaeans about whom Homer spins a tale in his epic poems, the *Iliad* and the *Odyssey*. The *Iliad* narrates the story of the 10-year Trojan War, which took place c. 1400 BC. The *Odyssey* tells of Odysseus's adventure-filled 10-year journey home to his faithful wife, Penelope, after the war. The Trojan War probably helped the Mycenaeans forge a common Greek identity since it brought them together to fight a common enemy.

## Heinrich Schliemann Discovers Evidence of the Mycenaeans

Heinrich Schliemann, a self-taught German archaeologist, set out on his own odyssey to find the places that Homer referred to in his epic poems. Schliemann, the Indiana Jones of the late 1800s, was bolstered by the support of his Greek wife, Sophia, who shared his passion. In Mycenae, located in the Peloponnese, he found tombs that looked like beehives as well as deep grave shafts. Using a second-century travel book by the Roman Pausanias, he excavated graves that dated from 1800–1700 BC. He marveled at his find of shrouded bodies adorned with diadems and gold. Masks of gold or electrum, a natural occurring alloy of gold and silver, covered their faces. Schliemann, when observing a mask, said, "I have gazed upon the face of Agamemnon."[1] The ruins later were found to be dated about 300 years before the time of the legendary king of Mycenae.

The ruins of Mycenae include a wall named after the Cyclops, giant mythological creatures with one eye in the middle of their foreheads. Since the walls were built with heavy boulders and huge bricks, the ancients thought only the Cyclops had the strength to build them.

## Troy

Heinrich Schliemann also excavated what some archaeologists believe to be the site of ancient Troy in Asia Minor (in present-day Turkey), the same city that Homer speaks about in the *Iliad* and the *Odyssey*.

Greece's 10-year war with Troy started after Paris of Troy abducted King Menelaos's wife, Helen (or maybe she willingly went with him). Her beauty, they say, "launched a thousand ships." Menelaos recovered his wife by winning the war. The Greeks, under the command of Menelaos's brother, Agamemnon, overcame the Trojans. The conniving Greeks presented the Trojans with a gift of a huge carved horse. After it had been brought in the city gates, Greek warriors crept out of it, opened the gates for fellow warriors, and defeated the Trojans. Thus the saying "Beware of Greeks bearing gifts."

One of the heroes of the *Iliad*, Achilles, was fatally wounded while fighting the Trojans. According to Greek mythology, the Fates informed Achilles's mother, the sea nymph Thetis, that her infant would die in battle. In an attempt to make him immortal, she dipped him in the River Styx, holding him by his heel. He died when a poison arrow pierced his heel, the only part of his body left unprotected. Thus the term "Achilles' heel" to refer to a vulnerable point.

The poetry of Homer investigates the human condition and how Odysseus survives in the most adverse circumstances, fighting off beasts and sirens, death, and the promise of immortality. During his 10-year journey, Odysseus falls for the beautiful Kalypso. Kalypso offers him a choice. He can either live forever, without dying, on the island with her or be a mere human. Odysseus chooses the life of a mortal and returns to Penelope and to his kingdom.

Traveling bards like Homer entertained their audiences with tales of gods and kings. The Greeks had been scattered throughout Greece, Asia Minor, and the area of the Black Sea as well as southern Italy, southern France, and North Africa. The recounting of the history of the ancients year after year helped the Greeks establish a common bond. The bards, like the troubadours of medieval Europe or the griots of West Africa, kept the culture and traditions of their ancestors alive.

Although there is some consensus that there was a Trojan War, scholars debate whether what Homer related about the Trojan War actually happened. They also debate whether the poems were actually written by Homer. Some even dispute whether the city that Schliemann discovered in Anatolia, Turkey, actually is Troy.

## DARK AGES OF GREECE, 1200–750 BC

The rich culture of the Mycenaeans was followed by a period of stagnation that some historians have labeled the Dark Ages. For a period of about 400 years, the cultural achievements of the Mycenaeans disappeared. Any of the following may have contributed to this decline: invasion of a Greek people called the Dorians from the north, civil strife, and natural disaster.

C. 1200 BC, the palaces of the Mycenaeans were either destroyed or abandoned. Writing as a skill seems to have disappeared and did not reappear again in another form until around 750. The wealth and the mode of living in city centers appears to have ceased. There were no more palaces or large structures. The people probably lived in tribal units and supported themselves through agriculture or a nomadic lifestyle.

Pottery making continued but with a simpler geometric motif as decoration. Gone were the figurative drawings of the earlier period. An innovation was the switch from bronze to iron. Although softer than bronze, iron had the advantage of weighing and costing less.

Until more recently it was thought that the Greeks of the Dark Ages had abandoned their trading. For the most part that seems likely. However, during recent excavations of Lefkandi in Euboea, a collection of imported items dating from the tenth century were found. They include earthenware and bronze jugs from Egypt, bowls from Phoenicia, and scarabs and seals.

## BEGINNING OF CITY-STATES, 750–500 BC

From 750 to 500 BC, the Greeks began to settle together in *poleis* (city-states). By the fifth century, over 1,000 city-states existed throughout the Mediterranean area. The city-state consisted of a major city center and the area surrounding it. City-states were not large, however. The city-state of Athens, including the outlying area, was the size of Rhode Island. The city-states acted independently of each other, developing their own systems of government, laws, and foreign policy. Each decided whether to go to war, took care of its own coinage and treasury, followed its own calendar, and decided which deities to worship. The citizens of the city-states owed allegiance only to their city-state. They did not think of themselves as the nation of Greece, although at times they came together as allies for war, when they fought an outside enemy such as the Persians. At other times they fought each other. An example of this was the 27-year Peloponnesian War (called the 30-Year War) between Sparta and Athens. As a result of the wars, some of the city-states, such as Plataea and Sybaris, were completely destroyed.

The disparate city-states did have a common language and often worshipped the same gods. The Greeks gathered together every four years from 776 to 393 BC at Olympia to compete in athletic contests in honor of the God Zeus. The stadium at Olympia where the athletes participated still exists. In 2004, the shot put events were held there.

Hesiod and Homer probably lived in the eighth century BC. Through their poems, we have knowledge of Greek mythology. Hesiod also wrote about farming, economic thought, astronomy, and timekeeping.

People came throughout the Greek world to seek the counsel or prophetic opinion given by a priestess at Delphi. C. 586 BC, in a demonstration of religious solidarity, a group of 12 city-states came together to protect the Delphic Oracle.

Since there were not enough resources to support the population on the Greek mainland, the city-states established colonies. Beginning in the eighth century BC, colonists settled in the northern Aegean, then on the shore of the Sea of Marmara (known then as Propontis), and on the Crimean shore of the Black Sea. Greeks also emigrated to western Sicily and southern Italy. Remnants of the Greek colony called Magna Graecia can be found in Calabria and Sicily, Italy. Some people in the area continue to speak a Greek dialect related to ancient Greek. Greeks also settled by the Bay of Naples and in the area now known as the French Riviera. The Greeks, in general, kept apart from the natives and continued their contact with the homeland.

During this period, trade developed again, especially with the colonies. The Greeks also traded with the Etruscans, who had settled in Italy. Greek influence can be observed in the Etruscans' sculpture and ceramic art. The city-states remained relatively independent, and frequent warfare continued between rival leagues.

King Darius I expanded the Persian Empire into Greek Ionia (present-day Asia Minor, Turkey, on the coast of the Aegean Sea). In 499 BC, the Ionians revolted against Persia. Athens sent 20 shiploads of soldiers to assist. Eretria, which was located on the Aegean Island of Euboea, sent five. They advanced inland, but in short order the forces of Eretria and Athens returned home. The Ionians on their own could not beat their Persian masters. They lost a naval battle off the island of Lade, near Miletus.

The Persians burned Miletus and transplanted part of its population to the mouth of the Tigris River 1,000 miles away. Phrynichus captured the pathos in his drama *The Capture of Miletus*. After he reduced his Athenian audience to tears, he was fined for making them so sad and forbidden to show the play again.

## GREEKS VICTORIOUS AT THE BATTLE OF MARATHON, 490 BC

The Athenians, under the command of Miltiades, won the Battle of Marathon in 490. Pheidippides ran 25 miles and dropped dead after delivering the message, "We have been victorious." Although this legend is probably not true, the marathon of the modern Olympics is based on the run by Pheidippides.

The continuing threat of Persia led the city-states to band together to fight this common enemy. In 481, they established the League of the Greeks, with Sparta as the leader. Athens became the real powerhouse, however. Under the leadership of Themistocles, the Athens navy was built up and a wall was erected around Piraeus Harbor.

After Darius died, his son Xerxes inherited the throne. Not forgetting the defeat of his father's forces at Marathon, Xerxes came back 10 years later with a vengeance. Herodotus, a Greek historian who wrote c. 440 BC, gives this description of Xerxes's forces:

> The army included not only his Medes and Persians dressed with iron-scaled armor, but Assyrians who wore brass helmets and Moschians who wore wooden ones; straight-haired eastern Ethiopians with helmets of horses' scalps and curly-haired western Ethiopians who dressed in leopard and lion skins and painted their bodies half chalk, half vermilion. The Indians in the line of march wore cotton dresses and carried bows of cane, while the Scythes were clad in trousers and tall, pointed

caps and fought with bow, dagger, and battle axes. The Thracians dressed in long cloaks of many colors. But the most spectacular unit in the army was the Ten Thousand, a body of picked Persians sometimes called the Immortals because when one fell in battle he was immediately replaced by another. They marched glittering with gold decorations and were followed by servants and women.[2]

## XERXES AND HIS FORCES DEFEAT SPARTANS AT THERMOPYLAE AND SET FIRE TO ATHENS, 480 BC

Xerxes and his forces fought Leonidas and his troops in 480 BC at the Battle of Thermopylae, on the southern border of Thessaly. The historian Herodotus reports that just before the Battle of Thermopylae, a Spartan warrior named Dieneces was told that the Median archers would "darken the sky" with their arrows. He replied, "Good, then we shall have our fight in the shade."[3]

The brave warriors lost the battle when a Greek traitor showed Xerxes a pass in the mountains that enabled his soldiers to strike the Greeks from the rear. Leonidas, when he saw the Persians advancing, sent most of the army back, but he kept 300 of his own men along with a group of allies and tried to hold the pass. He was killed early in the battle, and all his men were slaughtered. The movie *300* celebrates this battle. Although the Greeks lost the heroic struggle, the bravery of the warriors lives on in modern imagination. After Athens was evacuated, the Persians burned the buildings on the Acropolis as well as much of the rest of the city.

## PERSIANS SUFFER DEFEAT, 480–479 BC

Finally, at the Battle of Salamis in 480 BC, the Greek fleet defeated the Persians, even though they were greatly outnumbered. Both the Greeks and the Persians used galley boats called triremes, powered by three tiers of sweaty, muscular oarsmen rowing in unison. The Greeks defeated the Persians again at the land battle which took place near the city of Plataea in 479 BC.

## DELIAN AND SPARTAN LEAGUES

In 478 BC, the Athenians and their allies created a new anti-Persian alliance, separate from the Spartans and their allies, who organized their own league. The league organized by the Athenians was called the Delian League. Their treasury was on the island of Delos until it was relocated to Athens in 454 BC. The league started with about 100 member states and grew to nearly 200. The member states were mainly located in the northern Aegean region, Asia Minor, Ionia, and the islands. Each of the city-states agreed to contribute either money or ships. Athens soon took over leadership. Because it contributed practically all of the ships, it compelled those not providing ships to contribute money.

With the money collected through the Delian League, Pericles commissioned the building of the Parthenon and the other buildings of the Acropolis. From the charred ruins of the war with the Persians arose magnificent edifices in honor of Athena—to glorify the goddess for the victory she had given them over the Persians.

## ATHENS, 500–336 BC

The emergence of the city-state of Athens formed the foundation for the flowering of civilization that took place during the Golden Age (500–336 BC). The Greeks developed a form of writing that used vowels as well as consonants, making it easier for the commoners to read. Greek statesmen, philosophers, and artists communicated their thoughts and poetry in an elegant language, the vestiges of which can be noted in today's modern Greek. Brilliant and creative men sowed the seeds for the development of modern-day democracy, philosophy, science, literature, drama, and art. The creative spirit that arose out of the Golden Age is credited for being the foundation of Western civilization.

### Solon

When he was elected to the office of chief magistrate, Solon (c. 638–559 BC) worked to bring order to the chaos that gripped Athens because of the collapse of the economy. When small farmers went into debt, they could be forced into slavery if they had borrowed on the security of their person. His cancellation of the mortgages and debts of these farmers angered the landed class. Under Solon's governance, the class system of Athens continued. However, to those freemen without property he gave the privilege of taking part in the public assembly and acting as judges, although they could not hold office. This led to government by all free men. Solon instituted a rule of law that applied to marriage, adoption, farming, and the calendar. He canceled numerous laws of his predecessor, Dracon. The draconian laws punished even minor offenses, such as stealing a cabbage, with death.

### Cleisthenes

Cleisthenes governed in a more democratic manner than his predecessors. In 507/508 BC, he established legislative bodies run by individuals chosen by lottery rather than by kinship or heredity. Instead of four tribes based on family, he organized 10 tribes based on residence. He reorganized the *Boule* (council of citizens appointed to run everyday affairs) to consist of 500 members rather than the 400 members under Solon. There were 50 from each of

10 tribes. Thus governance was put in the hands of male citizens rather than a few families.

He may have been responsible for ostracism. With the vote of 6,000 male citizens, each one voting on a shard of pottery, a person could be exiled for 10 years. This system lasted about 100 years.

### Democracy

About 150,000 people lived in the city-state of Athens during the Golden Age. Pericles (495–429 BC), a gifted leader, furthered the development of democracy. Under his rule, the assembly of citizens met 40 times each year to decide how the city should be governed.

However, only a minority of the population of Athens could actually vote—only males who were free and whose fathers were born in Athens. Females, slaves, and foreigners had no voice in the governance of Athens.

### Slaves

Slaves constituted one-third of the population in the city-state of Athens. Slaves were either born into slavery or taken through piracy or as bounty from conquest. Slaves varied in terms of education and skill. They could be nurses, teachers, artisans, or laborers. Slaves could be owned by individuals (rich households had many slaves) or the state. The Athenian state used archers from Scythia as a police force. Some slaves worked and earned enough to buy their freedom. Citizen-slaves, who had been in bondage because of non-payment of debts, were freed during Solon's rule.

### Women

Women in Athens had no right to vote or to own land. They were under a guardianship of either the closest male relative or a husband. Shortly after puberty, they usually entered into arranged marriages. They managed the household and bore children. They ventured out in the street only to attend funerals or to participate in special women-only religious festivals or in women-only athletic competitions. Other than these occasions, prostitutes or poor working women would be the only women out on the streets. Only courtesans, not respectable women, would socialize with men, entertaining them with talk or music, much like Japanese geishas. Some historians believe that Aspasia, Pericles's mistress, was a courtesan. He revered her and sought her counsel. It is likely that she became his wife after he divorced his first wife.

### Socrates

Among the sayings of Socrates (c. 469–399 BC), whose words of wisdom were committed to writing by his pupil Plato, were these: "To know, is to

Greek *evzones* dressed in the traditional *foustanellas* (kilts) stand in front of the Acropolis of Athens. (Photo by Nick Thomopoulos)

know that you know nothing. That is the meaning of true knowledge"; "It is not living that matters, but living rightly"; "Let him that would move the world first move himself"; "The greatest way to live with honor in this world is to be what we pretend to be."[4]

Socrates taught his students by asking a series of questions that encouraged them to think critically in order to better understand the subject being discussed. Socrates was condemned to death by poison for "corrupting youth" and "impiety." Some historians believe the charges were political in nature—that he encouraged his students to think critically about the democratic governance of Athens. A couple of pupils brought him dishonor. Critias became a brutal tyrant who ruled briefly in 404 and 403 BC before he and the other tyrants were overthrown and democracy restored. Another student, Alcibiades, joined the Spartans in their fight against the Athenians.

## Art and Architecture

The Minoans and Mycenaeans used an abstract, stylized manner to depict humans, animals, and plants. The Dorians departed from this style and used simple geometric shapes to decorate their pottery. However, by 500 BC, artists had developed a naturalistic style, showing people in action.

Phidias, who was appointed by Pericles, designed the decorations and sculptures of the Parthenon on the Acropolis of Athens. The Parthenon and other buildings of the Acropolis were dedicated to the goddess Athena 2,500 years ago. Towering above the city's other buildings, they stand as a testimony to those ancient times. The Parthenon contained a 38-foot statue of Athena that was covered in ivory and gold. A replica of the Parthenon and the lost statue is in Nashville, Tennessee.

Phidias was acquitted of the charge of stealing gold from the statue of Athena. However, he was jailed because of sacrilege—accused of inserting portraits of himself and Pericles onto Athena's gold shield.

The Parthenon was completed in 438 BC. It has 46 marble columns, each slanted slightly inward, and gives a feeling of height, of grandeur. The 524-foot frieze, as well as the base reliefs on the pediments and metopes, each tell a story. The frieze chiseled on the upper cella depicted a lively procession containing 378 people and 245 animals.

At the outdoor theater of Dionysos, on the southern gradient of the hill, the tragedies by Aeschylus, Sophocles, and Euripides, as well as the comedies of Aristophanes and Menander, were performed. Their plays continue to be performed worldwide today, their themes still relevant.

## ADVANCES IN SCIENCE

Many Greek scientists made important advances in science and mathematics. Pythagoras (c. 580–500 BC), who was from Samos, believed that the world was mathematical in nature. He applied mathematics to music as well as to astronomy. He developed the Pythagorean theorem.

At the time of Hippocrates (c. 460–377 BC), doctors thought vengeful gods caused diseases. Hippocrates, who was born on the Greek island of Kos, is known throughout the world as the father of medicine. He believed that each disease had a natural cause, and by finding the cause, physicians could cure the disease. He advised his patients to eat a healthy diet, get plenty of rest, and have clean surroundings. Upon graduation, many of today's medical students take a modern version of the Hippocratic Oath, which is based on his guidelines for honorable conduct.

Aristotle (c. 384–322 BC), who was born in Stagira in northern Greece and became a student of Plato, founded the Lyceum in Athens. In his work he made careful observations, collected various specimens, and summarized and classified them. This became the basis for the scientific method. He wrote treatises on logic, the heavens, metaphysics, physics, politics, ethics, and natural sciences. His works exerted a major influence on Western thought. Aristotle also had a tremendous influence in the shaping of Muslim science and philosophy.

## FOOD

Food in classical Greece included olives and olive oil, cheese, wheat, barley, bread, peas, beans, lentils, onions, garlic, cabbage, lettuce, apples, pears, quinces, pomegranates, figs, grapes, fish, goat, sheep, fowl, honey, and wine mixed with water. Much of the same food continues to be served today, except the wine is not watered down.

## THE SPARTANS

In 725 BC, Sparta conquered the Messenians and made them their slaves. The helots, as they were called, had no civil rights and worked hard tilling the land for the Spartans. Since they were forced to give much of the profits to the owners of the land, barely enough remained for their families to survive. They could be killed with impunity. In 640 BC, with the assistance of the city-state of Argos, the Messenians rebelled against the Spartans. The Spartans were not defeated, but this battle alerted them to their vulnerability at the hands of the helots, who outnumbered the Spartans 10 to 1. In response to the threat of rebellion, the Spartans turned themselves into a military state. Thus they could keep control over the helots as well as defend themselves against any other adversaries. They instituted a political and educational system that instilled in its citizens service to the state and preparedness for the rigors of war.

The word Spartan conjures the image of a simple and sparse lifestyle of self-denial. Since the Spartans centered their life on the state, luxuries for themselves were not important. They valued physical prowess and endurance, qualities that were crucial in a country that relied on a strong army.

Newborn babies who were weak and handicapped were left outdoors to die. Starting at age seven, boys were taken from their homes to live in the barracks, where they followed a rigorous training that prepared them for warfare. They served in the army until they turned 50 and in the reserves until age 60. Their training included physical exercises, survival tactics (they were expected to steal food), and how to endure pain. Plutarch described this incident in his book *Lycurgus*, written c. AD 75: "So seriously did the Lacedaemonian [Spartan] children go about their stealing that a youth, having stolen a young fox and hid it under his coat, suffered it to tear out his very bowels with its teeth and claws and died upon the place, rather than let it be seen."[5] Males lived in the barracks and ate in common mess halls until they turned 30, when they were required to marry and allowed to live in their own homes with their wives and children. They were assigned land by the state when they turned 30, but helots took care of the land so that they could be free to go to war.

For Spartan warriors, death in battle was celebrated. Illustrating the Spartan command "Come back with your shield or on it" is the following quotation from Xenophon, the ancient historian who chronicled the Battle of Leuctra, which took place in 371 BC.

> What they did was to deliver the names of those who had fallen to their friends and families, with a word of warning to the women not to make any loud lamentation, but to bear their sorrow in silence; and the next day it was a striking spectacle to see those who had relations among the slain moving to and fro in public with bright and radiant looks, whilst of those whose friends were reported to be living, barely a man was seen, and these flitted by with lowered heads and scowling brows, as if in humiliation.[6]

Spartan women, like men, were brought up to be strong and hardy. Besides learning to read and write, they participated in vigorous physical education, such as learning how to throw quoits (heavy disks). They also participated in footraces and staged battles. They needed to be strong, to bear strong children and to defend the land when their husbands were away. The spinning and weaving were done by the helots. Even care of the children was put in the hands of the helots. Unlike the Athenian women, the Spartan women could go out into the streets, and they had power within the household. Although they could not vote, they could own land.

Spartan society included three classes: the native Spartans, the helots, and the *perioeci* (foreigners). The helots and perioeci could not serve in the army or have the full rights of the native Spartans. However, the perioeci had more rights than the helots, who were like slaves and could be killed with impunity. The perioeci carried out most of the trade or commerce.

The assembly of male Spartan citizens voted for the council that had the most power, the *ephors,* which consisted of 5 men. There was also the *gerousia,* which consisted of 30 men over the age of 60. It included two monarchs as well as 28 nobles.

Lycurgus (c. 800–730 BC) set up the Spartans' system of governance and laws. Whether he actually existed is debated among historians. However, the ancient historian Plutarch writes this account of him:

> He commanded that all gold and silver coin should be called in, and that only a sort of money made of iron should be current, a great weight and quantity of which was very little worth; so that to lay up twenty or thirty pounds there was required a pretty large closet, and, to remove it, nothing less than a yoke of oxen. With the diffusion of this money, at once a number of vices were banished from Lacedaemon; for who

would rob another of such a coin? Who would unjustly detain or take by force, or accept as a bribe, a thing which it was not easy to hide, nor a credit to have, nor indeed of any use to cut in pieces? For when it was just red hot, they quenched it in vinegar, and by that means spoilt it, and made it almost incapable of being worked.[7]

## PELOPONNESIAN WAR, 431–404 BC

Sparta and its allies fought Athens and its allies from 431 to 404 BC in the Peloponnesian War. The first phase of the war lasted until 421, when a peace accord was agreed to. However, in 418, fighting renewed at the Battle of Mantinea with Argos and Athens and their allies fighting Sparta and her allies. The Spartans emerged victorious. In 413, the Athenians intervened in Sicily, to come to the aid of their allies, but were once again defeated with a complete destruction of their expeditionary force. Their navy was defeated in the harbor of Syracuse. Although the Athenians had some victories in the next phase of the war, they lost their navy in 405 BC and surrendered to Sparta in 404 BC. Thucydides, a participant in the war, wrote the history of the war by collecting eyewitness accounts and examining documents and sites of battles.

## THIRTY TYRANTS, 404–403 BC

After Sparta defeated the Athenian Empire, Athens came under control of a repressive government known as the Thirty Tyrants. Their reign of terror resulted in hundreds of their opponents being executed by being forced to drink an extract from the hemlock plant. They were defeated in 403 BC in a battle at Piraeus.

By 378 BC, Athens had regained its spirit and gathered the Aegean states into a league to combat the Spartans. However, Sparta no longer was a threat after it was defeated by the city-state of Thebes at the Battle of Leuctra in 371 BC. Persia also disappeared as a threat. After a series of revolts, the confederacy crumbled.

## NOTES

1. "Mask of Agamemnon," Archaeologies of the Greek Past, a course with Christopher Witmore, http://proteus.brown.edu/greekpast/4917.

2. C. M. Bowra, *Classical Greece* (New York: Time-Life Books, 1970), 72.

3. Sir Henry Creswicke Rawlinson, ed., *The History of Herodotus: A New English Version*, vol. 4 (London: John Murray, 1860), 188, http://books. google.com/books?id=k4kOAAAAQAAJ&pg=PA497&dq=Sir+Henry+Cre

swicke+Rawlinson,+ed.,+The+History+of+Herodotus:&hl=en&ei=vo_xTc_
LLeTV0QG2iJSmBA&sa=X&oi=book_result&ct=result&resnum=1&ved=0C
C4Q6AEwAA#v=onepage&q&f=false.

4. "Socrates," BrainyQuote.com. Xplore Inc., 2011, http://www.brainyquote.
com/quotes/authors/s/soctrates_2.html.

5. Plutarch, *Lycurgus*, trans. John Dryden, Internet Classic Archive, http://
classics.mit.edu/Plutarch/lycurgus.html.

6. Ida Carleton Thallon, *Readings in Greek History, from Homer to the Battle
of Chaeronea: A Collection of Extracts from the Sources* (Boston: Ginn, 1914), 495,
http://books.google.com/books?id=wt0aAAAAYAAJ&printsec=frontcover
&dq=Readings+in+Greek+history,+from+Homer+to+the+Battle+of+Chaero
nea&hl=en&ei=44EATvDHEseXtweTrqSSDg&sa=X&oi=book_result&ct=res
ult&resnum=1&ved=0CCoQ6AEwAA#v=onepage&q&f=false.

7. Plutarch, *Lycurgus*.

# 3

# The Hellenistic Age Followed by Roman Rule

## PHILIP II OF MACEDON

The Peloponnesian War had weakened the Greek city-states and left them vulnerable to an invader from the north—Philip II of Macedon. His well-trained, formidable army of professional soldiers fought bunched together in dense rectangles, holding *sarissas,* pikes that were as long as 18 feet. He soon had the Greek city-states under his rule and organized them, with the exception of Sparta, into the League of Corinth. By 346, at the festival held in Delphi in honor of Apollo, Philip sat in the presidential chair.

Philip had several wives; thus he made political alliances. His wife, Olympias, bore his son and successor, Alexander. In 336 BC, while celebrating his daughter's wedding, Philip was killed by Pausanius, his bodyguard. Thus, Philip, who had survived three serious battle wounds, met his demise. After his father's death, Alexander rounded up all the suspected accomplices and executed them. In 1977, archaeologist Manolis Andronikos discovered what is believed to be Philip of Macedon's tomb in Vergina, Greece. Its elaborate gold and silver objects show the artistry and splendor of the kingdom.

## ALEXANDER THE GREAT

Upon the death of his father, Alexander assumed the throne. He was well prepared. As a 16-year-old, he had served as regent during the absence of his father. While still a teenager, Alexander led an expedition to modern-day Bulgaria, where he subdued a rebellion. Alexander received tutoring from Aristotle and thus became well schooled in the Greek language, arts, and philosophy.

What his father had started, Alexander finished in grand style. In the 13 years of his rule (336–323 BC), the empire expanded to North Africa, Afghanistan, and India. With his conquest, the disparate city-states, such as Athens, Sparta, and Thebes, became a more coherent whole. Greek language and culture spread throughout the empire.

Alexander proved an able leader and an outstanding commander on the battlefield. He acted with cunning, force, and sometimes brutality. In 335, when Thebes threatened to become independent, he quashed the rebellion and had its inhabitants slaughtered or sold into slavery. He ordered that the whole of the city be razed, except for temples and the house of Pindar, the Greek poet he revered. Seeing the destruction of Thebes, Athens quickly came into line.

Alexander battled Greece's ancient enemy, Persia, defeating the army of Darius III. After the conquest of the Persian Empire, Alexander turned to India. In northwest India, he met a dangerous foe, a powerful army with 130 or more elephants trained for war. After Alexander gave orders for his bowmen to kill the elephants' drivers, the elephants panicked. Alexander's army successfully outmaneuvered King Porus's army, even though they had been greatly outnumbered.

Alexander had intended to forge ahead and invade Arabia, but death awaited him instead. He rapidly succumbed to fever, dying in 323 BC, a young man of 33 years.

In his reign of 13 years, Alexander spread Greek learning and culture throughout his empire and beyond. The influence of Greek art can be seen in India, Persia, China, and Afghanistan. In Gandhara (in present-day Pakistan and Afghanistan), a school of religious art was established that used the art and techniques of classical Greek artists. Buddha statues dressed in Greek clothes assume Greek poses.

## AFTER ALEXANDER'S DEATH

After Alexander's death, the empire broke apart. India was governed by its own rulers, with the remainder of the empire divided among his generals. The divisions included the kingdom of Macedonia; the kingdom of Antioch, ruled by the dynasty of the Seleucids; and the kingdom of Egypt, which was ruled by the dynasty of the Ptolemies.

Greek culture and language continued to blossom even after the death of Alexander in what is called the Hellenistic Age. This era lasted from the time of Alexander the Great in 336 BC to the defeat of the Ptolemaic Kingdom of Cleopatra, which fell to the Romans in 30 BC.

One of the centers of Greek learning during the Hellenistic Age was Alexandria in Egypt, which had been founded by Alexander the Great in 331 BC. Its glory was a magnificent library built after his death at the beginning of the third century BC, during the Ptolemy dynasty.

## GREEK SCIENTISTS

During the Hellenistic Age, Greek scientists and scholars became influential throughout the Middle East as well as in Europe. Their discoveries became the foundation of modern science. Although his birthplace is unknown, Euclid (c. 330–270 BC) lived in Alexandria, a center of culture and learning. The *Elements of Geometry* by Euclid was used as a textbook for more than 2,000 years. His book, which summed up the teachings of early mathematicians, included plane geometry, proportion, properties of numbers, and solid geometry. He proved that the number of prime numbers is infinite.

Archimedes (c. 287–212 BC), who was born in the Greek colony of Syracuse, Italy, used mathematical concepts to investigate the world. He developed formulas for finding areas and volumes of spheres and cylinders and built inventions. Farmers continue to use an irrigation method he invented. Shaped like a large screw, it draws water from rivers. His experiments with the lever resulted in his statement of the law of simple machines. He served under the patronage of Hieron II, the king of Syracuse, who challenged him to drag a barge out of the water single-handedly. He did so with a compound pulley. The king also challenged him to determine whether a new crown was made of pure gold. He used the law of buoyancy, which he discovered while taking a bath. While leaping from his bath, he shouted, "Eureka!" ("I have found it!").

Eratosthenes (c. 276–196 BC) was from Cyrene, an ancient Greek colony in present-day Libya. He wrote about mathematics, astronomy, geography, history, and literary criticism. The map he compiled of the world, which extended from the British Isles to Sri Lanka and included countries bordering the Mediterranean Sea, was used for 200 years. Upon determining that the Egyptian solar calendar fell short one day every fourth year, he suggested adding an extra day every four years. Most significant, he calculated the circumference of the earth at 25,000 miles, remarkably close to the measurement calculated today: 24,902 miles.

## ROMAN EMPIRE VICTORIOUS OVER GREECE

In 281 BC, Pyrrhus of Epirus began the confrontation between the Greeks and the Romans. A strong warrior, he fought a series of battles against the Romans in southern Italy; in some of them he emerged victorious. Yet, his forces were weakened despite the victories. From this comes the term "Pyrrhic victory."

The Romans got the upper hand in subsequent battles. In 148 BC, Macedonia fell to the Romans, thus becoming a Roman province. In 86 BC, the Roman general and statesman Sulla sacked Athens.

The remnants of Alexander's empire were finally incorporated into the Roman Empire in 30 BC, after the Battle of Actium on the western shore of Greece. This battle between two Romans, Octavian and Mark Antony, ended years of civil war and determined who would take control of Rome.

Shakespeare and Hollywood have made the love story of Antony and Cleopatra famous. According to one of several legends, Antony was the lover/ husband of the Egyptian pharaoh Cleopatra VII, who was from the Hellenistic dynasty founded after the death of Alexander the Great. Cleopatra's ships joined with Antony's navy in fighting the forces of Octavian at the Battle of Actium. When Cleopatra and 60 of her ships departed for the open sea in the midst of the sea battle, Antony and 40 of his ships joined her. After his forces were defeated, he committed suicide. Cleopatra, according to the legend, then took her life by being stung by a poisonous snake, an asp. The defeat at Actium and the death of Cleopatra signaled the end of the last successor state of Alexander the Great's empire. The dynasty of the Ptolemies came to an end. Within three years of the battle, Octavian proclaimed himself Augustus Caesar. The Greek world came under his control.

## GREEK SPIRIT SURVIVED AFTER ROMAN CONQUEST

The Romans admired and learned from the Greeks. Greek scholars, artists, and architects continued their work and wealthy Romans as well as Greeks supported them. In AD 161, Herodes Atticus, a Greek aristocrat, built an odeum in memory of his wife on the south slope of the Acropolis. It continues to be used for performances. Hadrian's Arch, built by the emperor Hadrian, is a landmark of Athens. Hadrian also finished the Temple of Olympian Zeus in Athens, which had been started many centuries before. It was dedicated in AD 132.

The Romans even practiced the Greek religion, with the 12 major gods and numerous minor gods adopting Latin names. Also, the Latin language had a foundation in the Greek alphabet and Greek root words, especially in regard to scientific vocabulary. Much of the Greek language found its way into our current English language.

Greek scientists continued to innovate. Galen (c. AD 130 to 200) believed "a physician needs to study the body, as an architect needs to follow a plan."[1] He set the groundwork for modern anatomy and neurology by studying human skeletons, dissecting animals, and observing humans in his work as a physician.

## RELIGIOUS FREEDOM GRANTED, AD 313

Christianity had first been introduced to mainland Greece by St. Paul c. AD 50. During the next two centuries, the number of worshipers of Christ had continued to grow throughout the Roman Empire, despite persecution by some of the Roman emperors. In 313, Emperors Constantine and Licinius granted freedom in the exercise of religion, thus enabling Christians to practice their religion without fear of death.

## NOTE

1. John Hudson Tiner, *100 Scientists Who Changed the World* (Milwaukee, WI: World Almanac Library, 2003), 14.

# 4

# The Byzantine Empire Followed by Ottoman Rule

"Byzantine Empire," a term used by a 16th-century scholar, now describes what had previously been called the Eastern Roman Empire. Some scholars date the start of the Byzantine Empire to the year AD 330, when Constantine established the capital of the Roman Empire in Byzantium, which was renamed Constantinople. Others date it to the collapse of the Western Roman Empire in AD 476.

Even after the collapse of the Western Roman Empire, the Eastern Roman Empire continued to flourish. The practice of Christianity was at its core. Theodosius I established the Christian religion as the official religion. In the late fourth century, he employed Draconian methods to stamp out the pagan practices of religion. He terminated the Olympic Games, which had been celebrated in honor of Greek gods. Many temples were destroyed; for instance, the Temple of Apollo was broken up and used for the construction of churches, houses, and other buildings. Pagans were persecuted and even killed.

Although the practice of the ancient Greek religion was halted, the Greek language thrived during the Byzantine era. Greek soon became the official language of the empire. The everyday language of the people of Byzantine times, koine, lives on in the Greek language used in Greek Orthodox churches today. The Byzantine era's influence can also be found in the music and iconography of present-day Greek Orthodox churches.

Despite the discouragement of emperors such as Theodosius, scholars of the Byzantine Era continued studying the ancients such as Socrates, Plato, and Aristotle, and thus perpetuated that heritage.

In the fifth and sixth centuries, Byzantine scholars living in Persia translated scientific texts into Syriac. They in turn were translated into Arabic in the ninth century. Greek texts were also translated directly from the Greek into Arabic. According to scholar Elspeth Whitney, "Byzantine outposts in Italy and possibly North Africa were sources for Greek medical and other texts in the sixth century and again in the eleventh and twelfth centuries."[1]

The translations of the Greek texts eventually made their way to Muslim Spain. In Spain, the works of Archimedes, Galen, Hippocrates, and Aristotle were translated into Latin. Thus the knowledge of the Greeks was transferred to Western Europe.

## RELIGIOUS CONTROVERSIES

In the early days of the Christian church, the practice of the Christian religion had been a contentious and often dangerous experience. The Roman Empire persecuted and slaughtered Christians. After the Christian religion became accepted by the Romans, controversy continued within the church.

### Controversy over Use of Icons

Controversy over the use of icons in the church reached a climax when Emperor Leo III ordered icons destroyed beginning in 726. In 843, Empress Theodora restored the veneration of icons. Each year Eastern Orthodox churches around the world celebrate this as a holiday. As part of the service, priests and altar boys reverently proceed down the aisles of the church, each holding an icon.

### Schism between the Eastern and Western Churches, 1054

The early church was made up of five autocephalous Patriarchates: Antioch, Jerusalem, Alexandria, Constantinople, and Rome. In 1054, the original Christian church split into two parts: the Roman Catholic Church and the Eastern Orthodox Church. The break resulted from a gradual estrangement over many centuries because of cultural, political, and theological reasons. One of the theological differences was regarding the divinity of God. The church's beliefs about the divinity were formulated and agreed upon at two ecumenical councils—one convened in Nicaea, Asia Minor, in 325 and the other in Constantinople in 381. These beliefs were stated in the Nicene Creed.

Without consulting the other Patriarchates, Rome changed the creed by inserting the Latin word *filoque* (from the son). Thus, instead of reading that the Holy Spirit proceeds from the Father, it read that the Holy Spirit proceeds from the Father and Son. This was anathema to the other Patriarchates. Another major difference was the Roman Church's belief in the infallibility of the Pope. The Eastern Orthodox Church (made up of the dioceses of Antioch, Jerusalem, Alexandria, and Constantinople) relied on a council of bishops and was opposed to one man, the Roman pope, making decisions. Because of these and other differences the Roman Catholic Church and the Eastern Orthodox Church remain separated today.

The Eastern Orthodox Church today numbers about three hundred million worldwide. To the original four Patriarchates of the Eastern Orthodox Church were added Serbia, Moscow, Romania, and Bulgaria. There are also several autocephalous churches, of which the Church of Greece is one. The Ecumenical Patriarch, who is based in Istanbul (formerly Constantinople), has presided throughout the years in historical honor among all Orthodox Primates as "first among equals." According to the website of the Ecumenical Patriarchate of the Eastern Orthodox Church, "He also traditionally serves as the spokesman for Orthodox Church unity, convening inter-Orthodox councils, as well as inter-church and inter-faith dialogues."

## JUSTINIAN'S RULE, 527–565

The strength of the Byzantine Empire went up and down depending on the leader. Two powerful leaders were Justinian and Basil II (Basil the Bulgar Slayer).

Justinian, who ruled from 527 to 565, took on the daunting task of revising Roman law. He also put down a rebellion, known as the Nika riots, following the advice of his wife, Theodora, who encouraged him to take charge rather than flee the city. His forces killed 30,000 members of the opposition and quelled the rebellion. In the wake of the fires that were started in the weeklong Nika riots, parts of Constantinople were destroyed, including the Church of Hagia Sophia. It was rebuilt from 532 to 537. After the capture of Constantinople by the Ottomans in 1453, the building was used as a mosque. Atatürk opened the building to the general public as a museum in 1935.

## BASIL THE BULGAR SLAYER'S RULE, 979–1025

Basil II, who ruled from 976 to 1025, expanded the territory of the Byzantine Empire. His empire stretched from southern Italy to the Balkans (including Greece and Bulgaria), Georgia, Armenia, and Mesopotamia.

Basil II overcame a civil war against powerful generals from the Anatolian aristocracy. He went on to a complete victory over the Bulgars and is known as the Bulgar Slayer. During the war with the Bulgars, Basil's army captured 15,000 prisoners. According to legend, 99 out of each 100 men were blinded. The sighted men led the rest of them home. Two days after their leader, Samuel, saw his pathetic troop of warriors returning, he died.

## CAPTURE OF CONSTANTINOPLE BY THE FOURTH CRUSADE, 1204

The Fourth Crusade ripped the Byzantine Empire apart and ravaged the city of Constantinople. Historian Steven Runsiman, in his book *History of the Crusades*, gives this description of the capture of Constantinople:

> For nine centuries the great city had been the capital of Christian civilization. It was filled with works of art that had survived from ancient Greece and with the masterpieces of its own exquisite craftsmen. The Venetians wherever they could seized treasures and carried them off.... But the Frenchmen and Flemings were filled with a lust for destruction:

On May 29, 1453, Constantinople fell to the Ottomans, after over 1,000 years of Byzantine rule. Emperor Constantine XI Paleologos was the last Byzantine emperor. He died in battle fighting the Ottomans. (Photo by Elaine Thomopoulos)

they rushed in a howling mob down the streets and through the houses, snatching up everything that glittered and destroying whatever they could not carry, pausing only to murder or to rape, or to break open the wine-cellars. Neither monasteries nor churches nor libraries were spared. In St. Sophia itself drunken soldiers could be seen tearing down the silken hangings and pulling the silver iconostasis to pieces, while sacred books and icons were trampled underfoot. While they drank from the altar-vessels a prostitute sang a ribald French song on the Patriarch's throne. Nuns were ravished in their convents. Palaces and hovels alike were wrecked. Wounded women and children lay dying in the streets. For three days the ghastly scenes continued until the huge and beautiful city was a shambles. Even after order was restored, citizens were tortured to make them reveal treasures they had hidden.[2]

Despite the destruction, the Byzantine Empire survived, although it was smaller in size. Theodore Lascaris established a Byzantine government-in-exile in Nicaea. In 1261, one of his successors, Michael VIII Paleologos, moved the seat of the empire back to Constantinople. The Byzantine Empire lasted for over 1,000 years, until the fateful day when the Ottoman Empire crushed Constantinople.

## OTTOMANS CONQUER CONSTANTINOPLE, 1453

Tuesday is a day that is burned into the memory of the Greeks. On Tuesday, May 29, 1453, Constantinople fell to the Ottomans. *"Elate na tin parete"* ("Come and take her"), Byzantine emperor Constantine XI Paleologos replied to the Ottoman sultan Mehmet II upon his demand to surrender Constantinople (present-day Istanbul). Constantinople fell. The Greeks held out in the Peloponnese a few years more, until 1460. Crete did not fall to the Ottomans until 1669, when the Ottomans took control from the Venetians. The Ottomans had already taken over Thessaloniki from the Venetians in 1430.

The Ottomans organized their government into religiously based communities called *millets.* They governed through written charters between the Ottoman authorities and the various millets. The largest non-Muslim millet was the Eastern Orthodox Christian (also referred to as Greek Orthodox or Rum millet). The Ecumenical Patriarchate was responsible for this millet. After several moves following the loss of Hagia Sophia (Church of the Holy Wisdom) to the Ottomans, the Patriarchate moved its headquarters to the Phanar district of Constantinople in 1601, where it remains today.

The Patriarch, the highest religious leader of the Orthodox Christian millet, was responsible not only for ethnic Greeks, but also for other ethnic groups belonging to the Eastern Orthodox Church. This included Albanians, Vlachs,

Romanians, Serbs, and Bulgarians. In 1870, when the sultan awarded the Bulgarians their own church community, the Patriarchate declared the new Bulgarian church schismatic. The Bulgarian Church was not welcomed back until 1945.

The Patriarch was selected by the Orthodox of Constantinople, but he held office only at the discretion of the Ottoman government. He was responsible to the Ottomans for the loyalty of the community to the Sultan and for keeping law and order within the community. The Patriarch and the church courts handled marriage, divorce, adoptions, and testaments. By the 18th century, the church and its courts also became involved in other civil disputes. They did not hear criminal cases, however, or cases involving a Muslim and a non-Muslim. The millet also took on the responsibility of collecting taxes.

Because of the millet system, the Greeks, as well as other Orthodox people of various ethnicities, coalesced around the Greek Orthodox Church. The millet system enabled the Greeks to retain their language and religion during the 400 years of Ottoman rule.

It was commonly believed that during Ottoman rule children had to learn the Greek language in secret, at night. Present-day Greeks remember the ditty that they were taught in school:

My little moon so bright and cool,
Light me on my way to school,
Where to study I am free,
And God's word is taught to me.[3]

However, modern historians point out that the Ottomans did not discourage religious teaching or oppose the use or teaching of the Greek language, with very few exceptions.

There were obvious advantages to being a Muslim, such as not facing discrimination, not paying a head tax (a tax levied against each person), and being able to own firearms and ride horses. Some Christians became Muslims. Some believe that the Muslims in Turkey who speak a Greek dialect called Pontic are actually Greeks who had converted to Islam. The Muslims of Crete who had to leave Crete to go to Turkey during the exchange of populations in 1923 are also believed to be Greeks who converted en masse to Islam.

## PHANARIOTS

The Phanariots, a wealthy class of Greek merchants, emerged in the latter part of the 16th century. They tended to live in the Phanar district of Constantinople. They exerted considerable influence in the administration of the Patriarchate and the selection of the Patriarch.

The Ottomans used them in administrative and diplomatic positions. They were educated, had knowledge of commerce, and were fluent in several languages (the Ottomans were discouraged from learning foreign languages). They served in various capacities ranging from clerks to dragomans. Dragomans were interpreters-translators who at times became involved in political negotiations. Phanariots, from 1711 to 1821, also served as princes in the autonomous Ottoman principalities of Wallachia and Moldavia.

The Phanariots' support of Greek schools and students assisted in a revival of the Greek classics and an emergence of Greek pride. The Phanariots also played an important role in the Greek War of Independence against the Ottomans.

## JANISSARIES

Greeks suffered under the yoke of the Ottoman Empire. From the mid-14th century until 1683, the Ottomans seized up to a million young Greek and other Christian boys throughout the empire. The number of boys the Ottomans took varied depending on need. The boys converted to Islam and severed contact with their families. After extensive education, including reading and writing in the Ottoman-Turkish language and learning the Koran, they served in either the Ottoman army as janissaries (soldiers) or in government service. Many served in administrative posts in service to the sultan.

Some despondent Greek mothers maimed their sons so they would be spared from being taken by the Ottomans. Others welcomed the opportunity their sons had for a better way of life.

During the reign of Sultan Murad III (1546–1595), both Muslims and Christians began volunteering as janissaries. Thus, the need to take young Christian boys was not as necessary. By 1683, Sultan Mehmet IV stopped forcibly taking young Christian boys. By the beginning of the 19th century, the janissaries had outlived their usefulness to the Ottomans. In 1826, after the janissaries revolted, Sultan Mahmud II abolished the corps, slaughtering many of them.

## OTHER INVADERS DURING THE MIDDLE AGES

Besides the Ottomans, the Greek mainland and the islands of the Aegean and Ionian Seas were also subjected to the rule of other invaders. In the fifth and sixth centuries, the Slavs and Avars came. In 2010, Sandra Garvie-Lok, a professor in the department of anthropology at Alberta University who specializes in the study of bones, was called in to help solve a murder that occurred 1,500 years ago during the Slavic invasion. The remains of the middle-aged victim were found in a graffiti-lined stadium tunnel in ancient Nemea in the Peloponnese. She said, "The deceased possibly used the tunnel entrance as an escape from the invaders, where he died/was killed. The Slavs and Avars (another group of eastern European peoples) were pretty brutal. If he was hiding in that unpleasant place, he was probably in a lot of danger. So, he hid out, but he didn't make it."[4]

The Greek National Tourist Organization lists 60 castles, reminders of the foreign invaders of medieval times. In the old city of Rhodes stands the Palace of the Grand Master, which was built by the Sovereign Military Hospitaller Order of St. John of Jerusalem, of Rhodes, and of Malta. They took over the island in 1309, putting an end to Byzantine rule. They held it until 1522, when the Ottomans conquered the islands.

The Venetians conquered some of the Aegean Islands as well as the Ionian Islands. They took over the Ionian Islands in the 13th and 14th centuries. With the exceptions of Kefalonia, which was occupied by the Ottomans from 1479 to 1481 and 1485 to 1500, and of Lefkada (Lefkas), from 1479 to 1684, the Ionian Islands escaped the clutches of the Ottomans. The Venetians held the Ionian Islands until 1797, the end of the Venetian Republic. The islands were given to France, but in 1799 they were seized by a Russian-Ottoman fleet and came under Russian protection. In 1804, Russia returned the islands to France, and from 1809 to 1814, the British occupied all of the islands except Corfu. In 1815, the islands achieved some autonomy under British protection, as the United States of the Ionian Islands. They achieved union with Greece in 1864.

By 1687, the Venetians seized practically all of the Peloponnese from the Ottomans and held it until 1715 before they recaptured it.

Crete has had many masters. The island fell out of the control of the Byzantines c. 826 and remained under control of the Arabs until 961, when the Byzantines recaptured it. Soon after the fall of Constantinople in 1204, Crete was sold to the Venetians, who held it until the Ottomans took possession of most of the island in 1669, with complete control of the entire island in 1715. It was ceded to Greece in 1913, after the Balkan Wars.

## TRANSMISSION OF GREEK LEARNING TO SPAIN, ITALY, AND WESTERN EUROPE

During the 14th, 15th, and 16th centuries, Greek scholars, artists, soldiers, and merchants immigrated to European cities such as Venice, Rome, or Toledo. Some of the scholars who came to study and teach in the European universities brought Greek manuscripts with them.

By introducing the philosophy, science, literature, and art of the ancient Greeks to European scholars, these emigrants sowed the seeds for the flowering of the Renaissance. These intellectuals included Basilios Bessarion, Georgius Gemistos Plethon, and Marcos Musurus.

Basilios Bessarion, who became a Roman Catholic bishop in 1436 and a cardinal a few years later, contributed to the revival of interest in Greek letters in Rome by establishing a center for Greek learning. He commissioned fellow Greeks to translate Greek manuscripts into Latin. In 1468, he presented his library, which contained many Greek manuscripts, to the Venetian senate. It forms the nucleus of the library of St. Mark's.

Georgius Gemistos Plethon reintroduced the teachings of Plato to Western Europe after he attended the 1438–1439 Council of Florence. It was convened in an unsuccessful attempt to unify the Roman Catholic and Orthodox Churches. Because of his influence, Cosimo de'Medici founded the Platonic Academy.

Marcos Musurus in 1505 became a professor of Greek language at the University of Padua and also filled a similar post in Venice. He also established a Greek printing press.

One of the most famous emigrants was the world-renowned El Greco (Domenikos Theotokopoulos), who was born 1541 in Venetian-occupied Crete, where he had been an iconographer. He went to Venice, Rome, and Madrid and finally settled in Toledo. The expressionist paintings he created later in his life became the forerunner of modern painting. He died in 1614.

By the 18th century, the influence not only of Greek letters but of ancient Greek art and architecture on Europe was evident. The architects of the era tried to capture the purity of the ancients. Columns and simple lines reappeared rather than the heavy baroque and rococo styles. Painters used the painted vases of ancient Greece for inspiration and often used Greek myths as subject matter for their paintings.

## NOTES

1. Elspeth Whitney, *Medieval Science and Technology* (Westport, CT: Greenwood Press, 2004), 10.

2. Steven Runciman, *History of the Crusades,* vol. 3 (London: Folio Society, 1994), 104.

3. David Brewer, *The Greek War of Independence* (Woodstock, NY: Overlook Press, 2003), 6.

4. Jamie Hanlon, "The Ultimate Cold Case: Anthropologist 'Bones Up' on Site of Ancient Invasion," http://www.eurekalert.org/pub_releases/2010–06/uoa-tuc061810.php.

# 5

# Fighting for Independence

A precursor to the War of Independence was the Orlov Rebellion, which had the support of Russian czarina Catherine the Great. Russian count Aleksey Grigoryevich Orlov, after his brother Grigory had solicited the support of Greek leaders, landed a Russian fleet in the Peloponnese in 1770. The Ottomans, with the help of Albanian Muslim soldiers, defeated the outnumbered insurgents. The Orlov Rebellion ended with death, defeat, destruction, and even more repressive measures against the Ottoman's Christian subjects. From the date of the Orlov Rebellion, 50 years would come and go before the Greeks staged a full-fledged uprising against the Ottomans.

## ADAMANTIOS KORAIS

Adamantios Korais (1743–1833), a Greek scholar residing in Paris, published a library of Greek classics that included the works of Homer and Herodotus. Through his books, he raised Greeks' consciousness of their Hellenic heritage and paved the way for the revolution against their Ottoman oppressors. Korais introduced a revised Greek, later called *katharevousa*. Scrubbed *katharo* (clean) of foreign influences, this new language was a compromise between ancient Greek and modern spoken Greek (demotic).

## RIGAS VELESTINLIS

In the 1790s, the French Revolution triggered Greeks such as Rigas Velestinlis to political action. Velestinlis hailed from Thessaly in present-day Greece but resided in Bucharest and Vienna. He expressed his ideas about throwing off the Ottoman yoke and forming a new government in a 1797 pamphlet. It included his poem "Thourios" ("War Song"). He envisioned a Balkan Federation, consisting not only of Greeks, but of other Balkan peoples of various ethnicities and religions. He distributed his publication in Trieste. A Greek in Trieste betrayed him to the Austrians, who handed him over to the Ottomans. In Belgrade, in May 1798, the Ottomans strangled him and his compatriots and threw their bodies in the river. Before he died, he is reported to have said, "This is how brave men die. I have sown; soon will come the hour when my country will gather the harvest."[1]

An excerpt from his poem "Thourios" follows:


How long, brave warriors, shall we live in the narrow passes,
Solitary, like lions, on the ridges of the mountains,
How long shall we dwell in caves, gazing out on the branches.
How long shall we flee from the world because of bitter slavery,
Losing our brothers and sisters, our homeland, our parents
Our friends, our children and all of our kin,

[ ... ]

Better one hour of freedom
Than forty years slavery and prison.[2]


The last two lines served as a rallying cry to the Greek revolutionaries.


## PHILIKI ETAIRIA

Motivated by the martyr Rigas and bolstered by the success of the French and American Revolutions, three Greek merchants from Odessa met together in 1814 to plan for the revolution against the Ottomans. They were Nikolaos Skoufas and Athanasios Tsakaloff from Epirus and Emmanuel Xanthos from Patmos. They started with a small group, but by 1821 known membership increased to 1,093, with three-quarters of members recruited from abroad. They planned the revolution, solicited funds, and worked to secure the moral support of the Greeks of Europe and Asia Minor. The 1819 records of the Odessa branch delineated the occupations of 348 of the 452 members. The largest proportion was merchants and shippers.

An excerpt of the sacred oath that members of the secret society took follows: "Last of all, I swear by Thee, my sacred and suffering Country,—I swear by thy long-endured tortures,—I swear by the bitter tears which for so many centuries have been shed by thy unhappy children, by my own tears which I am pouring forth at this very moment,—I swear by the future liberty of my countrymen, that I consecrate myself wholly to thee; that hence forward thou shall be the cause and object of my thoughts, thy name the guide of my actions, and thy happiness the recompense of my labours."[3]

The members of the Philiki Etairia and their supporters decided that 1821 was an opportune time to stage their revolution. They felt that the populace supported a revolution; they misguidedly counted on the support of the Russians; and they noted that 500,000 of the Ottoman Empire's troops were tied up fighting Ali Pasha.

## ALI PASHA

Ali Pasha, a clever but brutal Albanian Muslim, had carved out a piece of Ottoman territory for himself. Pasha started his empire building in 1787, when he was awarded the pashalik of Trikala by the sultan in reward for his support for the sultan's war against Austria. From there he seized control of Ioannina, his center of government for the next 33 years. Area by area he gobbled up land for his own personal fiefdom. He took over areas of northwest Greece as well as parts of the Peloponnese. When Sultan Mahmud II came to power, he decided to put an end to Pasha's mini empire. In 1820, Mahmud's troops marched against Pasha. Pasha held out for 14 months. He was shot and killed, and his severed head was presented to the sultan in 1822. According to legend, as a sign of respect, the sultan kissed his beard.

Legends of Ali Pasha survive in folk songs. Vocalist George Dalaras sings about his brutal drowning of Kyra Frosini. Pasha's son had an affair with Frosini, a married woman. In 1801, she was accused of adultery. Pasha had her executed, along with 16 other women of supposedly ill repute. The women were bound to stone-laden bags and thrown off a boat in Lake Pamvotis. Pasha ordered that 250 pounds of sugar be thrown into the lake to sweeten the water for Frosini. According to local legend, on moonlit nights her ghost hovers over the lake.

Another folk song celebrates the courage of the women of Souli. In 1803, the Soulioti women defied Ali Pasha's Albanian Muslim troops by committing suicide rather than being taken captive. Because of the inaccessibility of their mountain villages in Epirus, the Souliotes had lived without domination by the Ottomans. However, they could not withstand the onslaught of Ali Pasha. Most of the Soulioti men were killed. To avoid being taken captive, the Soulioti women held their young children in their arms and one by one, while dancing a traditional line dance, they threw their children and themselves over a cliff of the Zalongo Mountain. Centenarian Vasiliki Scotes recalls the "Dance of Zalongo" she sang as a young woman growing up in Epirus:

A fish cannot live on dry land nor flowers on sandy shores.
So, too, the women of Souli did not learn to live as slaves.
Farewell to you springs of water, dales, mountains and high ridges.
Farewell to you poor, wretched world; farewell to you, life so sweet.
Farewell to you, our dear homeland; farewell to you forever.
As if bound for a festival, like a blooming lilac bush,
To Hades they were descending all laughter and all joy.
To Hades they were descending and in their arms the children.[4]

## DEVELOPMENT OF LEADERS

By 1687, the Venetians had taken over practically all of the Peloponnese. They held it until 1715. The Venetians gave the Greeks considerable autonomy. When the Ottomans regained the territory, they could not reestablish the control they had before. Officials ignored the prohibition about transfer of land to infidels. By the 18th and 19th centuries, powerful Greeks had taken over the feudal fiefs, assuming the leadership in their communities. Rich and poor, landowners and sharecroppers, lived together in small villages. Much as it does today, farmland surrounded the villages. Everyone living in close proximity forged strong bonds and contributed to a feeling of solidarity against the Ottoman oppressors. When the revolution started, the landowners, who were used to being in command, emerged as military and political leaders.

A group that lived in a remote region of the Peloponnese, the Mani, had been living autonomously for hundreds of years. Because of the inaccessibility of their mountain villages and their fierce nature, the Ottomans never ruled them. Their landowners/chieftains also took leadership positions in the revolution.

Other leaders developed out of the educated and wealthy class of Phanariots, many of whom had been educated in European universities. Two other groups that contributed leaders were the *klephts* (brigands), much experienced in guerrilla warfare, and the wealthy merchants/shipowners, islanders whose ships equipped the insurgent nation's navy.

## BEGINNING OF WAR

On February 24, 1821, Alexander Ypsilantis, former aide-de-camp to the Russian czar and leader of the Philiki Etairia, issued the proclamation, "Fight for Faith and Country" after he crossed the River Pruth from Russia to the Ottoman principality of Moldavia (present-day Romania). Enthusiastic Greeks, many of them students from Italy, Germany, and Russia, joined him in his struggle to gain independence from the Ottomans. This band of brothers was called the Sacred Battalion after the force that fought in Thebes in the fourth century BC. Together with the garrison of Moldavian prince Michael Soutsos, the insurgents advanced into Wallachia but met defeat at Drăgăsani. The forces that Ypsilantis had counted on from Tudor Vladimirescu, a Romanian, were not forthcoming. Nor did the Serbs or Russians support him.

Ypsilantis had asked the Russian czar: "Will you, Sire, abandon the Greeks to their fate, when a single word from you can deliver them from the most monstrous tyranny and save them from the horrors of a long and terrible struggle?"[5] In response, the czar denounced Ypsilantis. The Orthodox Patriarch Gregory V and 22 other bishops condemned the revolution.

Without the help he had counted on, within four months Ypsilantis's troops had been defeated. The Austrians held Ypsilantis in confinement for several years. He died in 1828, shortly after his release.

## REVOLT ON MAINLAND GREECE

According to a legend that has been proven untrue, Bishop Germanos of Patras raised the flag at the monastery of Hagia Lavra and gave his blessings to the Greek soldiers on March 25, 1821. Each year, on March 25, Greeks celebrate that date as Greek Independence Day. It has special significance since it is also a major church holiday, the Annunciation, which celebrates the day that the Archangel Gabriel told the Virgin Mary that she would bear the son of God, Jesus Christ. Greeks celebrate Greek Independence Day not only in Greece, but in cities and towns around the world. Children recite patriotic poems and adults give stirring speeches at public programs. The Greek diaspora communities of Chicago, New York, Boston, Baltimore, Detroit, Toronto, Melbourne, and Buenos Aires commemorate the event by parading down major city thoroughfares, with children dressed in colorful ethnic costumes, bands blasting, and city dignitaries at attention.

The Greek revolutionaries adopted the slogan "Liberty or Death." The Greeks forces fought hard and fierce for their freedom. A motley crew, they included two groups that considered themselves Greek—the Vlachs and the Arvanites—but they spoke languages that were different than Greek. The Vlachs spoke an eastern Romance language. The Arvanites, who migrated from the north between the 13th and 16th centuries, spoke an Albanian dialect. The two groups, the Vlachs and the Arvanites, claim to be related to the Greeks of ancient times.

Theodoros Kolokotronis, revolutionary war hero, scored major victories in the Peloponnese. He took pride in his role as leader of the Greek revolution. It has been reported that he had 400 pleats in his foustanella, one for each year that the Greeks were under Ottoman control. His statue, by Lazaros Sohos, stands in front of the National Historical Museum, which served as the parliament building from 1875 to 1935. (Photo by Elaine Thomopoulos)

Other than the philhellenes (friends of the Greeks) who came from Western Europe or America, the religious affiliation of the Greeks, Vlachs, and Albanians who supported the revolution was predominantly Greek Orthodox.

The freedom fighters included all classes of Greeks, poor illiterate peasants, rich landowners, European-schooled professionals, merchant shipowners, even black-robed priests who brandished pistols or swords.

Two groups of Greeks, the armatoloi and the klephts, had already had combat experience prior to the war. The armatoloi had been employed by the Ottomans to keep law and order—to ward off the roving bands of klephts who robbed rich and poor. Both the armatoloi and klephts were recruited into the army of the insurgents and made good soldiers. Greeks of today continue to sing folk songs that tell of the heroism of the klephts in the War of Independence. These former bandits became liberators.

The army of Greece mainly fought a guerrilla war. Like the klephts, they ambushed the enemy at mountain passes or attacked them while they were crossing a river, firing rifles from above. General Theodoros Kolokotronis, who had been a klepht, also had experience in the British service while he was in Zakynthos. Although he had been exposed to traditional warfare, he did not institute traditional warfare in the army of the revolution. He did bring some order to the armed forces by making sure that officers were appointed and given commissions and that there was a chain of command. He also insisted on keeping count of the number of men in a band. Thus captains couldn't so readily get excess rations, and men could not so easily desert. Sometimes Kolokotronis and other leaders took extreme measures to recruit soldiers. According to the historian David Brewer, Kolokotronis's son Panos was instructed to burn the houses of those who would not join the revolution and to distribute their goods to the revolutionary forces.

## VICTORIES FOR GREEKS AT THE BEGINNING

On March 23, 1821, Theodoros Kolokotronis's forces captured the weak Ottoman garrison in Kalamata. In April 1821, in retaliation for the uprising in the Peloponnese, the Ottomans hanged the Patriarch of Constantinople, Gregory V, even though he had cursed the revolution. His body was desecrated, dragged through the streets of Constantinople. A week later they hanged the former Ecumenical Patriarch Cyril VI and killed other prominent leaders.

These atrocities spurred the revolutionaries to even greater effort. They captured Monemvasia, Navarino (Pylos), Nafplion, and Tripolitsa (Tripoli) in the Peloponnese as well as Athens and Thebes.

A major victory occurred with the fall of Tripolitsa, on September 11, 1821. In Tripolitsa, Greek soldiers went on a rampage, butchering Jews as well as Turks, women and children as well as men. The harem of the Ottoman governor of the Peloponnese was spared. The legend is that Bouboulina, a heroine of the war, helped rescue them. The city had so many putrid unburied dead that a plague broke out. Some of the leaders of the War of Independence, such as Demetrios Ypsilantis and Alexandros Mavrocordatos, condemned the killing of thousands of Turkish and Jewish civilians. The philhellene Scotsman Thomas Gordon went home disgusted and did not return for another five years. The next year, Kolokotronis's forces went on to defeat the Ottoman army under Mahmud Dramali Pasha at Dervenakia.

At the beginning of the war, the navy had also been victorious. The Greeks prevailed in many of the sea battles because of their legendary fireships, ships loaded with explosives. The fireships, as with other warships of the Greek navy, had been privately owned merchant ships that had to be converted, at considerable expense to their owners, for the purpose of war. The captain and a small crew attached a fireship to the enemy ship. Before the ship exploded in flames, the crew escaped with their lives in a rowboat. The ships, as well as the sailors, came primarily from the islands of Hydra, Spetses, and Poros.

They contributed immensely to the war effort but suffered great losses during the War of Independence.

## MASSACRES OF THE GREEKS

The Ottomans massacred tens of thousands of Greek civilians in various towns and villages across Greece, Asia Minor, and Cyprus. The horrific slaughter of 25,000 or more civilians on the island of Chios in 1822 was captured in a painting by Eugene Delacroix. When exhibited at the Paris Salon of 1824, the painting stirred public opinion in support of the Greeks, in the same manner as the photos of the little naked girl burned by napalm and the slain students at Kent State swayed people in the United States against the Vietnam War. In June 1824, thousands of Greeks were slaughtered on the Aegean islands of Psara and Kassos.

In 1825, the Ottomans also laid siege to Messolongi, a city in western Greece. They had been unsuccessful at capturing the city in 1822 and 1823. Not giving up, they returned with a stronger army and navy. N. Kasomoulis describes this eyewitness account of the Greeks' survival strategies during the siege in Messolongi in February 1826:

> The partner of the typographer Mr. G. Mestheneas, who stayed at our place, slaughtered and ate a cat and made his errand boy Stornari kill another. He was the one that told the others to do the same thing and in a few days there were no cats at all. The doctor from Lefkas (P. Stephanitsis) cooked his with oil, of which there was plenty and praised it as the most tasty food.[6]

After a year facing continuous attack and starvation, on April 10, 1826, the Greeks of Messolongi decided on a mass exodus. The plan was betrayed. Few survived a subsequent massacre by the Ottoman-Egyptian troops.

These massacres of innocents helped gain support for the revolution among peoples of Europe, who in turn put pressure on their governments to help the revolutionaries.

## EGYPTIANS JOIN OTTOMANS

Things went well for the rebels in the first phase of the war. They gained control of areas in central and southern Greece. In 1825, things took a turn for the worse. Ibrahim Pasha, son of the leader of Egypt, Mehmet Ali, joined the Ottoman forces. By 1827, the Ottoman-Egyptian forces captured Modon (Methoni) and Corinth and recaptured Navarino, Messolongi, and Athens. The Great Powers, Britain, France, and Russia, tried to end the hostilities through the 1827 Treaty of London. However, the Ottomans were not interested in suspending the fighting since they were progressing well in the war.

## TURNING POINT—VICTORY AT BATTLE OF NAVARINO, OCTOBER 20, 1827

To fight an effective war, troops need arms and ammunition, food and clothes. To support their families, they need to be paid and not just rely on plunder taken after a battle. Wealthy merchant Greeks of the diaspora helped fund the war, merchant marines made their ships available, and philhellenes (European and American friends of the Greeks) gave their support, but that wasn't enough. The Greeks sought help from the countries of Europe.

In 1827, Britain, Russia, and France responded and turned the tide of the war. Since they were fearful of the Ottomans and Egypt getting control of Greece, they sent their combined fleet to Navarino Bay. The commander of the Great Powers fleet had issued orders that no one should fire upon the Egyptians. It is not known who fired the first shot. However, a musket shot escalated into a battle that resulted in the European fleet of 27 ships sinking 60 of the 89 Ottoman-Egyptian ships. Ottoman sultan Mahmud II found himself stripped of the forces that could defeat Greece and the Great Powers. A letter by Sir Robert Church describes the Battle of Navarino:

> The tremendous roar of the artillery of hundreds of ships of war, and the continual lightning of consuming fire, blazing awfully to announce the repeated peals bursting like thunder from thousands of heavy cannon will have already announced to many the glorious event of the destruction of the Turko-Egyptian fleet in the harbour of Navarino by the allied fleet of Britain, France and Russia under the supreme direction of His Exy Admiral Sir E. Codrington, and his noble supporters Admirals De Rigny and De Heyden—To those who from distance from the shores of Navarino could not have had the extreme delight of hearing the thunder of the Battle I have now the pleasure to communicate this signal interposition of divine Providence by the chastizing hands of the three Christian powers in favour of Greece.[7]

The sultan, upset about Russian participation in the Battle of Navarino, closed the Dardanelles to Russian ships. War broke out soon after, in April 1828. The outbreak of the Russian-Ottoman War diverted Ottoman troops from fighting the insurgents in Greece, thus influencing the outcome of the war. By 1829, Russia had defeated the Ottomans.

In 1828, a French expeditionary force came to help expel the Ottomans and Egyptians from mainland Greece. However, even prior to France's offer of help, Admiral Codrington and Mehmet Ali had agreed on the removal of Ibrahim's troops from the Peloponnese. The final battle, deciding Greek victorious, was the Battle of Petra in Boeotia, Greece, in the summer of 1829. The commander of the Greek troops was Demetrios Ypsilantis, brother of Alexandros Ypsilantis, who had started the revolution. Ypsilanti, Michigan, is named after Demetrios, and a bust of him stands in front of the water tower.

By 1829, the Greek quest for independence had been successful. Now all that remained was the question about boundaries and the form the new government would take.

## HEROES OF THE GREEK REVOLUTION

Heroes of the Greek revolution continue to be revered today. Their photos are displayed not only in the schools in Greece, but in the Greek schools of the diaspora as well. Here is a partial list of the heroes. Some of those previously mentioned, like Alexander and Demetrios Ypsilantis, are not included here.

### Odysseas Androutsos

On May 8, 1821, Odysseas Androutsos, with a band of about 100 guerrillas, held back a force of thousands (there is a report of 8,000) at Gravia in central Greece. In 1822, Ioannis Kolettis, Androutsos's political rival, accused him of being in contact with the Ottomans, and he was stripped of his command. In 1825, he was arrested and imprisoned in a tower on the Acropolis of Athens. He was found dead at the foot of the tower. The official report said that he fell while trying to escape, and an autopsy confirmed that his injuries were consistent with a fall. Years later a lawyer published an account of the murder of Androutsos that had been reported to him by a guard who had been on duty at the time. When four men approached the cell, the guard had been told to go to bed, but instead he hid. He heard a commotion and shouting. When he examined the dead body of Androutsos the next morning, he noted the swollen and bloody mouth and that the throat was bruised and bore fingernail marks.

### Markos Botsaris

Markos Botsaris, a Souliot, participated in battles in western Greece. He showed his mettle in combating the Ottomans in their attempted first siege of Messolongi in 1822–1823. On the night of August 21, 1823, he led the attack on Karpenisi in central Greece by 350 Souliots, against around 1,000 Ottoman troops. During this battle, Botsaris was mortally wounded by a shot to his head.

### Athanasios Diakos (Given Name, Massavetas)

Athanasios Diakos was a member of the Philiki Etairia and an ordained deacon (hence the nickname "Diakos") of the Greek Orthodox Church. He was arrested by the Ottomans following a battle at the bridge of Alamana in central Greece. According to popular legend, Diakos, who was wounded, was hauled before Omer Vryonis, the Ottoman commander. Vryonis offered to make him an officer in the Ottoman army if he converted to the Muslim religion.

Diakos replied, "Go you and your faith, you infidels, to destruction! I was born a Greek, a Greek will I die."[8] The next day he was impaled and died a terrible death. According to legend, as he was being led away to be executed he said, "Look at the time Charon chose to take me, now that the branches are flowering, and the earth sends forth grass."[9]

## Georgios Karaiskakis

Georgios Karaiskakis, the son of a nun and a klepht, was known as the Nun's Son and Gypsy (because of his dark complexion). At a young age, he became a lieutenant in a klepht band. When he was 15, Ali Pasha's troops captured him. Instead of being kept a prisoner, he rose through the ranks to become Ali Pasha's bodyguard. After he lost favor, he returned to life as a klepht. During the War of Independence, he helped in lifting the first siege of Messolongi and distinguished himself in the victorious battles at Arachova and Distomo. He was killed while he was trying to raise the Ottoman siege of Athens.

## Konstantinos Kanaris

Konstantinos Kanaris, from the island of Psara, served as an admiral in the Greek navy. With a fireship, he destroyed the flagship of the Ottoman navy off Chios. Kanaris led three successful attacks against the Ottoman fleet from 1822 to 1824. After liberation, Kanaris became prime minister.

## Theodoros Kolokotronis

Theodoros Kolokotronis was known as the "Old Man of the Morea" (the Peloponnese), since he commanded the revolutionary troops when he was in his 50s. As a youth, after his father was killed by the Ottomans, Kolokotronis joined a klepht band, and by the age of 15 had become leader of his own band. To escape the clutches of the Ottomans he went to the island of Zakynthos. There he served with the English for a couple of years and joined the Philiki Etairia. He demonstrated his military genius in the first year of the War of Independence with victories in the Peloponnese. In 1825, he was jailed by his political enemies in the provisional government under Petrobey Mavromichalis. However, a few months later, he was released to rejoin the war effort. In 1834, because of his opposition to the government under the king, he was tried for treason and given the death sentence. The king pardoned him in 1835.

### Ioannis Makriyannis (Triantaphyllou)

Ioannis Makriyannis, who was born at Avoriti in eastern Greece, partici-
pated in the battle at the Lerna Mills, south of Argos, along with Ypsilantis and
Petrobey Mavromichalis. With only 300 men, they held off the 4,000 troops of
Ibrahim Pasha. With the arrival of more troops they were able to defeat the
Ottoman-Egyptian forces. He learned to read and write so that he could write
his memoirs of the war and its aftermath.

### Alexander Mavrocordatos

Alexander Mavrocordatos, who was from a wealthy Phanariot family, contributed to the independence effort, both militarily and politically. The First
National Assembly, which convened in December 1821, elected him president.
He commanded the troops that advanced into western central Greece in 1822,
but the troops were defeated at Peta. He and his troops succeeded in resisting
the first of two sieges of Messolongi.

### Andreas Miaoulis

Admiral Andreas Miaoulis, who was born in Euboea and moved to Hydra,
became the captain of a commercial ship at age 17. He ran the British blockade
for the French during the Napoleonic wars. During the War of Independence,
he defeated the Ottoman Navy near Patra and the Ottoman-Egyptian Navy in
the Bay of Gerontas. He supplied Messolongi with provisions when they were
under siege. He retired from service when Edward Codrington of the British
Royal Navy took control of the combined English, French, and Russian fleets
at the Battle of Navarino.

In July 1831, in the civil war that followed independence, he tried to wrest
control of the Greek fleet. When Miaoulis was asked to surrender the fleet that
remained in his command, he destroyed part of the fleet instead.

### Papaflessas (also known as Gregorios Diakos)

Papaflessas was born in Messenia as Georgios Flessas. As a clergyman,
he was known as Papaflessas (*papa* means priest) and took the ecclesiastical
name Gregorios. He left Greece to escape a sentence of death by the Ottoman
authorities. He joined the Philiki Etairia, and he returned to spread the word
about the revolution. He showed his courage in the Battle of Maniaki against
Ibrahim Pasha's Egyptian troops, which took place in 1825. His outnumbered
troops were defeated, and he was killed.

### Petrobey Mavromichalis

Petrobey Mavromichalis was the leader of the Mani region of southern
Peloponnese for much of the first half of the 19th century. He scored an early

victory in the War of Independence when he liberated Kalamata on March 23, 1821. His clash with opposing political forces caused him to be imprisoned. After his release from prison and the enthronement of King Otto, he served in the senate of the new nation.

## Nikitaras (Nikitas Stamatelopoulos)

Nikitaras, nephew of Kolokotronis, was born in the Peloponnese. After serving in the English army based in the Ionian Islands, in 1821 he headed a band of freedom fighters. He achieved his fame in the Battle of Dervenakia, a major victory. In this battle, he is said to have broken four of the five swords he used. Because of his exploits in this battle, Nikitaras took the nickname of Tourkophagos (Turk-eater).

## HEROINES OF THE REVOLUTION

At the time of the War of Independence, a woman's place was in the home. Nevertheless, women did help with the war effort, not only by supplying food and clothing and giving jewelry and money, but by assuming leadership positions. Manto Mavrogenous and Laskarina Bouboulina excelled as leaders.

## Manto Mavrogenous

Manto Mavrogenous was born in Trieste, Austria (now part of Italy), to a Phanariot family of wealth and nobility. She went to college in Trieste, where she studied ancient Greek philosophy and history. She spoke French, Italian, and Turkish as well as Greek.

The family moved to Paros in 1809, and, after her father died, to Tinos. After the revolution started she moved to Mykonos, where her family had originated. She mobilized the islanders of Mykonos in repelling the Ottomans who had come to attack the island. She participated in the battle in Karystos in 1822 with a fleet of six ships and an infantry of about 800 men. Her men also participated in the Battles of Dervenakia, Pelion, Phthiotis, and Livadeia. She sold her jewelry to finance the equipment of men who fought the Ottoman fleet in the Cyclades. She also ventured to Paris and other European cities to persuade the women there to support the War of Independence.

After her fiancé, the revolutionary war hero Demetrios Ypsilantis, broke off their engagement, she became depressed. Although she was a stunning beauty, she never married. She died poor, having spent her money in the service of independence. Ioannis Kapodistrias's government honored her by awarding her the title of lieutenant general and gave her a home in Nafplion. Mykonos has named a town square after her, and the house in which she lived in Paros stands as an historical monument.

## Laskarina Bouboulina

Laskarina Bouboulina's revolutionary spirit must have been in her blood. Her father had been imprisoned in Constantinople for his participation in the Peloponnesian revolution against the Ottomans in 1769–1770, the Orlov Revolt. She was born while her mother was visiting her dying father in prison. She lived in Hydra for four years with her mother, and when her mother remarried she moved to Spetses. By the time she became involved with the revolutionary cause, she had been widowed twice (both of her husbands had been ship captains) and had seven children. Her eldest son was killed fighting in the War of Independence.

Bouboulina fought for her country, in command of her own vessels. On March 13, 1821, she raised a revolutionary flag of her own design on Spetses. On April 3, the island of Spetses revolted, followed shortly by Hydra and Psara. She supplied an army of soldiers from Spetses with food, weapons, and ammunition during the first two years of the war. Before the outbreak of the war, she had also constructed one of largest warships of the War of Independence, the *Agamemnon*, at her own expense, bribing the Turkish official so he would look the other way while the ship was being built. Her ships participated in blockades and battles at Nafplion, Monemvasia, and Navarino (Pylos).

General Ioannis Makriyannis (Triantaphyllou) led his men to victory in several battles against the Ottomans during the War of Independence. He learned to write in order to write his memoirs, which were written in demotic. Nobel Laureate George Seferis thought of him as one of the greatest masters of modern Greek prose. (Photo by Elaine Thomopoulos)

Theodoros Kolokotronis counted her as a friend. She was in Tripolitsa (she had supplied a contingent of 50 men) when he captured that city. Later, their children, Eleni Bouboulina and Panos Kolokotronis, married. Following the war, she lived in the capital, Nafplion. After being arrested twice, she was exiled to Spetses. In 1825, her life came to a tragic end. She died instantly when an unknown assailant shot her in the forehead as she stood on the balcony of her home. This occurred after her son had eloped with one of the daughters of the Koutsis family.

On the island of Spetses, Bouboulina's family maintains a museum dedicated to her. Throughout Greece, streets are named after her and songs commemorate this heroine who contributed so much so that Greece could become independent.

## PHILHELLENES (FRIENDS OF THE HELLENES)

Adventurous and committed philhellenes made an impact on the outcome of the revolution. Those with an education in the classics admired the Greeks for their contribution to Western civilization. In addition, the small Christian enslaved nation fighting off the large Muslim Ottoman Empire (like David with Goliath) attracted them to the cause. The massacres of civilians by the Ottomans also elicited the support of Europeans and Americans. The philhellenes contributed in a variety of ways, from writing poems, painting pictures, and raising money to actually fighting in the battles. About 1,200 are believed to have fought in the war. Philhellenes included Shelley, Goethe, Schiller, Victor Hugo, Alfred de Musset, Lord Byron, painter Eugene Delacroix, and banker Jean-Gabriel Eynard. The poet Percy Shelley said, "We are all Greeks. Our laws, our literature, our religion, our arts, have their root in Greece."[10]

Philhellenes raised money to help the Greek cause and generated public opinion in support of the Greeks' efforts. The London Greek Committee (composed of non-Greeks) extended loans to the insurgents and sent Lord Byron to Greece in 1823 to negotiate the first loan.

Lord Byron continues to be revered in Greece today. He helped in supplying cash, not only from the loan extended by the London Greek Committee, but from his own personal resources as well. More important, his poetry helped the Greek cause by arousing public support in Europe. One stanza of Byron's poem "The Isles of Greece" follows:

The mountains look on Marathon—
And Marathon looks on the sea;
And musing there an hour alone;
I dream'd that Greece might still be free;
For standing on the Persians' grave.
I could not deem myself a slave.[11]

In January 1824, just three months after his arrival in Greece, as he prepared to lead troops into battle, Byron died of a fever in Messolongi. His death rallied others to the cause.

Besides the London Committee, there were other Greek committees set up throughout Europe. "Greek fever" spread across the Atlantic Ocean to the United States. The revolutionaries wrote appeals to politicians in the United States. Edward Everell, who was a congressman and president of Harvard, said that the Americans should care about the Greeks because of their "common interest in Freedom and Virtue." Daniel Webster also supported the effort, bringing forth a motion in congress to send an envoy and to appropriate money toward the effort. On January 19, 1824, he said: "I have in mind the modern not the ancient, the alive and not the dead Greece . . . today's Greece, fighting against unprecedented difficulties . . . a Greece fighting for its existence and for the common privilege of human existence."[12]

The United States remained neutral and did not send any money, but an American-built warship, the *Hope*, renamed *Hellas*, was used by the Greek navy. Educational institutions and churches raised money by holding lectures, balls, and theatrical performances. Ministers appealed from the pulpit. An African American group helped by holding a ball in New York City.

Among the best known of the American philhellenes was George Jarvis, known as Captain Zervis. Also active was Captain Jonathan Peckham Miller of Vermont. True philhellenes, they learned to speak Greek and wore the traditional *foustanella* (kilt).

Dr. Samuel Gridley Howe served as a surgeon in the Greek army. He returned to the United States in 1827, where he raised $60,000 for the relief of refugees.

Volunteers came from Europe also. Some of them became commanders in the armed forces. Eleven ships sailed from Marseilles between the beginning of the revolution in 1821 and 1822, bringing 360 idealistic young volunteers to fight in the War of Independence. They most often supplied their own uniforms and arms.

## FIGHTING AMONG FREEDOM FIGHTERS

The leaders convened for their First National Assembly in Piada (near Epidaurus) in 1821. In January 1822, they declared their independence. An excerpt from their proclamation follows:

> For us the descendants of the wise and philanthropic Greek Nation, contemporary with the enlightened and favoured countries of Europe and spectators of the good acts which the latter enjoy under the unbreakable aegis of the laws, it was no longer possible for us to bear until

heartlessness and credulity the hard plague of the Ottoman State which already for about four centuries oppressed us harshly and was opposed to reason pretending that it knew of the law, persecuted and ordered everything in a tyrannical and arbitrary manner. After a long slavery we were finally forced to take up arms and defend ourselves and our country from such a horrifying and unjust—from the beginning—oppression, similar or capable of being compared to no other.

Our war against the Turks, far from being based on demagogic and mutinous or selfish principles of the Greek Nation, is a national war, a sacred war, the sole purpose of which is the regaining of the rights of our personal liberty, property, and honour.[13]

The First National Assembly elected Georgios Kountouriotis, a wealthy Hydriot sea captain, as head of the government. However, a faction led by Kolokotronis opposed him. In December 1822, Kolokotronis had captured the port city of Nafplion and put it under control of his son Panos. His son would not allow the Kountouriotis political faction to convene the Second Assembly there.

Finally the Second Assembly convened in Astros in the spring of 1823 and elected the wealthy landowner and chieftain from Mani, Petrobey Mavromichalis, as president. They revised the provisional constitution of the First National Assembly. The Greeks who came together agreed that they could no longer tolerate the reign of the Ottoman Empire, but they disagreed on how the nation should be governed and who should govern it. Like children playing "King of the Mountain," but dead serious, they killed to determine who would be in control.

In 1823 and 1824, civil strife continued between the two factions, one headed by Kountouriotis, which included maritime Greeks and Greeks of western Roumeli, and the other by Kolokotronis, which contained many from the Peloponnese.

In June 1824, the group in support of Kountouriotis defeated Mavromichalis at the mills of Lerna, a crucial loss since the mills supplied grain to Nafplion. After Kolokotronis's son abandoned Nafplion, Kountouriotis resumed his position as leader of the government and served in this position until 1827.

To rid himself of his rival, Kountouriotis imprisoned Kolokotronis, as well as some of the followers of Kolokotronis. However, after the Greek military defeat of New Navarino, he released these trained warriors so that they could fight the combined Ottoman-Egyptian forces.

The infighting continued. The Third National Assembly, which convened at Piada, was cut short by the fall of Messolongi. Because of disagreements, two rival groups met separately. The factions finally came together at Troezen. With 168 delegates assembled, in April 1827 they elected Count Ioannis

WESTERN THRACE
EASTERN THRACE
Black Sea
MACEDONIA
Sea of Marmara
EPIRUS
THESSALY
IONIAN ISLANDS
CENTRAL GREECE
AEGEAN ISLANDS
Izmir Smyrna
Aegean Sea
PELOPONNESE
Athens
Ionian Sea

Kingdom of Greece, 1832
Ceded by Britain, 1864
Ceded by Ottomans, 1881
Ceded after Balkan Wars, 1913
Ceded by Bulgaria, 1920
Ceded by unratified Treaty of Sevres, 1920; lost by Treaty of Lausanne, 1923
Ceded by Italy, 1948

DODECANESE
CRETE
Mediterranean Sea

**GREEK TERRITORIAL GAINS 1832-1948**

(Courtesy of Jeff Dixon) (In this map, boundaries between regions are not delineated.)

Kapodistrias, who had previously served in the Russian foreign service, to a seven-year term. In May, they approved a constitution. A cheering crowd greeted Kapodistrias when he arrived in January 1828. They had high expectations for the future of Greece at the hands of this distinguished leader.

## BECOMING INDEPENDENT

In 1829, with the help of the Great Powers, Greece won its independence. At that time, Greece was only a fraction of the size it is today. Then it was 18,346 square miles. Now it is 51,146 square miles. The total population in 1828 was about 800,000. In 2001, it was 10,964,020. The Greece following the War of Independence included central Greece (Sterea Ellas), southern Greece (the Peloponnese), the Aegean island of Euboea, and the Cyclades Islands in the Aegean Sea. The Cyclades includes the now popular tourist destinations of Santorini and Mykonos.

Various regions of what is now Greece were added in bits and pieces, most often with sacrifice and war. In 1864, Greece received the Ionian Islands from Britain. The acquisition of Thessaly and part of Epirus came after the Treaty of Berlin in 1881. After the two Balkan Wars (1912–1913), Greece, a victor, added the rest of the region of Epirus, Macedonia, Crete, and some of the other Aegean islands, including Samos, to its territory. After World War I, in 1920, Western Thrace joined Greece. It wasn't until 1948, with the addition of the Dodecanese Islands of the Aegean, that Greece pieced together the territory that now constitutes the nation.

## THE GOVERNANCE OF THE NEW NATION UNDER KAPODISTRIAS

On January 8, 1828, Kapodistrias arrived in Nafplion on the British frigate *Warstripe,* accompanied by a French frigate and a Russian frigate. Because of civil strife, a week later the government reassembled on the island of Aegina in the Aegean. In 1829, the government made Nafplion its capital and met in a former mosque.

Kapodistrias faced the challenge of a nation devastated not only by a hard-won War of Independence but also by a continuing civil war. During the War of Independence, up to 200,000 lost their lives. They lost their homes, livestock, and crops because of the battles, as well as the "scorched earth" policy of the departing Ottoman and Egyptian foes. In some areas, it was rare to find a house with both roof and walls intact. Disease and hunger devastated the people.

To stem the epidemics of typhus, dysentery, and cholera, Kapodistrias's government instituted quarantines. To help the food crisis, Kapodistrias had a shipment of potatoes sent to Greece. However, Greeks were reluctant to try them. According to legend, he then ordered that the potatoes be dumped on the docks of Nafplion and placed under guard. Rumors circulated that since the potatoes were so well guarded, they must be of great value. Before long someone tried to steal some of these "valuable" potatoes. Since the guards were told to ignore the stealing, it wasn't long before the whole shipment disappeared. The potato continues to be an important part of Greek cuisine today.

Kapodistrias tried to give the new nation stability through a strong central government. Instead of relying on the direction of the Senate, as envisioned in the constitution that the assembly had adopted the year before, he persuaded the Senate to let themselves be replaced by a 27-member Panhellenion appointed by him and under his control. He believed that a representative government was "like giving a child a razor. The child did not need it yet and might kill himself with it."[14] By appointing people loyal to him to the Panhellenion, Kapodistrias could direct the course of the new nation.

The new constitution provided for freedom of the press, but when a young man named Polyzoides set up the newspaper *Apollo* to present the views of the opposition, the first issue was confiscated, and the government took over the machinery and the plant. According to historian W. Allison Phillips, when Polyzoides questioned the government's action, Kapodistrias protested that he had no intention of interfering with the liberty of the press; but "liberty was no license, and that he reserved to the government the right of deciding when the bounds between the two had been overstepped."[15]

The popular poet Alexander Soutsos satirized Kapodistrias's policy:

My friend, the press is free—for him who spares the crowd
Of government officials and their friends,
Nor criticizes ministerial means and ends.
The press is free, my friend—but writing's not allowed.[16]

Kapodistrias worked long hours trying to bring order to the chaos following the War of Independence. However, many objected when he took control of the government rather than acting as a leader of a democratic nation as envisioned in the constitution. He offended some who felt they had been left out of leadership positions after all the sacrifices they had made. Each of the factions looked out for their own interests. The landowners objected to Kapodistrias's efforts for land reform. Many had already taken over much the land that the Ottomans had vacated. Neither did the merchant seamen like him. When they asked to be reimbursed for their considerable expenses during the war, Kapodistrias offered them a compensation they believed insufficient. The Mavromichalis clan of the Mani area of Peloponnese, with Petrobey Mavromichalis as its chief, also objected to not being reimbursed for expenses incurred during the war. Additionally they objected to paying taxes. The independent Mani chieftains had been accustomed to governing their own territory and had done so even under the rule of the Ottomans.

In December 1830, a rebel group asserted their independence from the state. They convened their own assembly and appointed Mavromichalis as president. Kapodistrias had Mavromichalis and other rebels arrested, and detained them without trial at Nafplion. A provisional government, which included Miaoulis, Mavrocordatos, and Kountouriotis, took possession of the island of Poros. They asked for the following: the convening of a national assembly; liberty of the press; and the release of certain prisoners, including Mavromichalis. Kapodistrias did not yield to their demands.

To curb the rebel group under Mavromichalis, Admiral Kanaris amassed a fleet at Poros in order to blockade the rebels. At the end of July 1831, the rebel Admiral Miaoulis seized some of the ships that Kanaris had gathered at Poros. When the Russian admiral Ricord asked Miaoulis to hand over the ships he commanded, he refused. Miaoulis blew up some of the ships, including the flagship *Ellas*.

## ASSASSINATION OF KAPODISTRIAS AND CIVIL WAR

On October 9, 1831, while Kapodistrias was on his way to attend liturgy at St. Demetrios Church in Nafplion, Mavromichalis's son Georgios stabbed Kapodistrias in the chest with a dagger, while his brother Konstantinos shot him in the back of the head. The president died immediately. Konstantinos was killed near the scene of the crime. A couple of weeks later, Georgios was executed. His father, Petrobey, was released from prison, and after King Otto assumed the throne, he served as vice president of the senate.

Following the death of Kapodistrias, civil war broke out between Kolettis's supporters and those who favored Augustinos Kapodistrias, the slain president's brother. He was supported by Kolokotronis and the Russians. Ioannis Kolettis had the backing of those from the area of Roumeli and the French.

Kolettis had gained control of Argos, Tripolitsa, and Nafplion and thus wrested control from Kolokotronis, who had held this area previously. The Kolettis group supported having King Otto, whom the Great Powers had selected as the monarch of Greece. However, Kolokotronis, although he had earlier supported the king, now opposed him.

Kolokotronis unsuccessfully attempted to set up a rival government. He offered the presidency of the rival government to Russian admiral Ricord, who declined. Kolokotronis attacked the Kolettis government by breaking up its assembly at Pronoia, near Nafplion. His group also attacked the French at Argos. On June 7, 1834, he was charged with treason, imprisoned at Nafplion, and sentenced to death. He received a pardon from the king in 1835.

## NOTES

1. David Brewer, *The Greek War of Independence* (Woodstock, NY: Overlook Press, 2003), 20.

2. Rigas Feraios, "New Political Constitution," original draft scanned from the collection of the Hellenic Parliament, http://www.hellenicparliament.gr/UserFiles/f3c70a23-7696-49db-9148-f24dce6a27c8/syn01.pdf. Translation by Elaine Thomopoulos.

3. George Waddington, *A Visit to Greece 1823–1824* (London: John Murray, 1825), xxvii, xxix, http://books.google.com/books?id=SX82AAAAMAAJ&pg =PR28&lpg=PR28&dq=oath+of+philike&source=bl&ots=TYG2OA6EoE& sig=ZrGk6t9xwmQ5JRN90zVXQWjzDVM&hl=en&ei=9bkFSpbJKIOR jAf1_Lj4BA&sa=X&oi=book_result&ct=result&resnum=6#v=onepage&q=o ath%20of%20philike&f=false.

4. Vasiliki Scotes and Thomas J. Scotes, *A Weft of Memory: A Greek Mother's Recollection of Songs and Poems* (Scarsdale, NY: Caratzas/Melissa International, 2008), 9. Used by permission.

5. Brewer, *The Greek War of Independence,* 54.

6. N. Kasomoulis, *Enthymimata stratiotika tis epanastaseos ton Ellinon, 1821– 1833* [Military Memoirs of the Hellenic Revolution, 1821–1833], vol. 2, ed. G. Vlachogiannis (Athens: 1940), 242. From the website "The Formation of the Hellenic State 1821–1897," http://www.fhw.gr/chronos/12/en/1821_1833/ sources/03.html.

7. C. W. Crawley, *The Question of Greek Independence: A Study of British Policy in the Near East, 1821–1830* (Cambridge, England: Cambridge University Press, 1930), 232, http://www.questia.com/PM.qst?a=o&d=4911867.

8. Alexander Eliot, *Greece* (New York: Time-Life Books, 1968), 63.

9. Douglas Dakin, *The Greek Struggle for Independence, 1821–1833* (Berkeley: University of California Press, 1973), 30.

10. Percy Bysshe Shelley, *The Poetical Works of Percy Bysshe Shelley,* vol. 2 (London: Edward Moxon, 1845), 286, http://books.google.com/books ?id=jGw-AAAAYAAJ&pg=PA286&dq=Shelley+We+are+all+Greeks&hl=en& ei=8SyETcmdKOea0QGB8dnjCA&sa=X&oi=book_result&ct=result&resnum= 6&ved=0CEQQ6AEwBQ#v=onepage&q&f=false.

11. "Modern History Sourcebook: Lord Byron: The Isles of Greece," http:// www.fordham.edu/halsall/mod/byron-greece.html.

12. George C. Chryssis, "American Philhellenes and the Greek War for Independence," Hellenic Communication Service L.L.C. http://www.hellenic comserve.com/greek_war_for_independence.html.

13. "The Proclamation of the First National Assembly," Formation of the Hellenic State, http://www.fhw.gr/chronos/12/en/1821_1833/sources/02. html.

14. Brewer, *The Greek War of Independence,* 338.

15. W. Alison Phillips, *The War of Independence 1821 to 1833* (London: Smithe, Elder & Co., 1897), 346. http://www.archive.org/stream/warofgree kindepe00philiala#page/n3/mode/2up.

16. Phillips, *War of Independence,* 347.

# 6

# Establishing an Independent Nation

Several conferences were held and treaties negotiated prior to ironing out the final agreement that recognized Greece as an independent nation in 1832. They included the 1829 Treaty of Adrianople, a settlement forged between the Russians and the Ottomans after the defeat of the Ottomans in the Russian-Ottoman War. The settlement contained the promise of autonomy for the fledging Greek nation. Then in 1830, the Great Powers (Britain, France, and Russia) met in London and adopted a protocol that declared Greece an independent state under their protection. They decided that in order to bring calm to the warring factions within Greece, the best course would be to appoint a monarch.

By 1832, after a meeting in Constantinople, the new country was recognized as the Hellenic Kingdom. The powers agreed on the following provisions:

- The borders of Greece would consist of the Greek mainland south of a line drawn from Arta to Volos and encompass the Greek mainland (Central Greece and the Peloponnese) as well as Euboea and the Cyclades Islands in the Aegean Sea.
- Greece would pay the Ottomans 40,000 piasters for the loss of its lands.
- Prince Otto of Bavaria would be king.
- Until the 17-year-old king became 20 years old, the nation would be ruled by three Bavarian regents.

King Otto (Othon in Greek) arrived in Nafplion on January 1833, along with the Bavarian regents and a Bavarian army of 3,500. Other Bavarians also followed him to Athens, including the brewmaster, Johan Ludwig Fuchs. His son, Carl Johan, established the Fix Brewery in 1864.

## KING OTTO

King Otto was from the House of Wittelsbach of Bavaria. He and his wife, Amalia, had no children. The six kings who succeeded him hailed from the House of Glücksburg of Denmark. Throughout Greece's history the monarchy has been dismissed and then reinstated. The monarchy ended in 1974.

In 1835, when King Otto became of age, he took over the leadership of Greece and ruled as an absolute monarch until 1843. He continued as a constitutional monarch until 1862, when he was forced to leave Greece.

King Otto faced many challenges in the three decades he served as king. During the War of Independence, many of Greece's people had succumbed to bloodshed or had been displaced from their homes. Many of the peasants lived in hovels and could barely eke out enough food from the earth to survive. The countryside had been torn up; forests burned; huge debts were due to the Great Powers; the economy was in shambles. Unfortunately, Greece's political parties did not come together to govern the country effectively. Each of the parties had its own agenda, and each was aligned with either Russia, France, or Britain.

## ATHENS AS CAPITAL, 1834

King Otto and the regents decided on Athens as Greece's capital, mainly because of its historic legacy. At the time, only about 12,000 people resided in Athens and the surrounding area. During King Otto's reign, the following neo-classical buildings were built: University of Athens, Old Royal Palace (now the Greek Parliament Building), and National Gardens of Athens. The buildings had a view of the Acropolis.

Unfortunately, by the time that King Otto became regent, the Parthenon of the Acropolis had been badly scarred. A sixth-century attempt to convert the Parthenon to a Christian church collapsed the west pediment. In 1687, in an attempt of Venetians to wrest control of Athens from the Ottomans, an explosion of powder housed in the Parthenon caused even more extensive damage. Just before the War of Independence, between 1801 and 1812, half of the surviving sculptures of the Parthenon, as well as objects from other buildings on the Acropolis, had been removed by Lord Elgin, who was the British ambassador to the Ottoman Empire from 1799 to 1803. The Parthenon marbles were purchased from Elgin by Britain in 1816 and are now on display in the British Museum.

Greece has questioned the legality of Britain holding the Parthenon marbles. Blank spaces highlight their omission from the New Acropolis Museum, which opened in 2009. Nicolai Ouroussoff, in an article titled "The New Acropolis Museum Is Missing the Elgin Marbles," said,

> A panel depicting the receding tail of one horse and the advancing head of another with an expanse of blank stone in between is breathtaking. But it's hard to picture how it originally fit into the Parthenon. The lack of context is only reinforced by Lord Elgin's decision two centuries ago to cut the works out of the huge blocks of stone into which they were originally carved, a cruel act of vandalism intended to make them easier to ship.
>
> In dismantling the ruins of one of the glories of Western civilization, Lord Elgin robbed them of their meaning. The profound connection of the marbles to the civilization that produced them is lost.
>
> Mr. [Bernard] Tschumi's great accomplishment is to express this truth in architectural form. Without pomp or histrionics, his building makes the argument for the marbles' return to Athens.[1]

## LANGUAGE: *KATHAREVOUSA* OR *DEMOTIKI?*

The leaders of the nation debated what to use as its official language. Modern spoken Greek, as any dynamic language, had been influenced by the myriad peoples who had inhabited Greece since ancient times. The Greek language had developed from the ancient Greek used by Homer to the *koine*, the language used as the lingua franca throughout the Roman Empire. Koine was the original language used in the New Testament and the Greek translation of the Old Testament, the Septuagint. Greek Orthodox churches continue to use the koine in their church services.

The language spoken by the newly liberated common people of Greece was different from koine. Adamantios Korais, an intellectual and a patriot, thought that the demotic language had been bastardized by the addition of Turkish, Latin, and Italian words. Early in the 19th century he introduced a revised Greek, which was later called *katharevousa*. Scrubbed *katharo* (clean) of foreign influences and using rules that were used in the language of Plato and Aristotle, this new language was a compromise between ancient Greek and modern spoken Greek (demotic) and was embraced by many of the educated upper classes.

Others such as Ioannis Psycharis, who in 1888 published his book *My Journey* in the *demotiki* (demotic), believed that the nation would be best served by use of the dynamic language of the common people. Both those who wanted katharevousa to be used and those who rallied for the demotic felt that the language used reflected their identity as Greeks. Those who lobbied for katharevousa took pride in their ancient heritage and wanted to retain the linguistic link to their ancestors.

Opponents of katharevousa felt that it enforced a class system to the detriment of the nation since it made the education of the ordinary people more difficult. They argued that those who had not gone beyond high school could hardly understand it, nor could they read a newspaper or book written in katharevousa. The debate about which of the two languages to use started from the birth of the nation. In 1834, katharevousa was adopted by the Greek government and continued until 1976, when demotic became the official language. The language question resulted in two riots. In 1901, there was a riot against A. Pallis's translation of the New Testament. In 1903, the use of the demotic in the National Theater's production of Aeschylus's *Oresteia* led to a riot.

The Greek language had five different types of accents. In ancient times, some of the accent marks indicated not only which syllable to accent, but also which pitch to use. In modern times the elaborate accent system no longer served its original function. Greek children celebrated when the accent system was abandoned in 1981. It is estimated that about 3,000 of 12,000 hours spent on grammar had been spent on learning this system. Now only one accent mark is used, indicating which syllable is to be stressed.

In 1833, the Orthodox Church of Greece declared itself autocephalous. However, the Patriarchate in Constantinople, which previously had direct jurisdiction over the church community in Greece, did not recognize the Church of Greece until 1850.

## CONSTITUTION OF 1843

The Greek Orthodox Church, as well as the populace, was upset that King Otto did not convert from Catholicism to Eastern Orthodoxy. Also, the people were critical of him because of the poor state of the economy and high taxes. The army, joined by the people, rebelled against his policies and autocratic rule. They gathered in Athens and demanded a constitution and a permanent national assembly. King Otto gave in to their demands. To commemorate the constitution, which was granted in 1843, the square across the Parliament Building was renamed Constitution Square. The constitution provided for two houses, one elected by universal male suffrage and the other appointed for life by the king. The constitution also specified that King Otto's successor be Orthodox.

## DON PACIFICO AFFAIR AND BRITISH GUNBOAT DIPLOMACY, 1847–1850

According to Don Pacifico, the former Portuguese consul-general to Athens, an anti-Semitic mob vandalized his home in Athens in the spring of 1847, and the Greek authorities did nothing to protect him. Don Pacifico, a Portuguese Jew who was a British citizen given that he had been born in Gibraltar, asked for the British to intervene. When Pacifico failed to get compensation from the Greek government, British foreign secretary Lord Palmerston took a drastic measure. In 1850, he sent a naval squadron to blockade the port of Piraeus. The navy seized Greek merchant ships, even though France and Russia objected.

## CRIMEAN WAR, 1853–1856

From 1853 to 1856, the Crimean War was fought between the Russian Empire and an alliance composed of the British Empire, France, the Ottoman Empire, and the Kingdom of Sardinia. When Russia sought support from Greece, King Otto encouraged soldiers to move across the borders of Greece (the Arta-Volos line) into Ottoman-occupied Thessaly. In short time, the Ottomans defeated the Greek troops. The British and French occupied Piraeus, Greece, to stop any further action Greece might take to help Russia. They also forced King Otto to declare neutrality and appoint another government.

## KING OTTO FORCED OUT, 1862

In February 1862, the garrisons at Nafplion and Athens rose in revolt against King Otto. A provisional government under Dimitrios Voulgaris was formed in October 1862, and the parliament voted that King Otto's rule should end. King Otto left Greece on a British ship "to avoid civil war," as he said. He lived for a few years in exile in Bavaria prior to his death in 1867. He continued to display his patriotism toward Greece by wearing the traditional *foustanella* (kilt). He also supplied the Cretans with funds for their unsuccessful 1866 rebellion against the Ottomans.

## KING OTTO'S ACCOMPLISHMENTS

King Otto loved his country and started the process of nation building. His administration set up the capital in Athens. They organized a free public education system, which included a university in Athens. Under his watch, Greece established a legal code and judicial system. After the Bavarian troops left, he replaced them with national armed forces.

When King Otto took power, much of the land was concentrated in the hands of wealthy landowners, with few of the farmers owning the land they farmed. After the War of Independence, the government seized vacated Ottoman estates. King Otto's land reform under the "Law for the Dotation of Greek Families" in 1835 helped thousands of farmers by extending low-cost

The Danish prince, George Christian William of the House of Glücksburg, was crowned king of the Hellenes in 1862 and served until 1913, when he was assassinated. (Courtesy of National Historical Museum)

loans. However, this did not have the success that was hoped for, because in many cases the loan amount did not provide enough money to buy a decent plot of land.

## THE 50-YEAR RULE OF KING GEORGE, 1863–1913

Prince Alfred of Great Britain was selected as king by an overwhelming majority in Greece's first referendum in November 1862. However, because he was from Britain, and the Great Powers had decided in 1832 that the monarchy should not come from one of their countries, he was not appointed king. Instead, the crown was offered to the 17-year-old Danish prince, George Christian William of the House of Glücksburg, after he was voted in by the Greek assembly. He was crowned King George in 1863 and served until his assassination in 1913—nearly 50 years. Subsequent kings included his son Constantine; Constantine's three sons (George II, Alexander, and Paul); and Paul's son (Constantine II).

King George was given the title king of the Hellenes, rather than king of Greece, the title that King Otto had. This new title implied that his responsibility did not stop with the newly declared nation but extended to the millions of Greeks who resided outside of Greece. It hinted at what was to dominate at the beginning of the 20th century—the *Megali Idea* (Great Vision). The vision of reclaiming lost lands had grown in the minds of the Greeks since the start of the nation. In January 1844, Prime Minister Ioannis Kolettis spoke to the National Assembly:

> The Kingdom of Greece is not Greece. It constitutes only one part, the smallest and the poorest....A Greek is not only a man who lives within the Kingdom, but also one who lives in Ioannina, Serres, Adrianople, Constantinople, Smyrna, Trebizond, Crete, in Samos and in any land associated with Greek history and the Greek race....There are two main centres of Hellenism: Athens, the capital of the kingdom, [and] "The City" [Constantinople], the dream and hope of all Greeks.[2]

## CONSTITUTION OF 1864 AND ANNEXATION OF THE IONIAN ISLANDS, 1864

During King George's rule, in 1864, Greece instituted a new constitution. It abolished the senate, which had been appointed by the king. Instead there was a one-chambered parliament. Male property owners 25 years of age and older elected the members.

In 1864, Greece expanded its territory. Britain handed over the seven Ionian Islands that it had ruled as a protectorate since 1815. They included Corfu (Kerkyra), Paxi, Lefkada (Lefkas), Ithaka (Ithaki), Kefalonia, Zakynthos (Zante), and Kythira. Kefalonia had revolted against British rule, starting in 1849. Although this and other revolutions were suppressed, anti-British feelings lingered. This unrest contributed to the Britain's decision to give Greece the islands.

## BRIGANDS

A few of the same men who had helped win the War of Independence, who had been praised and been the subject of patriotic songs, reverted to becoming brigands, terrorizing travelers and farmers. Their successors continued their misdeeds until the early part of the 20th century. In a year and a half, from January 1869 to June 1870, they had struck 109 times. The brigand problem received international attention in 1870 in what is referred to as the Dilessi murders. When they did not receive the expected ransom, the Arvanitakis band murdered four travelers, three Englishmen and one Italian. The opposition political party was accused of bungling the negotiations, such as encouraging the brigand leaders to seek amnesty from the king, which he was not empowered to grant. Seven of the brigands were captured and executed. The British press and politicians questioned the capacity of Greece to become a civilized society worthy of her illustrious ancestors.

Even after the uproar over this incident, brigands continued to play havoc. No wonder—they were well connected. They helped unscrupulous politicians get elected. Those not voting for the favored person could be terrorized by the brigands. Their connection with the community was demonstrated during a trial in Thessaly in 1894. The brigands "had shared their stolen goods with the Church and the local deputy and his two brothers."[3]

## KOUMOUDOUROS AND THE ADDITION OF THESSALY AND THE ARTA REGION OF EPIRUS TO GREECE

Alexandros Koumoundouros served as prime minister 10 times between 1865 and 1882. He alternated the premiership with Charilaos Trikoupis and Epameinondas Deligeorgis.

During his last administration, he achieved his greatest glory. At the Conference of Ambassadors in Constantinople, the Ottomans, under pressure by the

In 1870, seven brigands were executed by the government after they had killed three Englishmen and one Italian who had gone on a tour to Marathon. Until the early part of the 20th century, brigands terrorized travelers and farmers. (Courtesy of National Historical Museum)

Great Powers, yielded Thessaly as well as the Arta region of Epirus to Greece. After the territories were added in 1881, Koumoundouros called for new elections so that the citizens of these newly added regions could participate. On March 3, 1882, after the opposition party won the elections, he resigned. He died about a year later.

## CHARILAOS TRIKOUPIS

Charilaos Trikoupis, who is considered the father of modern Greece, recognized the brigand problem and sought to curb the "wild west" character of Greece. He attempted to bring order and economic and political stability to the country. He became prime minister in 1875 and was in and out of power until 1895.

In 1874, Trikoupis wrote an anonymous article, "Who Is to Blame," in the Athenian newspaper *Kairoi*. Trikoupis blamed the instability of Greece's government on the king exercising his right to appoint and dismiss governments. This perpetuated the existence of minority parties and the parties currying favors from the king, rather than concentrating on policies that were best for the country. There was bribery, patronage, and corruption. The article caused an uproar, and when Trikoupis claimed authorship of the article, he was arrested. After an outcry of public support for Trikoupis, he was held for only three days and acquitted.

His article had far-reaching consequences. In 1875, the king put into effect the principle of *dedilomeni*, which obliged the king to appoint the leader of the party with a plurality of parliamentary votes as prime minister. This encouraged Greek political parties to come together to form a majority. Thus the government gained more stability. In 10 years, from 1865 to 1875, there were seven general elections and 18 different short-lived governments. In contrast, after the institution of dedilomeni, only seven general elections were held in 25 years.

Trikoupis tried to modernize Greece. Under his administration, communication and transportation improved. By 1893, 569 miles of railway had been constructed, with another 305 in the process of being constructed. Another important infrastructure was the installation of 4,000 miles of telegraph line. He also initiated the construction of the Corinth Canal, which linked the Aegean Sea to the Ionian Sea. This enabled Piraeus, the port city near Athens, to gain prominence and encouraged the expansion of the Greek merchant marines. Under Trikoupis's administration, steamship tonnage grew. Merchants bought old steamships and expanded their markets.

Manufacturing also increased. By the early 1890s, Greece had 17 cotton mills and three large woolen mills. The drainage of Lake Copais by a British company added another 30,000 acres of arable land to Greece. Trikoupis also

Charilaos Trikoupis is seen as the father of modern Greece. His administration attracted overseas investors, built a railroad, and opened the Corinth Canal. In 1893, he announced to the parliament, "Regretfully, we are bankrupt." (Courtesy of National Historical Museum)

restructured and built up the armed forces and equipped them with the latest armaments.

Unfortunately, to fund these expenditures, Greece had to borrow heavily. By 1893, at least 40 percent of the annual budget was for the servicing of the loans. This, along with a worldwide depression and the drop in the price of currants (small black raisins) contributed to Greece's bankruptcy. Currants constituted the majority of the total value of the country's exports.

To try to balance the budget, the Trikoupis administration raised taxes and export duties on products such as tobacco and wine. There was a tithe on produce as well as taxes on sheep, goats, oxen, and donkeys. Taxes on land holdings were also increased.

When exports fell, so did the government's revenue. The taxes could not balance the budget. On December 10, 1893, Trikoupis announced to the parliament, "Regretfully, we are bankrupt."

## THEODOROS DELIYIANNIS

After the declaration of bankruptcy, it wasn't surprising that Trikoupis lost the election of 1895. Theodoros Deliyiannis became prime minister. Deliyiannis said, "I am against everything that Trikoupis is for."[4] Trikoupis focused on building the Greek nation from within, while Deliyiannis's government wanted to expand Greece's territory. Deliyiannis supported Crete's struggle to achieve *enosis* (union) with Greece, which resulted in the unsuccessful 1897 Thirty Day War with the Ottomans.

Deliyiannis served as head of the government during the following years: 1885–1886, 1890–1892, 1895–1897, 1902–1903, and 1904–1905. A professional gambler, Gherakaris, stabbed Prime Minister Deliyiannis with a dagger on the steps of the Parliament Building on June 13, 1905. He was upset with the rules that the prime minister had instituted against gambling houses. An emergency operation failed to stop Deliyiannis's internal bleeding, and he died shortly after the assault.

## MODERN OLYMPICS, 1896

Despite dire economic straits, Greece showed what it could accomplish by hosting the first modern Olympics, held in Athens in 1896. A Frenchman, Pierre de Coubertin, and a Greek, Demetrios Vikelas, worked tirelessly to make this happen. Vikelas became the first International Olympic Committee president. The idea of reviving the Olympics did not originate with either de Coubertin or Vikelas. Years before, the renowned poet Panagiotis Soutsos wrote poems about bringing back the Olympics to renew the glory of ancient Greece. In 1835, he wrote to King Otto. The king liked the idea but did nothing. Soutsos kept at it for decades.

Finally, Evangelis Zappas, a Vlach by descent, took the idea and ran with it, paving the way for the modern Olympics. War of Independence veteran Zappas had amassed a fortune as a merchant in Wallachia. He sponsored the games, held in a city square in Athens in 1859, which attracted athletes from throughout Greece and the Ottoman Empire. Zappas died in 1865. He had directed that his inheritance be used for the modern Olympic Games and that the Panatheniac Stadium, which had been used in ancient times for competitions in honor of the goddess Athena, be excavated and restored for future Olympics. The games of 1870 and 1875 were played in the restored stadium.

With the funds that Zappas had earmarked for the Olympics, the Zappeion Building was built and used for the fencing competition in 1896. Leonidas Pyrgos honored Greece by winning the master's foil competition. During the Olympics of 2004, the Zappeion was used as a press center.

Another wealthy Greek merchant also contributed to the 1896 games. George Averoff, who had been born in Epirus and made a fortune in Egypt, refurbished the Panatheniac Stadium. His statue stands at the entrance. The stadium, still in use today, sparkles with gleaming white marble quarried from nearby Mount Penteli.

The 1896 games attracted 15 nations. The Greeks celebrated when Spiridon Louis won the marathon. He received his prizes dressed in a spotless foustanella. An official report on the Olympic games captured that moment: "The Stadion resounded with cheers which seemed to take no end. Pigeons adorned, with ribbons of the national colours of Greece, were let flying across the Stadion; national flags and handkerchiefs were agitated in the air; nobody can even attempt to describe the joy, the enthusiasm of the Greek people."[5]

## CRETE'S STRUGGLE TO ACHIEVE UNION WITH GREECE AND THE GREEK-OTTOMAN WAR

Despite the depression, Greece still maintained interest in expanding its territories. Crete had not been part of the original Greece state as established in 1832. For many years, the Greeks of Crete had been revolting against the Ottomans to accomplish *enosis* (union) with Greece. The *Ethniki Etairia* (National Society), the secret society created in 1894 in favor of the Megali Idea, pressured the government to help Crete in its 1896 rebellion against the Ottomans. On February 13, 1897, Greek troops occupied Crete. The Great Powers instituted a blockade but were unsuccessful in preventing war between Greece and the Ottomans. On April 17, after an incursion of Greek irregular troops into the Ottoman territory of Thessaly and Arta, the Ottoman Empire declared war on Greece. Greek troops, under the command of Prince Constantine, suffered defeat. An armistice was signed on May 20, 1897.

As a result of the war, Greece lost a small amount of territory in Thessaly on its northern border, and it was forced to pay huge war reparations, despite the fact that it had declared insolvency in 1893. Greece accepted an International Financial Control Commission and diverted the income it received from state monopolies and port customs tariffs to the repayment of Greece's debts.

On the positive side, Crete achieved more autonomy than it had before. With the Great Powers' intervention, Crete was proclaimed an international protectorate but under Ottoman suzerainty. Prince George, second son of the king, was appointed high commissioner of Crete, and the Great Powers administered Crete.

A few years later, in 1905, Eleftherios Venizelos, president of the Cretan Assembly, announced Crete's union with Greece. However, Crete did not become recognized by the international community as part of Greece until the conclusion of the Second Balkan War, through the Treaty of Bucharest in August 1913.

## NOTES

1. Nicolai Ouroussoff, "The New Acropolis Museum Is Missing the Elgin Marbles," http://www.artknowledgenews.com/New_Acropolis_Museum.html.

2. Richard Clogg, *A Short History of Modern Greece*, 2nd ed. (Cambridge, England: Cambridge University Press, 1986), 6.

3. Richard Clogg, *A Concise History of Greece,* 2nd ed. (Cambridge, England: Cambridge University Press, 2002), 67.

4. Ibid., 240.

5. Sp. P. Lambros and N. G. Polites, *The Olympic Games BC. 776.–AD. 1896* (London: Grevel, 1896), 234, http://books.google.com/books?id=UyCCAA AAMAAJ&pg=PA1&dq=The+Olympic+Games+B.C.+776.%E2%80%93A.D. +1896&hl=en&ei=xLT_TbeCF4y3tgeq9_WoCQ&sa=X&oi=book_result&ct=re sult&resnum=4&ved=0CD0Q6AEwAw#v=onepage&q=The%20Olympic%20 Games%20B.C.%20776.%E2%80%93A.D.%201896&f=false.

# 7

# Immigration, Wars, and the Great Catastrophe

## IMMIGRATION TO THE UNITED STATES, 1890–1924

Between 1890 and 1917, about 450,000 Greek immigrants, including those from Asia Minor, went to the United States. From 1918 to 1924, an additional 70,000 immigrated. In 1924, the restrictive immigration policies of the United States essentially closed the door to Greek immigrants until after World War II.

The railroads, factories, and mines of America welcomed the young Greek males who came to work hard and return to Greece with money in their pockets. Around 30 to 50 percent did return. Many of those remaining in America established themselves in small businesses, such as restaurants or candy stores, often starting as peddlers. Once the men decided to stay in America, the women followed. Often marriages were arranged by letters sent back and forth across the ocean.

Money sent home by the immigrants helped relatives in Greece, but the tearing apart of families was a dear price to pay. Bitter tears were shed on both sides of the ocean.

Marie Thomopoulos immigrated to Chicago in 1920, when she was 25. She did not see her siblings again until 42 years later. Nick, her Chicago-born son, describes his mother's reunion with her sister in Athens:

The lady who came out also looked like my mother—so I knew she was my aunt. She saw us and said several times, "Who are you? Who are you?"

My mother started crying and said, "I'm Marie. I'm your sister."

Startled, Aunt Diamantia took a few moments to get her composure, and then all began screaming, crying, hugging, and kissing, and she exclaimed, "It's been so long you were away, Marie."[1]

Also touching was Thomopoulos's 1965 reunion with his paternal aunt, who had not had contact with her deceased brother's family since the 1930s. He tells his story, which starts with a conversation with villagers in Keri, Zakynthos:

"My father was from this village; his name was Nick Thomopoulos and a long time ago went to Chicago, started a family and soon after died in Chicago. We are his family and have no contact with the family. Is there anyone with that name in this village?"

They shook their heads, no. They did not know anyone. But it was a long time ago and most did not remember much from so far back. One lady said, "There is a village lady who had a brother, and he died in America—maybe it was him." So I asked, "Where could we find this lady?"

A boy from the village said he would show us. . . . The boy pointed to a lady tending her goats on a hilly area about 150 feet away. This woman looked like she was in her 90s and had a very long skirt on with a scarf and long sleeves. I proceeded up the hill to talk to her. I was fearful that if she was my father's sister, the shock of seeing relatives that she didn't know existed might cause her to faint or something. As I approached she looked at me intently and seemed a bit frightened. She kept saying, "What do you want? Who are you?"

I told her, "My father was Nick Thomopoulos, and he came from this village many years ago and died in Chicago. Did you know him?"

Startled, she started screaming, did the sign of the cross, thanked the lord for this day and was crying as she asked if I was really her brother's son. After I assured her I was, she exclaimed, "He was my brother." We hugged and cried and started kissing on the cheeks. I pointed below and told her my sisters, wife, niece, and nephew were there.[2]

Some fathers left their wives and children behind in Greece, feeling that America was not a good place to raise a family. The fathers traveled back and forth every few years to see their wives and children. Many families were separated during World War II and the civil war, when travel was impossible.

## RIOTS IN THE EARLY 1900s

Several uprisings rocked the country from 1901 to 1905. The *Evangelika* (gospel) riots broke out in November 1901 after the poet Alexandros Pallis, with the support of Queen Olga, translated the scriptures into demotic Greek. The rioters burned copies of the newspapers that supported the translation. Three demonstrators were wounded by shots fired by police. The next day, Bloody Thursday, saw the death of 8 to 10 people.

In the Sanidika Riot of 1902, Deliyiannis's supporters used *sanides* (planks) from buildings under construction as weapons. After an election that failed to produce a majority, supporters of Deliyiannis demanded that he be declared prime minister. King George gave in to their demands and swore in Deliyiannis as prime minister on November 24, 1902.

A few months later an uprising of peasants protested the deplorable state of the rural economy in the Peloponnese. The army intervened to restore order. In 1903, students demonstrated against use of the demotic by the National Theater in their presentation of Aeschylus's play *Oresteia*. Still another demonstration occurred in 1905 when guild members besieged the palace demanding an audience with the king to protest the government's tax hikes.

## MACEDONIAN STRUGGLE, 1903–1908

Pavlos Melas, the son of a prominent Athenian family, was killed on October 13, 1904, as he participated in the Greek struggle against Bulgarians in Macedonia. He became a larger-than-life folk hero who motivated volunteers throughout Greece to join the Macedonian struggle. The pro-Greek units had some success in defeating pro-Bulgarian units. However, the Ottomans continued to rule Macedonia until 1913, when the Greeks gained their present territory in Macedonia.

In his book *Claiming Macedonia,* George Papavizas summed up the struggle: "Through the years 1903 to 1908 the conflict over domination in Macedonia by Bulgarians or Greeks, still under Ottoman rule, was marked by extreme brutality and gross violations of human rights by both sides. The Macedonian struggle was not a declared war between sovereign countries, but guerrilla warfare between two ideas, Hellenism and Bulgarism, reflecting two ethnic entities loathing each other under the umbrella of a foreign conqueror [the Ottomans] entrenched in the sorry land for four hundred years."[3]

## GOUDI REBELLION IN 1909 AND VENIZELOS GOVERNMENT

The summer of 1909 was hot, not only because of the temperature but because of a conflagration generated by the military in what is known as the Goudi Rebellion. The Military League, under the leadership of Colonel Nikolaos Zorbas, issued its demands for reform to King George I at the Goudi army barracks on the outskirts of Athens. In response to the demands, King George I replaced Prime Minister Dimitrios Rallis with Kyriakoulis Mavromichalis. After a month, upset that the new government under Mavromichalis did not meet its demands, the Military League staged another large demonstration, which included not only military men but the general public as well. Finally, Eleftherios Venizelos was called in as the new prime minister and proceeded to institute some of the reforms that had been demanded.

The reforms that Venizelos instituted during the early years he served as prime minister included the following:

- The right to expropriate land and property for the national interest. Thus, big estates could be distributed to tenant farmers or small landowners.
- The creation of a labor relations board.
- Prohibition of child labor and night-shift work for women.
- The legalization of trade unions, and the prohibition of management-controlled unions that employees had to join.

Eleftherios Venizelos served as prime minister several times between 1909 and 1920 and then again from 1928 to 1933. Venizelos and King Constantine disagreed about Greece's entry into World War I. Venizelos wanted to join the Triple Entente, but the king didn't. This began a long-term struggle between those who supported Venizelos and those who supported the monarchy. (Courtesy of National Historical Museum)

- A six-day workweek, with Sunday a holiday and no stores open.
- The abolishment of the law of summary seizure for the collection of debts.
- Compulsory and free elementary education until the sixth grade.

Although compulsory education for four years of grammar school had been instituted in 1834, illiteracy was the norm. Venizelos's policies made schooling more accessible, and they seemed to have been effective. In 1907, illiteracy of men and women totaled 63 percent, with male illiteracy at 43.1 percent and female illiteracy at 82.5. By 1920, the total illiteracy for men and women was 48.5 percent, with the rate for males 27.9 percent and the rate for females 68.8 percent. (This was the rate for the old boundaries, i.e., excluding territories added to Greece after the Balkan wars and World War I.)

Unfortunately, although there was compulsory education, many people did not attend school or attended school for just a few years, especially in the rural areas. In rural areas, high schools were a distance away, and to attend, children would need to board in the town where the high school was located. Girls in the rural areas were not encouraged to go to school. Being a good *nikokyra* (housewife) was deemed to be more important than becoming educated.

## FIRST BALKAN WAR, 1912

During his first term in office (1910–1915), Venizelos basked in Greece's victory in the Balkan Wars. As a result of the wars of 1912 and 1913, Greece increased its territory. During the First Balkan War, which started on October 18, 1912, Greece, Bulgaria, Serbia, and Montenegro defeated the Ottomans. The Ottomans were outnumbered by the combined troops. Forty-five thousand Greeks who had immigrated to the United States returned to fight in the Balkan Wars. Some of them trained at Hull House, a settlement house established by Jane Addams in Chicago.

Both the Greeks and Bulgarians coveted the thriving seaport city of Thessaloniki. The Greeks captured Thessaloniki on October 26, 1912, according to the old calendar, just hours before the Bulgarians reached the city. In 1913, the Greeks captured Ioannina. The Treaty of London, which was signed on May 30, 1913, ended the first Balkan War.

In the midst of the war, on March 18, 1913, the anarchist Alexandros Schinas shot King George in the back while he was walking in the streets of Thessaloniki. The king died a half hour later. Schinas did not name any accomplices. Two months after the assassination, Schinas supposedly committed suicide by jumping off a balcony while he was in police custody. After the death of King George, his eldest son, Constantine, assumed the throne.

This undated photo was taken during either the First or Second Balkan War. As a result of its victories during the Balkan Wars of 1912–1913, Greece added the rest of the current region of Epirus, Macedonia, Crete, and some of the other Aegean islands to its territory. (Courtesy of National Historical Museum)

## SECOND BALKAN WAR, 1913

On June 16, 1913, Bulgaria, dissatisfied with its gains after the First Balkan War, attacked its former allies Greece and Serbia. Greece, Serbia, Montenegro, Romania, and the Ottoman Empire fought Bulgaria in the Second Balkan War. The war concluded on August 10, 1913.

As specified in the Treaty of Bucharest, Bulgaria ceded much of Macedonia to Greece and Serbia. Bulgaria retained Western Thrace, including the Aegean outlet at the port city now known as Alexandroupolis. It did not retain western Thrace long. It lost control of it under the 1919 Treaty of Neuilly, and it became part of Greece in 1920.

After victories in the Balkan Wars of 1912 and 1913, Greece added a major part of Epirus, Macedonia, Crete, and some of the other Aegean islands to its territory. Greece expanded its territory by 68 percent, adding valuable agricultural land and gaining the cities of Thessaloniki and Ioannina. The population nearly doubled, from 2,800,000 to 4,800,000. The newly added territory included not only those of Greek ancestry but also Slavs and Jews who inhabited Macedonia.

## AUTONOMY OF NORTHERN EPIRUS

Greece evacuated her troops from that part of Epirus (to the north of Greece) that was awarded to Albania by the Florence Protocol of December 17, 1913. Greeks continue to refer to this area as Northern Epirus. Albanians object to this term since it is located in the southern part of present-day Albania. Although the Greek nation withdrew her troops from this area, the guerrilla war between the Greeks and Albanians of Northern Epirus continued.

The Greeks in Northern Epirus set up a self-governing entity on February 28, 1914. The International Control Commission, which included representatives of Britain, France, Germany, Austria-Hungary, Russia, and Italy, met together with the Albanians and the Greeks of Northern Epirus. In May, the Protocol of Corfu, which was signed by both Albanian and Greek Epirot representatives and approved by the International Control Commission, granted autonomy to Northern Epirus. For a few months, the region had its own administration and self-government under Albanian sovereignty. This continued only until October 17, 1914. When World War I broke out in 1914, Albania collapsed. At various intervals, Northern Epirus came under the control of France, Italy, and Greece. At the end of 1921, the Conference of Ambassadors, an executive body of members of the Entente formed after World War I, decided that Albanian's claim to northern Epirus would prevail.

## WORLD WAR I

Shortly after the Balkan Wars, World War I broke out. Austria-Hungary believed that the Serbs were behind the assassination of Archduke Franz Ferdinand and his wife. The assassination became the spark that lit the raging firebomb of World War I. On July 28, 1914, Austria-Hungary declared war on Serbia. The Triple Entente (France, Britain, and the Russian Empire) fought against the Central Powers (Austria-Hungary, Germany, and Italy).

### Great Schism: Venizelos versus the Royalists

Venizelos was at odds with King Constantine regarding Greece's entry into World War I. Venizelos wanted to join the Triple Entente, but the king wanted to remain neutral. The king's wife, Sofia, was the sister of Wilhelm II of Germany.

The disagreement about whether to enter the war began the Great Schism, a long-standing struggle between those who supported Venizelos and those who supported the crown. Because of his differences with the king, Venizelos twice resigned in 1915.

On October 5, 1916, after a revolt by officers, a rival Greek government was established under Venizelos. The Government of National Defense, which governed northern Greece and Crete, declared war on the Central Powers in November 1916.

The Greek government in Athens remained neutral. The French and the English were concerned that the Greek government might help the Entente. They asked Greece to agree to the following demands: control of railways to the north, the surrender of some of their warships, disarmament of batteries at Salamis and Piraeus, and the departure of enemy legations. At first the king agreed, but he reneged on this agreement. Thinking the king might respond to force, the French and British entered Piraeus and Athens on December 1, 1916. Shooting broke out between their troops and the Greek government troops based in Athens. The French and British forces had the support of those Greeks who backed Venizelos. This altercation resulted in casualties for the British and French and forced their retreat. Demanding reparations, the British and French then instituted a blockade of southern Greece, which lasted more than 100 days. They officially recognized the Venizelos government.

King Constantine, under pressure from France and Britain, left Greece in June 1917 but did not formally abdicate. His second son, Alexander, succeeded him.

By June 27, 1917, Venizelos returned to Athens and reinstated the parliament of two years earlier. It became known as the Parliament of Lazarus. After the parliament gave him a unanimous vote of confidence, Venizelos became prime minister. Civil war had been averted.

However, the division between the monarchists and those who supported Venizelos continued for decades. Whichever faction came to power used its power to purge the government and civil service of the rival faction. Blood was spilled over their differences. Even across the Atlantic Ocean in America, the schism played out in inflammatory newspaper articles in the ethnic press, in divided churches that were either for Venizelos or for the Royalists, in heated arguments, and in fistfights.

This description from the anti-Venizelos press shows how the opposition demonized Venizelos: "Venizelos, son of the Devil, grandson of Beelzebub, great-grandson of Eosphorus, great-great-grandson of Satan. A well-known maniac injected with rage. He married a viper."[4]

A few days after Venizelos arrived in Athens, he reiterated his declaration of war on the Central Powers. However, Greece wasn't ready to mobilize for full-scale war until several months later, when nine divisions were sent to the Macedonian front. They fought, together with the Entente forces, to eject the Central Powers from Macedonia. They then advanced into Serbia and Bulgaria. By September 30, 1918, the Bulgarians asked for an armistice. By November, the Central Powers surrendered. With their ships anchored in the Bosphorus, the Greek troops, along with other Entente forces, triumphantly marched into Constantinople. During the 18 months it was at war, Greece mobilized 230,000 troops and lost about 8,000 of its troops in combat-related deaths.

## FIRE IN THESSALONIKI, 1917

Shortly after Venizelos returned to Athens, a terrible fire consumed Thessaloniki. A fierce wind spread the fire, which started August 6, 1917, to over 250 acres. The inferno destroyed 9,500 houses and most of the city's religious institutions, schools, printing presses, banks, hotels, and shops. Of the 72,000 people left without homes, two-thirds were Jewish.

Poet Yiorgos Vafopoulos in "Pages from an Autobiography" describes the scene:

> There where once the labyrinthine alleys of the Jewish district had spread out, were now only stones and smoldering ashes. In the other quarter, where the grand shops and hotels tower, tragic ruins reminded one of their former glory. And all these sad remains of a rich big city were swathed in heavy clouds of smoke. Deep in their basements the embers glowed for several months after the fire and, as we discovered later, so great was the force of the fire that all the glassware melted and amidst the debris of the pastry shops one could make out the jars of sweets transformed into a mass of burnt sugar and glass. The tremendous expanse covered by this catastrophe took the name of the *Kammena* (burnt areas). The whole district had been transmuted into a new Pompeii, where by day teams of excavators labored and by night the bums, criminals, and lovers found refuge.[5]

## TREATY OF NEUILLY, 1919

Western Thrace not only became part of Greece as a result of the Treaty of Neuilly, but the following provision of the treaty was also put into effect on November 27, 1919: "Within a period of two years from the coming into force of the present treaty, Bulgarian nationals over 18 years of age and habitually resident in the territories assigned to Greece in accordance with the present treaty will be entitled to opt for Bulgarian nationality....Persons who have exercised the above right to opt must within the succeeding twelve months transfer their place of residence to the state for which they have opted."[6]

Statistics on the number who participated in the exchange of populations vary. From 50,000 to 92,000 Bulgarians moved out of Thrace and Macedonia in Greece. Greece, in turn, welcomed from 25,000 to 50,000 ethnic Greeks from the coast of the Black Sea in Bulgaria.

## TREATY OF SEVRES, 1920

The Treaty of Sevres awarded Eastern Thrace as well as Imbros and Tenedos, two islands commanding the Dardanelles, to Greece.

Greece was to have administered Smyrna and the surrounding area for a five-year period, after which the local parliament, by a majority vote, could have asked the League of Nations for the area's incorporation into Greece. According to the treaty, the League of Nations had the right to request a plebiscite as a preliminary.

The Treaty of Sevres was not ratified by the new Turkish government and thus became a dead issue. The 1923 Treaty of Lausanne superseded it. None of the territory specified by the Treaty of Sevres became part of Greece.

## DEATH OF KING ALEXANDER AND RETURN OF KING CONSTANTINE, 1920

In October 1920, King Alexander died of an infection caused by the bite of a monkey from the gardens of the summer palace. In November 1920, Venizelos, who had survived a shot by an assassin's bullet in August, lost the election. The supporters of former King Constantine gained control of the government. They conducted what the Venizelos supporters termed a rigged plebiscite on whether the monarchy should remain; the vote was overwhelmingly in favor of the monarchy: 999,960 to 10,383. King Constantine, who had been forced to vacate the throne in 1917, returned to Athens on December 19, 1920.

## TURKISH OPPRESSION OF CHRISTIAN MINORITIES DURING THE EARLY 1900S

In 1908, the revolutionary group referred to as the Young Turks forced Sultan Abdul-al-Hamid II to grant a new constitution that promised justice, freedom, and dignity. However, by 1913, three pashas took control and established a military dictatorship. What followed was not justice, freedom, and dignity, but slaughter and exile of Christian Greek, Armenian, and Assyrian minorities in Turkey and confiscation of their property.

Beginning in the summer of 1914, young Greek men from Thrace and western Anatolia were conscripted into labor battalions in which hundreds of thousands died. In his memoirs, Henry Morgenthau, the U.S. ambassador to the Ottoman Empire between 1913 and 1916, wrote: "Everywhere the Greeks were gathered in groups and, under the so-called protection of Turkish gendarmes, they were transported, the larger part on foot, into the interior. Just how many were scattered in this fashion is not definitely known, the estimates varying anywhere from 200,000 up to 1,000,000."[7] Women and children were included in the forced relocation. Thousands died in traveling from one area to another.

Turks forced the child Sano Halo, her family, and thousands of others from their homes in the Pontos region by the coast of the Black Sea on a death march toward the Syrian Desert. Her story of suffering and survival during the spring of 1920 is told in *Not Even My Name,* written by her daughter, Thea Halo. An excerpt follows:

> We had been on the road for about four months when my shoes wore out completely. Walking though this barren land with bare feet was like walking on pitted glass. The food we had brought was also gone. Each day brought another death, another body left to decompose on the side of the road. Some simply fell dead in their tracks. Their crumpled bodies littered the road like pieces of trash flung from a passing cart, left for buzzards and wolves.... The sound of crying was a constant companion for the first few months, but even that had diminished as our bodies grew weaker, our minds numbed, and our eyes focused only on the road ahead.[8]

The Turkish government is reluctant to acknowledge the slaughter of the Christians. In February 2010, a U.S. congressional panel adopted a resolution that recognizes the World War I–era deaths of Armenians under Ottoman rule as "genocide." Anger about the resolution caused Turkey to withdraw its ambassador from the United States.

## GREEK-TURKISH WAR, 1919–1922, AND THE COLLAPSE OF THE MEGALI IDEA

The Greek-Turkish War lasted from May 1919 to October 1922. In 1919, the Greek army entered Smyrna (Izmir) with the approval of the Allies and under the provisions of the Treaty of Sevres, which in Article 71 stated: "The Greek Government shall be entitled to maintain in the city of Smyrna and the territory defined in Article 66 the military forces required for the maintenance of order and public security." The Greek troops were there to protect the Greeks living in Smyrna and the surrounding area. Greece took control of Smyrna but was not content with that. The Greek armed forces ventured inland, toward Ankara, an ill-conceived plan. The Greeks attempted to take over lands that they believed rightfully belonged to them. They dreamed that their small country would eventually encompass all the lands of the former Ottoman Empire where Greeks resided, including Constantinople and Smyrna.

By end of March 1921, Greek armies had reached the Sakarya (in Greek, Sangarios) River, 40 miles from Ankara. However, the tide turned. The Greeks had counted on the support of Britain, as Prime Minister Lloyd George had led them to believe. Instead, Britain proclaimed itself neutral, and the Greek armed forces were not able to purchase arms from Britain. On the other hand, Turkey was fortified by arms supplied by Russia, France, and Italy.

Commander of the Turkish troops Mustafa Kemal launched an offensive on August 26, 1922, and routed the Greek forces. On September 8, the army evacuated the city of Smyrna. The Megali Idea died with the defeat of the Greeks. In 1923, Kemal was elected the first president of the Republic of Turkey. The Turkish Grand Assembly named him Atatürk, meaning "Father of Turks."

## THE GREAT CATASTROPHE OF SMYRNA, SEPTEMBER 1922

After their defeat, the Greek troops retreated to Smyrna. By September 8, they had been picked up by Greek ships. Left behind were thousands of Greek civilians. The city of Smyrna was flooded with thousands who had fled from the interior of Turkey to Smyrna.

On September 13, 1922, a fire swept the Greek, Armenian, and Frankish (European) sections of the city, destroying homes, shops, and churches and killing thousands. The fire started in the Armenian section of the city and spread to the area where the Greeks lived. Just a few of the Greek neighborhoods avoided the destruction. The area that housed the Turks and the Jews was spared. Giles Milton compiled eyewitness testimonies of what the Greeks call the Great Catastrophe or the Asia Minor Catastrophe. In *Paradise Lost: Smyrna, 1922* he presents this account:

> One of the first people to notice the outbreak of fire was Miss Minnie Mills, the director of the American Collegiate Institute for Girls. She had just finished her lunch when she noticed that one of the neighboring buildings was burning. She stood up to have a closer look and was shocked by what she witnessed. "I saw with my own eyes a Turkish officer enter the house with small tins of petroleum or benzine and in a few minutes the house was in flames." She was not the only one at the institute to see the outbreak of fire. "Our teachers and girls saw Turks in regular soldiers' uniforms and in several cases in officers' uniforms, using long sticks with rags at the end which were dipped in a can of liquid and carried into houses which were soon burning."[9]

The American doctor Esther Lovejoy, an eyewitness, tells of scenes on the quay:

When I arrived at Smyrna there were massed on the quays 250,000 people—wretched, suffering and screaming with women beaten and with their clothes torn off them, families separated and everybody robbed...heartrending were the cries of children who had lost their mothers or mothers who had lost their children. They were herded along through the great guarded enclosure, and there was no turning back for lost ones. Mothers in the strength of madness climbed the steel fences fifteen feet high and in the face of blows from the butts of guns sought the children, who ran about screaming like animals.[10]

Without the intervention of Asa Kent Jennings, the refugees would probably have perished. An unassuming hunchbacked man of five feet, three inches, he possessed courage, a caring spirit, and a quick intellect. After seeing the desperate faces of the refugees waiting day after day for ships to rescue them, Jennings decided to take things into his own hands. He negotiated with Atatürk for the evacuation of the refugees and for safe passage for the ships that would come into the bay to take them to safety. He had to act quickly because Atatürk told him that he had only seven days to accomplish this herculean task. He later got an extension of four more days.

He offered to pay the captain of an Italian cargo liner to transport about 2,000 refugees to Mytilini. When Jennings reached the Greek island, he noticed that the ships that had evacuated the Greek army were still there. Jennings sent the Greek government the following cable: "In the name of humanity, send twenty ships now idle here to evacuate starving Greek refugees from Smyrna without delay."[11] It was signed, "Asa Jennings, American citizen." When the Greek government asked his position, he replied that he was chairman of the Relief Committee in Mytilini. When they asked what protection the ships would have, Jennings replied that American destroyers would accompany them. He did not directly reply to the question about whether the destroyers would protect the Greek ships if the Turks attempted to seize them. He telegraphed: "No time to discuss details. Stated guarantee should be satisfactory."[12]

When the Greek government failed to act upon this request, Jennings cabled back that "if he did not receive a favorable reply by six that evening he would wire openly, without code, so that the message could be picked up by anyone in the vicinity, that the Turkish authorities had given their permission, that the American Navy had guaranteed protection, and that the Greek government would not permit Greek ships to save Greek and Armenian refugees awaiting a certain death or worse."[13] The Greek government gave their OK, making Jennings admiral of the fleet that flew the American flag. Jennings not only assisted the refugees from Smyrna, but he also saved those from other areas of Turkey.

He could not help Greek and Armenian males of military age. As the refugees boarded the boats, Turkish soldiers grabbed any males of the age to serve in the military. Thousands of them were forced to go to the interior to work on public projects such as roads. Many perished en route to the labor camps or while in the camps.

In her novel *Old Gloves: A 20th Century Saga,* Beatriz Badikian-Gartler tells of this incident based on her grandparents' reunion in Greece after his release from imprisonment in Turkey:

> A bearded haggard-looking man faced her, a faint smile on his lips. *I have nothing to give you. Go away,* she said in a loud, angry voice. His clothes in tatters, his face smeared gray, his hand extended, she looked at his fingernails, brown and long. *Go Way,* she repeated and moved back to close the door.
>
>   Then he said, *It's me, Evgenia, your husband. It's me, Odyssea.*[14]

The refugees arrived in Greece tattered and torn, hungry and forlorn. The American Red Cross arrived in Greece on October 1922 to help and remained for eight months. They trained Greeks, mostly women, to take over after they left. The Red Cross team provided food for 500,000 people during the eight months they were situated in Greece. Another American-based relief organization, the Near East Relief, evacuated about 25,000 Greek and Armenian orphans and brought them to Greece. Also helping in the resettlement effort was the High Commission for Refugees. It had been established by the League of Nations under the direction of the Norwegian-born explorer, scientist, and diplomat Fridtjof Nansen.

Some of the refugees lived in makeshift shantytowns or squatted in factories, at times without the owners' consent. Those not settled in the farms desperately tried to make a living as peddlers, shoeshine boys, or beggars. Some had taken with them only the clothes on their backs. They were seen in old sacks, with shoes crafted from old tires.

In cooperation with Near East Relief, Dr. Esther Lovejoy and her colleagues from the American Women's Hospitals treated the refugees in the hospitals of the Aegean islands.

Despite the help from various agencies and the government, food and water were in short supply. Starvation and disease stalked the refugees. Some had died on the journey from Turkey to Greece. On the ships, mothers cradled their dead infants as if they were alive, not wanting them to be tossed into the ocean. They waited to reach land so their children could be given a proper burial.

## TREATY OF LAUSANNE AND EXCHANGE OF POPULATIONS, 1923

The Treaty of Lausanne was signed on July 24, 1923, by the British Empire, France, Italy, Japan, Greece, Romania, and the Serb-Croat-Slovene State of the one part, and Turkey of the other part. It delineated Greece's current borders, with the exception of the Dodecanese Islands, which did not become part of Greece until 1948. Greece gave up whatever hope it had to claim Smyrna, Imbros, Tenedos, and Eastern Thrace as part of its nation. Greece retained Western Thrace, which it had added to its territory in 1920 after the conclusion of World War I.

A tragedy for both Greeks living in Turkey and Turks living in Greece was the agreement signed by both Turkish and Greek representatives six months earlier, on January 30, 1923, at Lausanne, Switzerland. The "Convention Concerning the Exchange of Greek and Turkish Population" changed the character of both the Greek and Turkish nations. The first four articles read:

> As from the 1st May, 1923, there shall take place a compulsory exchange of Turkish nationals of the Greek Orthodox religion established in Turkish territory, and of Greek nationals of the Muslim religion established in Greek territory. These persons shall not return to live in Turkey or Greece respectively without the authorization of the Turkish Government or of the Greek Government respectively.
>
> The following persons shall not be included in the exchange provided for in Article 1: a) The Greek inhabitants of Constantinople, b) The Muslim inhabitants of Western Thrace.
>
> All Greeks who were already established before the 30th October, 1918, within the areas under the Prefecture of the City of Constantinople, as defined by the law of 1912, shall be considered as Greek inhabitants of Constantinople. All Muslims established in the region to the east of the frontier line laid down in 1913 by the Treaty of Bucharest shall be considered as Muslim inhabitants of Western Thrace.
>
> Those Greeks and Muslims who have already, and since the eighteenth October, 1912, left the territories the Greek and Turkish inhabitants of which are to be respectively exchanged, shall be considered as included in the exchange provided for in Article 1. The expression "emigrant" in the present Convention includes all physical and juridical persons who have been obliged to emigrate or have emigrated since the eighteenth October, 1912.
>
> All able-bodied men belonging to the Greek population, whose families have already left Turkish territory, and who are now detained in Turkey, shall constitute the first installment of Greeks sent to Greece in accordance with the present Convention.[15]

After the convention was signed, Greece and Turkey agreed that the Albanian-speaking Muslim Chams of Epirus were also to be exempted from the population exchange.

The population exchange took a terrible toll on displaced Greeks and Turks alike, but many more of the Greeks were affected. The International Mixed

Commission established by Article 11 of the Lausanne Convention reported that it had transferred under its auspices 189,916 Greeks to Greece and 355,635 Muslims to Turkey during 1923–1926.

However, by the time the convention went into effect most of the Greeks of Asia Minor had fled, especially the Greeks from Smyrna and Cappadocia and surrounding areas. Also, many of the Muslims from Greece had also immigrated to Turkey. The total number of Muslims who left Greece is estimated at 450,000. Greek refugees numbered about 1.2 million.

Greeks had come not only from Turkey but from other areas as well. A 1926 report undertaken by the League of Nations listed the number of refugees, which can be found in Table 7.1.

Along with the Greeks, there were about 70,000 Armenians who entered Greece to escape Turkish persecution. From Greece, many of them later immigrated to other countries.

Ernest Hemingway, in an October 1922 issue of the *Toronto Star*, covered the movement of Greeks from Eastern Thrace (in Turkey) to Western Thrace (in Greece) in the wake of the Turkish victory. He reported: "Twenty miles of carts drawn by cows, bullocks and muddy-flanked water buffalo, with exhausted, staggering men, women and children, blankets over their heads, walking blindingly along in the rain beside their worldly goods. It is a silent procession. Nobody even grunts. It is all they can do to keep moving."[16]

The refugees were a motley crew, peasants as well as aristocrats, educated as well as illiterate, farmers as well as merchants and tradesmen. Even the languages they spoke varied. Most spoke Greek. Those from the Karaman and Cappadocian regions of Turkey, however, spoke Turkish, and Pontian Greeks from the Black Sea area spoke a Pontic Greek language that was not intelligible to the native Greeks.

Most of the refugees settled in Macedonia (which includes Thessaloniki) and Central Greece and Attica (which includes the cities of Athens and Piraeus). The percentages of the total refugee populations that settled in each of the regions according to the 1928 census are listed in Table 7.2.

Greece experienced a population surge. Greece's population from 1920 to 1928 rose by 12 percent, from 5,536,375 to 6,204,684. The cities, especially,

## Table 7.1  Number of refugees in Greece in 1926

| | |
|---|---|
| Greeks from Asia Minor, including the Pontos | a little over 1,000,000 |
| Greeks from Eastern Thrace | 190,000 |
| Greeks from the Caucasus in Russia | 70,000 |
| Greeks from Bulgaria | 30,000 |
| Greeks from Constantinople in Turkey | 70,000 |

increased in size. The 1920 census reported that 36.3 percent of Greeks lived in urban or semi-urban areas, while the 1928 census reported that 45.6 percent of Greeks lived in urban or semi-urban areas.

The percentages of the refugees within the general population according to the 1928 census can be found in Table 7.3.

The ratio of female refugees to male refugees was 58 percent to 42 percent, since men of the age to serve in the military had been detained to serve in the labor battalions of Turkey, where many perished.

Greece became even more "Greek" because of the population exchange. The Turks from the northern regions of Macedonia, from some of the islands, and even some from Western Thrace, although they were exempt from the move, had moved to Turkey. Macedonia, where Thessaloniki is located, had previously been multicultural. In 1912, the Macedonian Region included 42.6 percent who identified themselves as Greek. By 1926, with the expulsion of the Turkish and Slav residents and the massive immigration of the Greek refugees, it became 88.8 percent Greek. The population rise of Greeks in Macedonia might have been partly caused by land reform that stipulated that only married couples could receive land.

There were both positive and negative results resulting from the flow of Greek refugees. At first the Greeks welcomed their compatriots. However, soon their presence put a damper on traditional Greek *philoxenia* (welcoming of strangers). When the refugees started arriving from Turkey with typhus, smallpox, and cholera, the Greek government put a temporary stop to their arrivals. Some of the refugees lingered in disease-ridden boats offshore. A ship arriving in Piraeus from Samsun, on the north Turkish coast, in January 1923

## Table 7.2 Percentage of Total Refugee Population in 1928

| | | |
|---|---|---|
| Macedonia | 638,253 | 52.2 percent |
| Central Greece and Attica | 306,193 | 25.1 percent |
| Thrace | 107,607 | 8.8 percent |
| North Aegean Islands | 56,613 | 4.6 percent |
| Thessaly | 34,659 | 2.8 percent |
| Crete | 33,900 | 2.8 percent |
| Peloponnese | 28,362 | 2.3 percent |
| Epirus | 8,179 | 0.7 percent |
| Cyclades | 4,782 | 0.4 percent |
| Ionian Islands | 3,301 | 0.3 percent |
| **Total** | **1,221,849** | **100 percent** |

## Table 7.3 Percentage of Refugees within General Population in 1928

| | |
|---|---|
| Thessaloniki | 48 percent |
| Athens | 40 percent |
| Piraeus | 25 percent |
| Mytilini | 10 percent |

carried 2,000 people, 1,600 of whom had typhus, smallpox, or cholera. Two of the three doctors on board were sick.

Also, the refugees drained the scant resources of the Greek state. By 1928, Greek refugees constituted one-fifth of the Greek population at that time. So many refugees within such a short period put a terrific burden on Greece. To care for them, Greece borrowed money, which added to the debt.

On the positive side, the refugees added new vitality to the economy because of their intellectual and creative skills as well as their enterprise. The refugees were of various social strata and educational levels. They included merchants, industrialists, bankers, doctors, lawyers, small businessmen, artisans, laborers, shepherds, and farmers. On the farms where they settled, they raised silkworms and grew tobacco, maize, and other vegetables and fruits.

Skilled iconographers brought back the traditional Byzantine style. They painted stylized, elongated, brightly colored two-dimensional figures and turned away from the Westernized lifelike figures then popular. The refugees also brought their unique cuisine, folk music, and dance. The rebetico music they brought from Smyrna and Constantinople blended together with the indigenous rebetico of Greece that had been played since the 19th century. The rebetico of the 1920s and 1930s became part of the underworld culture, and the lyrics of the songs reflected the experiences of life, including poverty, drink, drugs, disease, and death as well as work, love, and marriage.

After the refugees arrived, there was a rise in agricultural production, brought about by the government policy that distributed land to the refugees. Thus arable land increased by 55 percent. Also from 1923 to 1927, there was a significant rise in the payment of income taxes.

Life was difficult for the refugees. Besides the economic hardships they faced in their struggle to start a new life in a strange land, they had to cope with prejudice. The established Greeks called them *Tourkosporoi* (Turkish seeds) or *Yiourtovaftismenoi* (baptized in yogurt). They got ridiculed with the latter term because they used yogurt in their cuisine.

It was especially difficult for the refugees who could not speak Greek. Those from the region of Karaman spoke Turkish, although they wrote the Turkish words with the Greek alphabet. At the time of the exchange of populations in

1923, it was estimated that there were as many as 400,000 of them. Although those who originated from the Pontos area spoke a Greek language called Pontic, this language could not be understood by the Greeks living in Greece.

The Asia Minor Greeks felt the burning prejudice of the "old Greeks" and mourned the loss of their homeland. This loss has been felt even into the third or fourth generations.

## Pontians

The Pontians came from both Asia Minor and Russia. A brief history of the Pontians from the eighth century BC to AD 1923 follows.

The Pontians are believed to be descendants of Greeks who in the eighth century BC had moved from the Ionian cities located in the islands and shores of the Aegean Sea, in what is now Turkey, to the area of the Black Sea called Pontos (*pontos* is an ancient Greek word for "sea"). The Pontians retained their culture and the Greek language until modern times. After they became Christians, they also retained their religion, despite persecution. Their Hellenic language developed differently from that of mainland Greece, making it impossible for the Pontians and modern Greeks to understand each other.

Although the Christian Pontians have left the Pontos area, there are Muslims in Pontos who continue to speak the Pontic language. Although they identify themselves as Turks, many of them may be Pontians who converted from Christianity to Islam generations ago.

Some in Ottoman-controlled Pontos as well as in other areas of the Ottoman Empire became crypto-Christians (secret Christians). They pretended to be Muslims but actually practiced their Christian religion in secret.

In the 19th century, the Pontians who had settled around the Black Sea excelled in the shipping, banking, tobacco-growing, and manufacturing industries. During this time, Greek culture flourished. Teachers trained in Constantinople and Athens opened schools and taught not only about Byzantium but about ancient Greece as well, inspiring nationalistic feelings in their students. The Greeks achieved high positions and used their wealth in cultural pursuits.

However, persecution during the rule of the Turks drove some of the Pontians out of the Black Sea area. The wars that the Eastern Orthodox Russians fought in the Balkans and in the Caucasus with the Muslim Ottomans created tensions between the Pontian Greeks and the Ottomans. As noted by Neal Ascherson in his book *The Black Sea*, "After the Russian-Turkish war of 1828–9, some 42,000 Greeks, almost a fifth of the Pontian population, followed the withdrawing Russian armies. More Pontians left after the Crimean War, settling mainly in Georgia and Crimea, and another emigration took place after the 1877–8 war between Russia and Turkey. By about 1880, nearly 100,000 Greeks had taken refuge under the Christian protection of the tzar."[17]

At the beginning of the 20th century, many of the Pontians had established communities in various parts of the former Soviet Union. Many had settled there following World War I, after Russia had occupied Trebizond for two years (1916–1918). The Greeks followed the Russians when they withdrew from Trebizond, fearing repercussions.

Other non-Pontian Greeks settled in southern Russia, around the northern shores of the Sea of Azov, in or around the port of Mariupol, in southeastern Ukraine. Catherine the Great of Russia had persuaded 30,000 Greeks from mainland Greece and some of the islands to move to Russia in 1779, promising 30 years without taxation and the ability to retain their Greek language, Greek Orthodox religion, and customs. They spoke a Greek dialect that was different from Pontic Greek.

In 1919, Greece joined the Ukraine in an attempt to squelch the Communist Revolution. Greek soldiers fought in Odessa and Sevastopol. Fearing retaliation after the Greek army had departed, hundreds of thousands of Pontian Greeks escaped to Georgia as well as to Greece.

From 1919 to 1924, about 50,000 Greeks from the Soviet Union immigrated to Greece. In 1924, an agreement between Greece and the Soviet Union allowed 70,000 additional Greeks to come from the Soviet Union, in exchange for allowing Armenian refugees in Greece to settle in Soviet Armenia.

Not only the Pontians in Russia but also the Pontians who remained in the Pontos suffered a harsh fate. Thousands of Pontians in Turkey were killed or allowed to die of starvation and disease in death marches instituted by the new Turkish government following World War I. The Turkish authorities forced them to march from the Pontos region south for seven to eight months, through the mountainous regions of northern Turkey and arid plains to exile in the Syrian Desert.

In 1923, in the midst of the chaos that followed the defeat of Greece in the Greek-Turkish War, Metropolitan Chrysanthos of Trebizond led 164,000 Greeks of Pontos to safety in Greece.

## GREECE AFTER THE GREEK-TURKISH WAR

The nation reeled from the tragic turn of events in Asia Minor: the loss of lives of both soldiers and civilians, the storming of the refugees into the country, and Greece's toppled hopes for a greater Greece. In September 1922, in response to the defeat, a group of military men formed a group known as the "Revolutionary Committee." They included colonels Nikolaos Plastiras and Stylianos Gonatas as well as General Theodoros Pangalos. The Revolutionary Committee demanded the abdication of King Constantine, the resignation of the Royalist government, and the punishment of those responsible for the military disaster. They forced the king to abdicate, and his firstborn son, George II, succeeded him.

Within a few weeks, the administration convened a special military tribunal. This dark phase of Greek history is known as the Trial of the Six. Nine of those who were thought to be responsible for the military disaster were arrested. In a trial that lasted for two weeks, they were tried for high treason. Six were convicted and sentenced to death. These unfortunate ones included five who had served in the overthrown administration as well as the last commander in chief of the Asia Minor campaign. They were executed by firing squad on November 15, 1922, a few hours after the tribunal had sentenced them.

The tribunal convicted three others, but they were not sentenced to death. They included the son of King George I, Prince Andrew, who was sentenced to banishment from Greece. Prince Andrew's infant son, Philip, accompanied his father, mother, and sisters to France. Prince Philip married Queen Elizabeth II of England.

## OCCUPATION OF CORFU BY ITALY, 1923

In 1923, Italy bombarded and then occupied the island of Corfu for a month. This happened during the administration of Stylianos Gonatas and started with a boundary dispute between Greece and Albania. A commission authorized by the League of Nations was created to determine the boundaries, and a small detachment of soldiers from several countries was sent to assist the commission. On August 27, 1923, unknown assailants murdered Italian general Enrico Tellini and three Italian soldiers within Greek borders. Italy demanded reparations from Greece and the execution of the killers. Greece could not identify the killers and did not respond to the demands. Benito Mussolini took quick action. On August 31, he ordered the bombardment and occupation of Corfu. The resolution of the dispute was handed over to the Conference of Ambassadors. After Greece paid reparations to Italy on September 27, as was suggested by the Conference, Italy left Corfu. Incensed by Italy's act of aggression, the Corfiots stopped playing Italian operas at their theater.

## LEONARDOPOULOS-GARGALIDIS MILITARY COUP RESULTS IN KING GEORGE'S EXILE, 1923

King George II is said to have remarked that the most important tool for a king of Greece is a suitcase. A year after assuming the throne, he had to leave. During October 1923, another military coup was staged, this time by midlevel military officers who were loyal to the crown. They included the lieutenant generals Georgios Leonardopoulos and Panagiotis Gargalidis, and Colonel Georgios Ziras. The coup failed, and with it the hopes of the royalty to remain in power. Following the coup, King George II and his wife Elisabeth of Romania left Greece. Ioannis Metaxas, who had been involved in the coup and who was later to become prime minister, followed them into exile.

## SECOND HELLENIC REPUBLIC

The Second Hellenic Republic denotes the period between 1924 and 1935 when Greece did not have a king. During this period, a conflict raged between those who wanted the monarchy returned and those who did not. The republic had been proclaimed on March 25, 1924, by the new prime minister, Alexandros Papanastasiou. This was confirmed by plebiscite on April 13. Thus, King George II, who was living in exile, was deposed. The Papanastasiou government lasted only about four months. Between 1924 and 1928, prime ministers were in and out of office 10 times, three general elections were held, and the military participated in 11 coups or ultimatums.

An important change for Greece occurred in 1923. The parliament adopted the Gregorian calendar, which had been in use by much of Europe since Pope Gregory XIII introduced it in 1582. It replaced the Julian calendar. Because of this change, a group of Greek Orthodox Christians known as the Old Calendarists broke away from the Church of Greece.

The constitutional powers of the parliament under the new republic were short-lived. General Theodore Pangalos instituted a bloodless coup, and in June 1925 he seized power. By January 1926, he had suspended the constitution and assumed dictatorial powers.

During his administration, Greek soldiers fought Bulgarian soldiers in the War of the Stray Dog. The strange-named conflict lasted from October 19, 1925, to December 15, 1925. Supposedly a dog wandered over Greece's border into Bulgaria. The Greek soldier who chased after the dog was gunned down by a Bulgarian sentry. Pangalos responded by sending Greek troops into Bulgaria. The League of Nations decided that Greece should pay a fine to Bulgaria for violating Bulgarian territory and that Bulgaria pay damages for the shooting of the Greek soldiers.

Pangalos did not last long. He instituted censorship of the press and other repressive laws. One law dictated that the length of women's skirts be no more than 14 inches above the ground. A cartoon of that era pictures a policeman measuring the space between a woman's dress and the street.

In August 1926, another coup overthrew Pangalos. A short-lived government, from August to December, headed by Major General Georgios Kondylis, another military dictator, took over. Alexander Zaimis became prime minister in 1926 and served until 1928. During his administration, a new constitution, which had been started two years prior, was finally approved.

## VENIZELOS RETURNS, 1928

In the 1928 election, Venizelos's Liberal Party won an overwhelming victory, bolstered by the support of the Asia Minor refugees. Venizelos took over the post of prime minister and held that office until 1932. During his last term in office, he had to cope with the Great Depression, which ravaged not only Greece, but the entire world.

Greece's economy failed in the wake of the economic crisis that hit the United States and Europe in 1929. By 1932, Greece could no longer service its huge debts. It had the burden of the reparations to pay to Turkey after the Greek-Turkish War. Also, it could not pay off the loans given by Washington and London from 1928 to 1930 for various public works including water supply, land drainage, and road construction. Added to that was the cost of settling more than one million refugees. Greece's income had dropped because of the lagging sale of tobacco, currants, and olive oil. Exports of these items fell drastically.

In prior years, young men had gone to the United States when Greece could not support them. However, the traditional safety valve of immigration closed in 1924 because of restrictive immigration laws. Adding to the economic woes, remittances from the United States stopped coming because of the depression. Many immigrants returned to Greece with empty pockets. Around 30 percent to 50 percent of the first wave of American immigrants eventually repatriated.

In the area of foreign relations, Venizelos attempted to strengthen relations between Greece and the new nation of Turkey under Kemal Atatürk through the Treaty of Ankara, which was put in effect in 1930. However, the Asia Minor refugees strongly objected to the treaty since they had to give up rights to their properties. This dashed their dream of going back to lost homelands or seeking remuneration for lost property. With this treaty, Venizelos lost the support of the refugees. Instead, many turned to the Greek Communist Party, which had been formed in 1918. In 1929, Venizelos adopted measures against the Communists by introducing the *idionymon* law. The law was applied to the person "who tries to apply ideas that have as an obvious target the violent overthrow of the current social system, or who acts in propagandizing their application." The law shut down workers' organizations and curtailed strikes.

Because of the depression and also because of the Treaty of Ankara, Venizelos lost his hold on the populace. After Venizelos resigned in 1932, two unsuccessful military coups followed. In March 1935, Venizelos fled to Paris after participating in an unsuccessful coup.

## DIFFICULTIES FOR GREEKS REMAINING IN TURKEY

By 1928, 50,000 Greeks from Constantinople had left the city, even though most had been exempt from the population exchange of the Lausanne Convention. Despite Venizelos's attempt to make things better between Greece and Turkey, the government of Turkey continued repressive measures against the Greeks living in Turkey. A 1932 law barred non-Muslims in Turkey from working in a series of 30 trades and professions. Tailors, carpenters, doctors, lawyers, and many others could not practice their professions. Besides this, in 1942, taxes that discriminated against non-Muslims made life difficult for the Greeks.

## RESTORATION OF THE MONARCHY AND APPOINTMENT OF GENERAL METAXAS AS PRIME MINISTER

In the November 1935 plebiscite, over 95 percent of the voters supported restoration of the monarchy. After 12 years of exile, King George returned. *Time Magazine* described what it considered this rigged plebiscite in its November 18, 1935, issue: "As a voter one could drop into the ballot box a blue vote for George II and please General George Kondylis, the Dictator who is bringing him back to Athens, or one could cast a red ballot for the Republic and get roughed up."

In 1936, just prior to Ioannis Metaxas becoming prime minister, there had been a strike of tobacco workers in Thessaloniki, which escalated when joined by railway and tram workers. The number of strikers reached 25,000 and resulted in a clash that killed 12 and wounded about 200. At the time, Konstantinos Demertzis was the head of the caretaker government in the absence of a majority government or a coalition. When he died in April 1936, the king appointed Ioannis Metaxas prime minister; parliament ratified the appointment.

A general strike was called for August 5. Metaxas set himself up as a dictator on the 4th of August 1936, using the excuse of labor unrest and fear of a Communist takeover.

The Metaxas regime is called the Fourth of August Regime. Metaxas dreamed of setting up the Third Hellenic Civilization, following in the footsteps of the ancient Greek and Byzantine civilizations and combining the best of both. Members of opposition parties, such as the Communist Party of Greece (KKE), were jailed or went into exile. Strikes were prohibited. He took full control by suspending parliament and various articles of the constitution. He banned political parties and censored the media, as well as theatre and the cinema. Certain music was banned and music to be recorded needed to have the permission of the Directorate for Enlightenment of the Populus in the Ministry.

During Metaxas's dictatorship there were huge book burnings, which included the works of Heine, Shaw, Freud, Zweig, France, Gorki, Dostoyevsky, and Darwin. Censorship extended to certain plays of Greek classical theatre.

In 1938, a law was instituted that forbade the speaking of non-Greek languages even in private homes. In Macedonian localities, posters read "Speak

King of the Hellenes George II stands to the right of Ioannis Metaxas. Metaxas, who became prime minister in 1936, set himself up as a dictator, suppressing civil rights and persecuting suspected Communists. The people rallied behind him when he said "no" on October 28, 1940, to the Italian demand to occupy Greece. (Courtesy of National Historical Museum)

Greek." Adult evening schools taught the Greek language. Those who spoke languages other than Greek, such as Slavic, Vlach, Romani, or Ladino, could be fined.

Metaxas's dictatorship at times resembled those of the fascist nations in its appearance, although in contrast to Hitler, he had no desire to harm the Jews. Photos of him with soldiers or schoolchildren show them saluting him in the type of Roman salute given to Mussolini and Hitler, with the right arm extended in front. He formed the National Youth Organization (EON), which, like Hitler's youth groups, emphasized devotion to the nation. The supposedly voluntary youth groups were held on Wednesdays and Sundays. Lack of attendance at 20 meetings could result in being expelled from school. By October 1939, the youth groups had 750,000 members.

## NOTES

1. Nick Thomopoulos, *100 Years: From Greece to Chicago and Back* (Bloomington, IN: Xlibris, 2011), 115.
2. Ibid., 165.

3. George C. Papavizas, *Claiming Macedonia:. The Struggle for the Heritage, Territory and Name of the Historic Hellenic Land, 1862–2004* (Jefferson, NC: McFarland, 2006), 67, 68.

4. Constantine Tsoucalas, *The Greek Tragedy* (Baltimore: Penguin, 1969), 49.

5. "The Fire of Thessaloniki [in] 1917," Thessaloniki from the 18th to the 20th Century, Hellenic Macedonia, http://www.macedonian-heritage.gr/Hellenic Macedonia/en/C3.1.3.html.

6. "Treaty of Neuilly Treaty of Peace between the Allied and Associated Powers and Bulgaria, and Protocol and Declaration signed at Neuilly-sur-Seine, 27 November 1919," World War I Document Archive, http://wwi.lib.byu.edu/index.php/Treaty_of_Neuilly.

7. Henry Morgenthau, *Ambassador Morgenthau's Story* (Garden City, NY: Doubleday, Page, 1919), 325.

8. Thea Halo, *Not Even My Name* (New York: Picador USA, 2001), 136.

9. Giles Milton, *Paradise Lost: Smyrna, 1922* (London: Sceptre, Hodder and Stoughton, 2008), 306.

10. "Women Pictures Smyrna Horrors," *New York Times,* Monday, October 9, 1922, http://smyrnialbum.s5.com/The_New_York_Times.htm.

11. Marjorie Housepian Dobkin, *Smyrna 1922: The Destruction of a City* (New York: Newmark Press, 1998), 194.

12. Ibid.

13. "The Rescue," Hellenic Electronic Center, http://www.greece.org/hec01/www/arts-culture/palikari/history_outline.html

14. Beatriz Badikian Gartler, *Old Gloves: A 20th Century Saga* (Chicago: Fractal Edge Press, 2006), 43.

15. "Greece and Turkey—Convention Concerning the Exchange of Greek and Turkish Populations and Protocol," signed at Lausanne, January 30, 1923 [1925] LNTSer 14; 32 LNTS 75, League of Nations Treaty Series: 78–79, http://www.worldlii.org/int/other/LNTSer/1925/14.html.

16. Bruce Clark, *Twice a Stranger: Greece, Turkey and the Minorities They Expelled* (London: Granta, 2005), 48.

17. Neil Ascherson, *The Black Sea* (New York: Hill and Wang, 1995), 185.

# 8

# World War II and the Occupation

On August 15, 1940, an Italian torpedo hit a Greek warship, causing the death of 9 sailors, with 24 wounded. The *Elli* had been moored off the coast of the island of Tinos during the holiday of the Assumption of the Virgin Mary. Metaxas did not respond, trying to keep Greece out of World War II, which had started in 1939.

However, Metaxas had been preparing for the possibility of war. Between 1936 and 1939, the budget for defense comprised nearly one-third of total state expenditure. Metaxas also oversaw the construction of the Metaxas Line, fortifications along the border of Bulgaria.

## GREECE SAYS NO TO MUSSOLINI AND REPELS THE ITALIANS, 1940

Metaxas's wife, Lela, recalled the fateful day of October 28, 1940, that led to Greece's involvement in World War II. Count Emmanuel Grazzi, the Italian ambassador, arrived at the Metaxas home in the early hours of the morning, with an ultimatum asking for Italian access into Greece.

According to a handwritten note from Mrs. Metaxas, "Their conversation began calmly, but soon I heard an animated exchange, and an angry tone in

ΕΠΙ ΤΗΣ ΚΟΡΥΦΗΣ ΤΗΣ ΠΙΝΔΟΥ 28 ΟΚΤΩΒΡΙΟΥ ΕΩΣ 12 ΝΟΕΜΒΡΙΟΥ 1940

On October 28, 1940, the Italians crossed the Albanian border and invaded Greece just hours after Prime Minister Ioannis Metaxas said no to their ultimatum asking for access into Greece. By November 13, the Greeks had chased the Italian invaders out of Greece. This poster celebrates their victory. It says, "On the mountains of Pindos October 28 to November 12, 1940." The victory over the previously unstoppable Axis powers astonished the world. (Printed by Dimitri Dimitrakos in Athens. From the book *To Epos Tou '40* by the National Historical Museum.)

my husband's voice followed by a loud bang of the palm of his hand on the top of the desk. It was the exact moment of the 'OXI' ('NO'), and there followed Grazzi's departure. When he returned to our room Metaxas told me right away, 'We are at war; I must dress quickly.'"[1]

"Ohi" Day is celebrated throughout Greece and in Greek immigrant communities more than 70 years later. The Greeks take pride in their heroic stand against the Italians. Just hours after Metaxas said "No," the Italians penetrated the borders of Italian-occupied Albania into Epirus in northwestern Greece. The women of the Pindos Mountain, where the assault took place, assisted the Greek troops by clearing the snow from the mountain paths and carrying supplies that weighed up to 80 pounds. By November 8, the Greek armed forces had chased the Italian invaders out of Greece. Within six weeks of the beginning of the battle, they had pushed them deep into Albania. The victory over the previously unstoppable Axis powers astonished the world.

## GERMANY INVADES GREECE, 1941

The victory celebration of Greece's defeat of Italy was cut short. On April 6, 1941, Germany attacked, only a couple of months after Metaxas had died of an infection. Formidable German armored divisions descended through Bulgaria and Yugoslavia, and German aircraft bombed several targets. The Greeks lost 11 British and Greek ships during the attack on Piraeus. The Greeks, together with the British, Australian, New Zealand, and Free Polish divisions, held on for several weeks. The Germans took over Thessaloniki on April 9, 1941. They marched into Athens, the capital, on April 27, 1941. Despondent over the advance of the Germans into Athens, Prime Minister Alexandros Koryzis, who had taken over the helm of the Greek government after Metaxas's death, killed himself. He was replaced by Emmanuel Tsouderos.

Before the occupation of Athens, the Greek government, as well as Greek soldiers and gendarmes, had escaped to Crete. On May 20, 1941, German paratroopers landed on Cretan soil, with accompanying air strikes. Greek, British, Australian, and New Zealand troops, under Commander Major Bernard Freyberg, made a valiant stand against the Germans. Brave Cretan men, women, and children took up arms, whether guns or pitchforks, to save their island. Despite their efforts, in 10 days, on June 1, 1941, the Germans won the Battle of Crete. Many of the Cretans, together with the Commonwealth troops that had been left behind, continued fighting in the resistance.

Although they overcame the Greeks, the battle was a blow to the Germans. They lost half of their 8,000 elite troops, the Seventh Airborne Division. The loss was so bad that Hitler never again attempted to use paratroopers. Winston Churchill said, "Goering gained only a pyrrhic victory in Crete: for the forces he expended there might easily have given him Cyprus, Iraq, Syria, and even perhaps Persia."[2]

It took 218 days for the Greeks to succumb to the massive war machine of the Axis. They lasted much longer than any other European country. The bravery of the Greeks was acknowledged throughout the world. Winston Churchill said, "Until now we would say that the Greeks fight like heroes. From now on we will say that heroes fight like Greeks."[3]

Some historians believe that the unexpected victory of the Greeks over the Italians influenced the course of the war. The diversion of Nazi troops and equipment to Greece caused a six-week delay in the invasion of the USSR. Thus the Nazi troops had to face the harsh winter conditions that contributed to their defeat in the Battle of Moscow. According to artist and film producer Leni Riefenstahl, on March 30, 1944, Adolph Hitler told her, "If the Italians hadn't attacked Greece and needed our help, the war would have taken a different course."[4]

The bravery of the Greek troops during World War II improved the image of Greek Americans, who at that time were subjected to discrimination. Their image changed from swarthy and untrustworthy foreigners to that of heroic Greek freedom fighters who were worthy of their illustrious ancestors.

## DARK SHROUD OF OCCUPATION

In his book of poems *Cries and Whispers,* Dr. Chrys Chrysanthou remembers the day that the Germans marched into Athens. Although he was just a young student, he recalls the message from the Radio Athens broadcast just before German troops entered the city: "When the barbarians enter not a single person should be seen in the streets."

This excerpt from his poem "Invasion of Athens" creates a picture of that dreadful day:

The dark shroud of occupation
Spread ominously over the eternal city
and the rhythmic cluck of black boots
reverberated terrifying nightmares
in the silent streets.[5]

When the Germans marched into the city, they ordered the removal of the blue and white Greek flag from the Acropolis so that it could be replaced with the Nazi swastika. According to an article reported in the June 9 edition of the *Daily Mail,* a London newspaper, the Germans asked Konstandinos Koukidis, an *evzone* (member of elite Greek troops), to remove the Greek flag. Wrapping the blue and white flag around his body, he hurled himself from the Acropolis to his death. Although there is a plaque at the base of the Acropolis commemorating this event, no documentation has been found to verify its occurrence.

On May 30, 1941, 18-year-old university students Manolis Glezos and Apostolos Santas defied death when, under cover of night, they snatched the swastika flag from the Acropolis. They were sentenced to death in absentia. Thankfully they fled the clutches of the Germans. Both participated in the resistance during World War II, but after the occupation, they were imprisoned by the Greek government for their leftist activities.

From 1941 to 1944, German forces controlled Athens, Piraeus, Thrace, Western Macedonia, Crete, and most of the Aegean islands. Italy controlled the Aegean Islands of Samos and Syros, the Ionian Islands, Epirus, Thessaly, Central Greece, and the Peloponnese until 1943, when Italy surrendered to the Allies. Bulgarian troops were stationed in central and eastern Macedonia. The Bulgarians closed Greek schools and brought in Bulgarian teachers. They replaced Greek

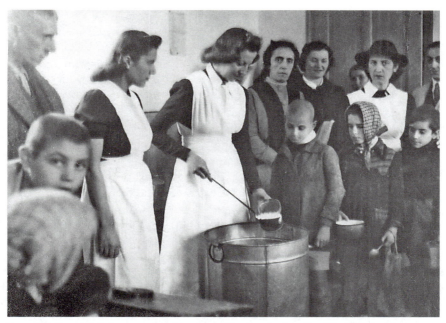

Soup kitchens fed thousands of hungry Greeks during the World War II occupation by Axis forces. About 5 percent of the Greek population died because of famine. (Courtesy of National Historical Museum)

priests with Bulgarian priests. To further lay claim to the area they occupied, they brought in Bulgarian settlers.

The quisling government based in Greece during the occupation was headed successively by General Georgios Tsolakoglou, Konstantinos Logothetopoulos, and Ioannis Rallis. Rallis created the Security Battalions. Under control of the Nazis, their function was to keep order and to fight against ELAS, a Communist-dominated resistance group. They were responsible for the death of thousands of fellow Greeks they believed to be Communists.

After the defeat of Crete, the Greek government officials, the king, and the armed forces left Crete in haste. The Greek government in exile, from 1941 to 1944, was set up in Egypt as well as in South Africa, London, and Caserta, Italy. Prime ministers of the Greek government in exile included Emmanuel Tsouderos, Sophocles Venizelos, and Georgios Papandreou.

## FAMINE, DEATH, AND DESTRUCTION

The Occupation from 1941 to 1944 resulted in terrible hardship, with thousands starving to death or killed in brutal attacks by the Axis occupying forces. Up to 5 percent of the Greek population, from 250,000 to 500,000, died because of famine. Greece was especially hard-hit during the first winter of the occupation—1941–1942. In Athens, trucks regularly combed the streets, and corpses were loaded onto them

The famine was caused by various factors. The British had instituted a blockade that prevented needed supplies such as wheat and medicine from reaching Greece. Britain's purpose was to weaken Germany, but thousands of Greek people starved as a result. Another factor was the decreased production of food because of the weather. Also adding to the problem was the Axis requisitioning, or taking food from the farmers in order to feed their troops. Greeks depended on cows, sheep, goats, mules, donkeys, and horses to feed themselves, to work the farms, or for transport. The animals had been depleted first in their use for Greece's fight against the Axis powers and then by the Axis themselves after they had occupied Greece. Also, in Thessaloniki, refugees fleeing Bulgarian-occupied sectors further depleted limited food supplies in that city.

Historian Violetta Hionidou says that the food crisis prevailed not only during that first winter of the occupation, but throughout the occupation and that it evolved, depending on conditions, into full-blown famine at different points and times. She delineates a variety of reasons for the variations within Greece, including "local food production levels; patchy relief provision; limited communications with the rest of Greece; employment levels; inflation; and destruction by military operations."[6]

The Greeks of the diaspora, most of them worried about relatives in Greece, organized a countrywide effort to help relieve the suffering. They collected money and goods through the Greek War Relief Association (GWRA). The organization, headed by Archbishop Athenagoras, primate of the Greek Orthodox Church in America, and Spyros Skouras, president of 20th Century Fox, enlisted the assistance of the Greek American churches and organizations throughout the nation. Thousands of Greek restaurateurs put out collection boxes. Faye Mezilson Machinis of Chicago remembers collecting money for the Greek War Relief effort outside of the McVickers Theatre in Chicago. Even non-Greek celebrities, such as Judy Garland and Frank Sinatra, joined the effort.

The British did not lift their blockade until February 22, 1942, and the first ship left from New York on March 27, 1942. Three years later there was a total of 100 fleet missions by the GWRA, with the value of goods received reaching $100,000,000. In 1941, before the blockade had been officially lifted, the Turkish ship *Kurtulus*, with the OK from Britain, made several trips across the sea to deliver goods that had been purchased with funds collected through the GWRA.

## ATROCITIES DURING WORLD WAR II

During the war, many lost their lives because of massacres by Axis powers. The Germans are estimated to have killed 21,000 Greeks, the Bulgarians

40,000, and the Italians 9,000. Most of these massacres of innocents occurred in retaliation for partisan activities. A decree issued on October 25, 1943, stated that 50 Greeks would be executed for every murdered German soldier and 10 for every wounded German soldier.

A few of the many atrocities committed during World War II are detailed as follows:

## Bulgarians Massacre Civilians as Reprisal for a Revolt in Macedonia

A revolt in Drama, Macedonia, against Bulgarian domination resulted in reprisals by the Bulgarian occupying forces. The brutal killings of Greek citizens by machine-gun fire took place during September 28 and 29, 1941, in Drama and the surrounding region (Doxato, Choristi, Adriani, Prossotsani, Kallithea). Altogether the casualties were estimated to be as high as 3,000.

## Kommeno Massacre by Germans

The joyous all-night celebration of a wedding in the village of Kommeno on August 16, 1943, ended brutally. German soldiers shot the bride, groom, and wedding guests dead. The massacre of the civilians of Kommeno started at 5:30 A.M. and finished at 12:30 P.M. The soldiers murdered 317 of the 680 inhabitants of the village. They slaughtered children as well as adults—74 of them, ages 1 through 10.

## Machine-Gun Murder of the Men of Kalavryta by Germans

In retaliation for the killing of German soldiers by the resistance, on December 13, 1943 the 117th Jäger Division herded villagers of Kalavryta into the local school. They marched males over age 12 into a hollow of a nearby hill and brutally machine-gunned 696 of them to death. Only 13 survived. They locked the women and children in the school. The Germans set the school on fire, but the women and children escaped when the soldier ordered to guard the school opened the doors. The town was burned to the ground, as was the monastery of Hagia Lavra; only eight houses out of nearly 500 were left standing. The statue erected in the schoolyard in 1998 depicts a grieving woman dragging the body of her husband, her two young children by her side.

## House-to-House Slaughter of Greeks by Germans in Distomo

"This pain will never heal,"[7] said George Koutriaris, a survivor of the German massacre in Distomo, Greece, that occurred on June 10, 1944, during the German occupation of World War II. Survivors recall the hot, terror-filled afternoon when German soldiers stormed the village in retaliation for German soldiers being killed. After they shot a group of 60 to 70 innocents in the village square, the soldiers went on a horrific house-to-house rampage for two hours. They left 218 of the 1,000 inhabitants of the village dead. Almost all of the homes were torched, and the carcasses of animals, shot by the Germans as they departed, lay everywhere on the fields. Eyewitness accounts describe human bodies hanging from trees and brutal sights such as a swastika cut into a slaughtered baby's cheeks. However, not all the soldiers followed their orders to kill. In Distomo, one of the soldiers spilled animal blood instead of human blood. Another shouted *kaput* (dead) to his commanding officer, sparing the lives of the frightened family.

Today, the skulls and bones of the victims are displayed in the Mausoleum of Distomo. Each year a commemorative event is held, in which German children have participated.

Greek poet Yiannis Ritsos honors the victims so that they and the tragedy of man's inhumanity to man is not forgotten:

Here, the bitter soil of Distomo.
Oh, you, traveler, wherever you tread, take care.
Here, the silence aches; the stones of every road give pain,
Because of the sacrifice,
Because of the cruelty of man.
Here, a simple marble column covered with the names of good people who
Glory lifts sob by sob, step by step, up the majestic ladder.[8]

## Germans Kill Italian Soldiers at Kefalonia and Kos Islands

Italy signed an armistice with the Allies on September 8, 1943. After the armistice, the Italians on the island of Kefalonia celebrated. The celebration was cut short when the Germans came and demanded that the Italians surrender their arms. Rather than surrender, the Italians unsuccessfully revolted against the Germans. The Germans rounded up their prisoners and in groups of 4 to 10 shot them and left their bodies to rot. Some of the Italian soldiers who were being transported to Germany for forced labor perished when their ships were blown up by mines. Altogether some 9,500 Italian soldiers died.

Another smaller-scale but just as horrific massacre of Italians occurred on the island of Kos in the Aegean on October 4, 1943, when the island was taken over by German forces. The Germans imprisoned the British and Italian soldiers. The order was given to execute all the Italian officers. The 102 officers killed by gunfire were buried in mass graves.

## Meligalas Massacre by ELAS Forces

One of the most brutal of massacres occurred not at the hands of the Axis forces but through the slaughter of fellow Greeks by the Communist-dominated ELAS guerrilla forces. It took place after a battle in September 1944 between ELAS and the Security Battalions. The Security Battalions were special forces that had been set up by Rallis's collaborationist Greek government to keep order and to go after any suspected Communists.

In the armed conflict that occurred in Meligalas, Greece, ELAS troops got the best of the Security Battalions, and they agreed to a ceasefire. Rather than being taken as prisoners, men of the Security Battalions were slaughtered. Hundreds of dead and wounded were thrown in a well. Many of those killed may have been collaborators, but innocent civilians were slaughtered as well.

Tasos Antonopoulos, who was 18 when the ELAS forces came to Meligalas, reported the following in his book *The Calvary of Meligalas:*

> In one of the groups we saw Panayiotis Nezis. He was a teacher, an innocent citizen. He had not hurt anyone; on the contrary, he had helped many people. He was a politically uncommitted person, who happened to be outside of his house that day. It was enough to earn him a death sentence. His punisher made him walk past his house. His wife and children were all gathered, waving him goodbye, while he called to each one by name.[9]

## Cham Albanians from Filiatra Killed and Driven from Their Homes by EDES

Chams, who are Muslim Albanians, lived in dozens of communities in Epirus, in an area called Chameria. During World War II, the Greeks hated them because some of them had joined with the Italian forces in terrorizing the Greeks. Napoleon Zervas, the commander of the National Republican Greek League (EDES), the largest non-Communist resistance group, was encouraged by the Allied Mission, under its commander, Colonel Chris Woodhouse, to chase them out of their homes. Although Woodhouse believed they collaborated with the Italians, other sources say a group of Chams joined the resistance organization ELAS.

Zervas's troops not only chased the Chams out of their homes but massacred some of them as well, including an undetermined number of innocent civilians, women and children among them. About 30,000 fled their homes. Most went to Albania and some to Turkey. The Chams have campaigned for right of return to Greece and restoration or compensation of confiscated properties. As of 2011, this issue has continued to complicate Greek-Albanian relations.

## Jews of Greece Slaughtered by Germans

Few Greek Jews survived the Holocaust. Almost 80,000 Jews were residing in Greece before World War II. After the war, the population decreased to 10,000. Many of them had been fighting in the resistance or been in hiding, helped by their Christian neighbors. Others fled from Greece to safety. The Spanish government rescued some of the Sephardic Jews by providing Spanish citizenship. Out of the 46,091 Jews deported to the extermination camps, only 1,950 returned alive—approximately 4 percent. After the war, about half of the Jews (5,000 Jews of the 10,000 in Greece) emigrated; many of them went to Palestine.

Jews had been living in Greece at least since the second century BC, as noted in ancient historical texts. By Byzantine times, the Jews became well integrated into the Hellenic community and spoke the Greek language. They were called Romaniote Jews (Jews of the Roman Empire).

When King Ferdinand and Queen Isabella expelled Jews from Spain in 1492 (and later from Sicily and Italy), the Ottomans welcomed them into their empire. Over 20,000 Sephardic Jews, including some who had converted to Christianity, arrived in Greece to join their Romaniote brethren.

Jews who resided in other areas of Europe also joined the Jews from Spain. They included Sephardic Jews from Portugal who were expelled by King Emmanuel of Portugal, who in 1496 ordered them to either convert or leave. Later, even the converts were forced to leave. During the 16th century, Jews also came from Provence, Poland, Italy, Hungary, and northern Africa.

Unlike the Romaniotes, who had adopted the language and many of the customs of the Greeks, the Sephardic Jews held on to their customs and their Judeo-Spanish language (Ladino) into the 20th century. The Greek they spoke had a distinct accent—a terrible handicap for those trying to hide from the Germans during World War II by pretending they were Greeks.

During the War of Independence (1821–1828), the Greek soldiers took revenge on the Jews for their being supportive of the Turks. The Jewish communities of Mystras, Tripolitsa, and Kalamata were decimated, and few Jews remained in Athens.

When King Otto came to Athens in 1834, Max Rothschild accompanied him. By the middle of the 19th century, a small Jewish community, which included Ashkenazi Jews and Jews from Turkey, had settled in the capital.

By the time of World War II, in 1940, the Jewish presence in Greece had reestablished itself. The nearly 80,000 Jews resided in 31 communities, with about 56,000 of them in Thessaloniki. For the most part, the Jews and Greeks lived harmoniously together. The peaceful coexistence was disturbed by the Campbell riots during the summer of 1931. An entire Thessaloniki neighborhood was burned to the ground, leaving one dead and 500 Jews homeless. Many in that neighborhood left for Palestine. Several leaders of the National Union of Greece, an anti-Semitic organization, were brought to trial in conjunction with the riot but were acquitted. A codefendant was the editor of the *Makedonia Newspaper,* which had fueled the fire by publishing falsehoods about the Jews.

According to Defense Ministry records, 12,898 Greek Jews—of whom 343 served in the officer corps—were called for active duty and fought during World War II; 513 died on the battlefields of northern Greece and 5,743 were wounded. Colonel Mordechai Frizis, a Jew from Chalkis, was one of the first Greek officers to die in battle. Jews also were active in the resistance when Germany, Italy, and Bulgaria occupied Greece.

After the Germans entered Thessaloniki, they started the mechanism for the "Final Solution." On July 11, 1942, the Germans ordered all Jewish males between ages 18 and 45 to assemble in Liberty Square. Throughout the hot and humid Saturday, their Sabbath, around 9,000 were forced to do gymnastics while the German soldiers humiliated and flogged them. By early 1943, they had herded the Jews into ghettos, confiscated property, forced them to wear the Star of David, and imposed a 5 p.m. curfew. The fate of the Jews of Thessaloniki was sealed when the chief rabbi, Zvi Koretz, handed over a list of the Jews of Thessaloniki to the Germans. He naively believed what the Germans told him, that his people would not be harmed but just resettled. Most of the Jews of Thessaloniki perished in Auschwitz. In 1943, the Nazis and their Greek collaborators destroyed the Jewish cemetery, which contained 500,000 tombs. In its location, buildings of the University of Thessaloniki have been constructed.

Jews from Bulgarian-occupied Greece, which included Kavalla, Drama, and Komotini, also suffered a dire fate. On March 3, 1943, about 5,000 of them were incarcerated in tobacco warehouses in Kavalla and then transported to Treblinka, across the Danube. Many perished in sealed cattle cars or capsizing ships before they even got to the camp.

The Jews of Athens fared better than those of Thessaloniki. Unlike Koretz, Elias Barzilai, the chief rabbi of Athens, did not give the Germans a list of names. Rabbi Barzilai joined partisans in the mountains of Greece.

The Church of Greece, based in Athens and under Archbishop Damaskinos's leadership, condemned Hitler's plans. He instructed priests to announce the church's position in their sermons, and through the church thousands of Jews were provided with false baptismal certificates. Damaskinos asked monasteries and convents to shelter Jews, and he informed his priests to encourage their congregations to hide Jews in their homes, even though that might result in death to the people who concealed them. More than 240 Jewish children were hidden by the Orthodox clergy alone.

On March 23, 1943, Archbishop Damaskinos sent a letter demanding that the Nazis stop the persecution of the Jews. An excerpt of the letter, which was cosigned by 27 prominent leaders of the Greek community, follows:

In our national consciousness, all the children of Mother Greece are an inseparable unity: they are equal members of the national body irrespective of religion... Our holy religion does not recognize superior or inferior qualities based on race or religion, as it is stated: "There is neither Jew nor Greek" and thus condemns any attempt to discriminate or create racial or religious differences. Our common fate both in days of glory and in periods of national misfortune forged inseparable bonds between all Greek citizens, without exemption, irrespective of race.[10]

Chief of Police Angelos Evert did not comply with German orders to turn in the Jews. It is reported that Evert issued thousands of fake IDs.

None of the Jews of the island of Zakynthos faced death or deportation. As told on the website of the United States Holocaust Memorial Museum: "In 1944, Mayor Loukas Carrer was ordered at gunpoint to hand over a list of Jews residing on the island. The list presented to the Germans by Bishop Chrysostomos contained only two names: Mayor Carrer and Bishop Chrysostomos. The Bishop bravely told the Germans, 'Here are your Jews. If you choose to deport the Jews of Zakynthos, you must also take me so I will share their fate.'"[11] The Germans deported no one. The 275 Jews of Zakynthos were safely hidden in mountain villages, and no one revealed where they were. After Zakynthos suffered a devastating earthquake in 1953, Israel sent a ship with aid for the victims. With the ship came this message: "The Jews of Zakynthos have never forgotten their Mayor or their beloved Bishop and what they did for us."[12]

## OTHER HORRORS OF OCCUPATION

Jeanne Tsatsos, whose own husband, a university professor, was in hiding from the Germans, wrote a journal detailing the suffering experienced by Athenians from 1941 to 1944. Under the guidance of Archbishop Damaskinos, she organized a relief effort. She provided food to starving children, helped to hide those fighting in the resistance against the Germans, and provided succor and sustenance to wives and mothers of those who had been executed. She describes New Year's Eve 1941:

We closed the office in Byron Street late, and I started from home. I went ahead through the icy night. That darkness was thick. Here and there I heard something like weeping, like groaning. I imagined bony hands reaching out, searching for something which I was absolutely unable to give them. Nor is there the slightest cause for hope. The Germans are winning everywhere. And this hunger, like a mass extermination of the race, is killing us all.

I try to hurry home. But my flashlight has goes badly, and I am tangled up in obstacles...in a pit...in the trunk of a frozen tree.[13]

On May 27, 1942 she writes:

Yesterday the Nazis killed two wonderful young men, Angelos and Marinos Barkas. They were arrested at the very moment when they were cutting the German cables. I went to see the parents. Their mother keeps as a talisman a letter from her boys. She wept when she showed it to me.

The Barkas parents came to see me. By now all the wives and mothers of those who were executed have found their way to our door. When in my ignorance I undertook to stand by them, I did not know what an endless Golgotha is compassion.[14]

Greek women fought as soldiers during the resistance and the subsequent civil war. This photo was taken in 1944 at ELAS headquarters in Lamia. (Photo by Dmitri Kessel; courtesy of Hellenic Literary and Historical Archive—National Bank of Greece Cultural Foundation [E.L.I.A-M.I.E.T.])

George Chiagouris shared his experience of the occupation with interviewer Athanasios Tzouras of the Frank S. Kamberos Oral History Center, National Hellenic Museum:

> Partisans would blow up the trains, put dynamite in the rails, so when the train would go over it, it would blow up. So to slow the partisans down or to detract from it, they put a car in front of the engine pushing it, and it was full of Greeks from the villages. And every so often they would go to the villages and raid the villages and pick up men and take them to jail so they could be used for that purpose. That was the most terrifying thing that I could ever imagine, because they would come in the middle of the night. And of course in the village, you've probably seen the pictures in the village; you could see they had guards, would you believe. Some of the men would guard up there to see lights coming from Tripoli. And if they saw it they would blow off a siren. Of course all the men would leave and go up in the mountains, wherever they made it. I believe one thing, I never told this before to anybody, is that in our house, I could probably show you a picture, it's on a semi hill and on the one side there's a wall and a garden bay. So my brother and the next door neighbor, they were about 18 years old, they dug like a cave. So whenever that happened we'd go in the cave and hide and fill it up, and they would pass by and thought nothing. Nobody would see them. That was terrifying.

## RESISTANCE DURING OCCUPATION

Resistance was demonstrated by the thousands who came to the funeral of Kostis Palamas. At his funeral in February 1943, the lyric poet Angelos Sikelianos made a speech and recited a poem dedicated to the poet.

Editor and translator George Katsimbalis, close friend of both Palamas and Sikelianos, started singing the banned national anthem. Edmund Keeley captures this incident in his book *Inventing Paradise:*

> In mid-February exactly three years later, Lawrence Durell sent Henry Miller a report on Katsimbalis's version of this story as told to him....According to Katsimbalis's account, he shouted insults at the German Embassy representative laying a wreath on the tomb, then broke into the national anthem, which he pointed out, was banned under pain of death. Katsimbalis told his English friend that he was like a man in a nightmare, ten thousand people and nobody would sing along, while his voice was breaking on the top notes, his eyes bulging, then silence at the end of the first verse as he stood there trembling, his wife trying to

shut him up, Ioanna Tsatsos pulling at his arm. But on he went into the second verse, still singing alone, the Germans looking around angrily, he feeling "like a drowning man in the midst of that huge crowd," until suddenly he was joined by a fat Corfiot friend whose rich voice finished the second verse with him as a duet. And then, Katsimbalis reported, "as if you had thrown a switch, the roar of the crowd took up the hymn and sang along, the tears running down our faces."[15]

Resistance to the Germans also occurred in March 1943, when Germany tried to conscript civilians to work in the factories of Germany. A massive strike was held, which included telephone operators as well as schoolchildren. Demonstrations were held in the streets, and a fire was set at the Ministry of Labor.

From the moment the occupying forces came into Greece, underground resistance groups sprang up throughout Greece. Estimates of the number of groups range from 30 to 70. They included major organizations that were dispersed throughout a particular region, or even throughout the nation, as well as smaller groups, active mainly in Athens.

They resisted in various ways: sabotage, strikes, blowing up bridges and communication systems, cutting down telephone poles, attacking supply convoys, planting mines that looked like rocks in the highways, transporting supplies for the resistance organizations, and armed guerrilla attacks against the occupiers. Some worked in intelligence, relaying information about the Axis. From the beginning, the various resistance organizations acted independently of each other and at times fought each other, jockeying for control of the government after liberation.

Here is a list of some of the organizations:

## Leftist Organizations

The strongest resistance group, the National Liberation Front (EAM), was dominated by the Communist Party, although not all those who joined it were Communists. A description of leftist organizations follows:

### Greek Communist Party (KKE)

The Greek Communist Party (KKE) had been active in Greece since November 1918. Inspired by the Bolshevik Revolution, a small number of students and intellectuals got together to form the Socialist Labor Party of Greece. In 1920, they became known as the KKE and included workers from industry, such as the tobacco and railroad workers. After 1923, refugees from Anatolia bolstered their ranks. The KKE joined the Communist International (Comintern), which was founded in Moscow in March 1919 and followed Moscow's party line.

The KKE became influential in the Greek trade unions and strikes. In 1936, when Ioannis Metaxas took over Greece as dictator, they were suppressed and many of the leaders were jailed. They went underground and resurfaced during the Occupation, when they took a leading role in the resistance against the Axis occupying forces.

### National Liberation Front (EAM), United Panhellenic Youth Organization (EPON), and Aetopoula (Little Eagles)

The KKE established EAM in September 1941, in conjunction with other groups, such as the Greek Socialist and Agrarian Parties. EAM welcomed both men and women. Women even assumed leadership roles, uncommon in Greece at that time.

Beginning in 1943, EAM's youth branch, EPON, recruited teenage boys and girls to join their ranks. The youth participated in acts of sabotage or labor unrest in the cities and were given elementary military training. Some joined EPON to become soldiers. Children from the ages of 7 to 14 joined Aetopoula (Young Eagles). A photo shows them training with small wooden rifles. Estimates of the number who joined EAM and its youth affiliates vary from 500,000 to two million.

### Greek People's Liberation Army (ELAS)

ELAS, the military branch of the EAM, was ready for action by the summer of 1942. ELAS forces have been estimated to be between 40,000 and 70,000. Many resistance fighters joined this group, not because of leftist ideology but because of a patriotic duty to fight the Axis occupiers. ELAS fought not only the Axis occupiers but also rival resistance groups, anticipating who was to gain control of Greece after liberation.

### Greek People's Liberation Navy (ELAN)

ELAN, the naval branch of the EAM, operated small boats called caiques. They traveled back and forth between the mainland and the Ionian Islands transporting personnel and goods. Some of the boats were armed, creating a nuisance to German shipping.

### Organization for the Protection of the People's Struggle (OPLA)

The word *opla* means weapons in Greek. The reason for the creation of OPLA, the policing unit of EAM, was to defend the members of the EAM and its affiliates. OPLA killed those who they believed were Axis collaborators, whether or not they had proof, as well as those they felt were their opponents on the left. André Gerolymatos, in his book *Red Acropolis, Black Terror,* says, "The executioners of the OPLA, the dreaded security service of the Greek Communist Party, took particular delight in dispatching Archive Marxists by slicing their throats with the tops of tin cans, and they massacred at least 600 Archive Marxists during this tumultuous period."[16]

### Political Committee of National Liberation (PEEA)

In March 1944, the EAM organized the PEEA, a rival to the government in exile. As announced by radio, the aims were "to intensify the struggle against the conquerors, carrying it on by every means at our disposal within Greece at the side of our Allies and to strive for the expulsion of the German and Bulgarian invaders, for full national liberation, for the consolidation of the independence and integrity of our country.... To struggle for the annihilation of domestic Fascism and armed bands of traitors."[17]

The PEEA had its own elections and governing body. It helped local communities organize schools and supported traveling theater groups and musicians.

## Other Resistance Organizations

### National Republican Greek Organization League (EDES)

Napoleon Zervas, a former officer in the Greek army, organized the other major resistance organization, EDES. It became active as early as June 1942 in Zervas's native Epirus. By March 1943, they had about 6,000 men.

### National and Social Liberation (EKKA)

EKKA, which numbered about 1,000, was founded by Colonel Dimitrios Psarros in 1942. Psarros named it the 5/42 Evzones Regiment after the unit he had fought with while he was in the Greek Armed Forces. EKKA was active in central Greece. However, they disbanded after an ELAS attack on Easter Monday, April 17, 1944. Psarros was killed, and many of the other members were captured, tortured, and killed.

### Greek Intelligence Organizations

Greeks also functioned in intelligence, supplying important information, such as deployment of troops and Axis shipping and air defense. Some of the organizations, such as the Bouboulina group founded in 1941 by Lela Karagianni and her family, also worked helping Allied soldiers flee to the Middle East and Jews to flee to Turkey, as well as engaging in sabotage acts. Another group working to transport British troops to safe havens in the Middle East was the Maleas's group (named after Cape Malea in the Peloponnese). It was founded in late 1941 by navy captain Alexandros Levidis.

Two well-known agents, Odysseus and Prometheus II, had been enlisted even before the Axis powers entered Greece by the British Special Operations Executive (SOE), the highly trained British intelligence agency. Odysseus (Gerasimos Lexatos) was a professional smuggler well suited to this work. He made frequent trips to Turkey as a courier, carrying instructions and equipment. His team was the liaison between SOE and EAM.

Prometheus II (Charalambos Koutsogiannopoulos) and his team served as the liaison between SOE and EDES. The Germans captured him in February 1943. Another team, headed by Ioannis Peltekis, who had previously been part of the Prometheus II team, freed Koutsogiannopoulos from jail.

Ioannis Peltekis had fled to Turkey upon the Prometheus II team's destruction by the Germans and subsequently organized a new group called Apollo. It grew to over 800 agents, one of the largest in wartime Europe. It supplied the British with information on Axis shipping, air defenses, and aircraft deployments.

## ROLE OF RESISTANCE

The resistance groups hindered the Axis in the war effort. Because they were forced to use their troops against the resistance, the Axis was not as free to fight in other countries. The resistance also worked at shutting off communication systems and supply lines.

Working together with the British, two of the resistance groups destroyed the Gorgopotamos Railroad Bridge, a major supply line for the Axis in the Theatre of War in north Africa. The British Air Force dropped 12 men whose mission was to blow up the bridge. They were headed by Colonel Eddie Myers of the Royal Engineers. They planned to enlist EDES as well as ELAS. However, a team of eight of them had landed a hundred miles from the EDES camp. A shepherd who had lived in America and could speak English went to their aid. "Uncle Niko" Beis, assisted by local villagers, equipped them with food, cooking equipment, and mules.

On November 25, 1942, with the cooperation of both EDES, under the command of Napoleon Zervas, and ELAS, under the command of Aris Velouchiotis, the bridge was demolished. The destruction of the bridge inspired other Greeks to join the resistance.

In 1943, Myers, head of the British Military Mission to Greece, and C. M. Woodhouse, the second in command, operated along with Greek resistance fighters to carry out what was termed "Operation Animal." Their aim was to cut main communications throughout Greece at the end of June and for the first week in July so that the Axis would think the Allies were preparing for an invasion of Greece. Woodhouse, Myers, and another four British soldiers blew up the Asopos viaduct. They and Greek resistance fighters damaged road and railway lines and cut hundreds of telephone wires.

This intense activity in Greece was done in conjunction with "Operation Mincemeat." On April 30, 1943, the British had planted top-secret documents on a corpse who was given the I.D. papers of a fictitious "Major William Martin." The British carefully placed "Major Martin" in the sea so that he would wash up on a Spanish beach. The Spanish found the documents, which revealed false plans for an Allied invasion of Greece and Sardinia, and sent them to the Germans. The "top-secret" documents, as well as the flurry of activity in

Greece, convinced Hitler that an Allied attack on Greece was imminent. Germany diverted forces to Greece instead of fortifying Sicily. The Allies fought a successful battle in Sicily during July and August 1943.

## PLAKA AGREEMENT, FEBRUARY 1944

Resistance forces fighting each other weakened the resistance effort. The Allied Military Mission, wanting to put a stop to this, met with EAM-ELAS and EDES near the Plaka Bridge on the River Arachthos in Epirus. The river marked the dividing line between their respective territories. The EAM-ELAS and EDES signed what is known as the Plaka Agreement on February 20, 1944. Both agreed to join the Allied Military Mission in fighting the Axis and stop fighting each other, in return for arms and supplies from the Allied Military Mission. They agreed that they would occupy the positions they held at the time of the agreement. EDES retained control of part of Epirus.

## FIGHTING WITHIN GREEK ARMED FORCES IN EXILE IN EGYPT, APRIL 1944

The fighting between the groups in mainland Greece played out in the Greek army in exile. At the beginning of April 1944, the government in exile experienced an attempted mutiny by the air force, navy, and army. It lasted three weeks.

The mutiny occurred after the formation of a provisional government in Greece, the Political Committee of National Liberation (PEEA), which had been organized by the leftist-dominated organization EAM. Those soldiers and sailors in support of the PEEA demanded that the current government in exile be disbanded and a new government of national unity be formed. When a response was not forthcoming, they mutinied against the government in exile. They were overpowered by Allied troops, and about 8,000 were incarcerated in prison camps in Egypt, Libya, and East Africa. After the mutiny, officers were carefully screened to make sure they were not Communists. Thus about half of the military personnel in the Middle East were out of commission, and the ones that remained were mostly royalists. The men were kept in the camps throughout the war.

Prime Minister Tsouderos had been replaced by Sophocles Venizelos, who served for only a short time. On April 26, 1944, Georgios Papandreou took over the leadership of the Greek government in exile.

## COMPROMISE BETWEEN THE GROUPS: LEBANON CONFERENCE AND CASERTA AGREEMENT, 1944

On May 17, 1944, the resistance groups met in Lebanon, where they agreed to unify all guerrilla forces under one authority. Following the agreement, 6 of the 24 ministers appointed to the government were EAM members.

The Communist-dominated EAM organization compromised again in an agreement signed at Caserta, Italy, on September 24, 1944, just prior to the liberation of Greece. The agreement, which was signed by the Supreme Allied Commander in the Mediterranean, General Sir Henry Maitland Wilson; General Stefanos Saraphis of ELAS; and General Zervas of EDES said:

- All guerrilla forces in Greece place themselves under the orders of the Greek Government of National Unity.
- The Greek Government places these forces under the orders of General [Ronald] Scobie, who has been nominated as G[eneral] O[fficer] C[ommanding] Forces in Greece.
- The Greek guerrilla leaders declare that they will forbid any attempt by units under their command to take the law into their own hands. Such action will be treated as a crime and punished accordingly.
- As regards Athens, no action is to be taken save under the direct orders of General Scobie.
- The Security Battalions are considered as instruments of the enemy. Unless they surrender according to the order issued by the GOC, they will be treated as enemy formations.
- All Greek guerrilla forces, in order to put an end to past rivalries, declare that they will form a national union in order to coordinate their activities in the best interests of the common struggle.[18]

The agreement also specified that Zervas continue to operate within the territorial limit of the Plaka Agreement, with General Saraphis continuing to operate in the remainder of Greece, with some exceptions. The signatories to the agreement agreed that the "task of both commanders will be to harass the German withdrawal and to eliminate German garrisons."[19] As the territory was evacuated, both commanders were to be responsible for "maintenance of law and order in the territories where their forces are operating, prevention of civil war and killing of Greeks by Greeks, prevention of infliction of any penalty whatsoever and of unjustifiable arrest, assistance in the establishment of the legal civil authority and distribution of relief."[20]

By the time of liberation, EAM-ELAS had control of much of Greece. Historian L. S. Stavrianos reports: "When the British troops landed at Patras on October 5, 1944, they found EAM-ELAS in control of all of Greece except for a few square miles in Epirus held by Zervas."[21] As the Germans abandoned cities and towns, ELAS units in the surrounding countryside occupied them, usually several days before the British arrived.

After the German evacuation of Athens on October 12, the British took control of Athens and the surrounding area.

Prime Minister Georgios Papandreou, Archbishop Damaskinos, and other officials celebrate liberation. On October 12, 1944, the Germans evacuated Athens. On October 18, Papandreou returned from exile along with other government officials and the Greek army. (Courtesy of National Historical Museum)

## LIBERATION, 1944

On October 12, 1944, the Germans evacuated Athens. The Germans cleared out of the rest of Greece by November 1944 (except some who remained around Chania, Crete, until May 1945). On their way out, the Germans destroyed property, leaving Greece tottering on the brink of collapse.

The Greeks looked beyond the devastation that surrounded them. They were free! Tsatsos describes the jubilation when the Germans departed from Athens:

> And we see the German flag slowly, slowly descend, see it disappear as if the Sacred Rock had swallowed it. And there begins to rise in its place the beloved color of our sky. My brimming eyes can no longer see. But when I have managed quickly to dry my tears the Blue and the White waves proudly in the breeze.
>
> Greece is once more our own, our very own. We have won her with our blood, our toil, with daily privations, and above all we have won her

This building in Athens was destroyed during the clash between ELAS and the allied national and British troops that occurred in December 1944. (Photo by Dmitri Kessel; courtesy of Hellenic Literary and Historical Archive—National Bank of Greece Cultural Foundation [E.L.I.A-M.I.E.T.])

in the dark grief of all our years of slavery. Greece is once more our own. The People are mad with joy. They kiss each other. They weep. They wait for the English to come.[22]

The people of Athens celebrated again when the British troops, welcomed by a cheering crowd, entered the city a day after the Germans departed, and when Papandreou, the government, and Greek army troops arrived on October 18, 1944.

The honeyed taste of liberation did not last long, however. A bitter pill followed. The people who had suffered so much during the war had to cope with poverty, hunger, homelessness, and disease. Added to that was another war, a civil war between government forces and the Communist-controlled forces.

## AFTERMATH OF WORLD WAR II

The war left Greece in terrible economic shape. Not only were the Greeks forced to supply the Axis with raw materials, food, and livestock, but they also had to pay for the cost of the occupation and give a "war loan" to Germany.

As of 2010, the war loan had not been repaid in full. To keep up with these burdens, Greece kept printing more and more currency. Before long the Greek drachma became worthless. Greek architect Dimitri Augoustinos remembers that when he was a young boy in 1944 he threw his father's hard-earned Greek drachma bills from the window, watching them float to the ground.[23] As money became worthless, a barter economy developed, not only in the rural areas where it had existed for centuries, but also in the cities. Also, the black market was rampant. Corrupt officials even took goods from ships delivering supplies and sold them on the black market. Some farmers charged exorbitant prices to city folk for their produce or olive oil. Anyone who emerged from the war years with lots of money was suspected of dealing in the black market. The consequences of the war and occupation follow:

- 8 percent of the population (550,000 people) perished;
- between 1,400 and 1,770 villages were burned;
- 401,500 houses were completely destroyed;
- more than a million people were left homeless or displaced;
- 34 percent of the national wealth was destroyed;
- large harbors, including Piraeus, Thessaloniki, Volos, and Patras, were ruined;
- railway tracks, steam engines, telephone networks, civilian airports, and bridges were destroyed;
- 73 percent of cargo ship tonnage and 94 percent of passenger ships were sunk;
- 56 percent of rails were destroyed;
- 65 percent of private cars, 60 percent of trucks, and 80 percent of buses were gone;
- 60 percent of horses and cattle, and 80 percent of small animals were dead;
- 25 percent of the forests were burned; and
- cereal production fell by 40 percent, tobacco production by 89 percent, and currant production by 66 percent.

Unfortunately, rather than focusing on rebuilding the country, the people were thrown into a brutal civil war that followed soon after liberation.

## NOTES

1. "A Letter from Metaxas' Wife," Metaxas Project Inside Fascist Greece (1936 to 1941), http://www.metaxas-project.com/metaxas-wife/.

2. Winston Churchill, *The Grand Alliance* (Boston: Houghton Mifflin, 1950), 302.

3. "Greeks in World War II," http://students.ceid.upatras.gr/~akis/jotd33/att-0349/02.

4. Leni Riefenstahl, *Leni Riefenstahl: A Memoir* (New York: Picador, 1995), 295.

5. Chrys Chrysanthou, *Cries and Whispers* (Bloomington, IN: Xlibris, 2006), 46. Used by permission.

6. Violetta Hionidou, *Famine and Death in Occupied Greece, 1941–1944* (Cambridge, England: Cambridge University Press), 32.

7. Paul Wood, "Greek Bailiffs Size Up German Property," *BBC News*, August 10, 2000, http://news.bbc.co.uk/2/hi/europe/872532.stm.

8. The Greek version of this poem appears in "Massacre of Distomo," http://www.distomo.gr/history/massacre.htm. Translation by Elaine Thomopoulos.

9. Tasos Antonopoulos, *Calvary of Meligalas* (Chicago: Tom Anton, 2006), 29.

10. "Archbishop Damaskinos," International Raoul Wallenberg Foundation, http://www.raoulwallenberg.net/es/generales/archbishop-damaskinos/.

11. "The Holocaust in Greece: Zakynthos," United States Holocaust Memorial Museum, http://www.ushmm.org/museum/exhibit/online/greece/eng/zakyntho.htm.

12. Ibid.

13. Jeanne Tsatsos, *The Sword's Fierce Edge: A Journal of the Occupation of Greece, 1941–1944*, trans. Jean Demos (Nashville, TN: Vanderbilt University Press, 1969), 17.

14. Ibid., 24, 25.

15. Edmund Keeley, *Inventing Paradise: The Greek Journey 1937–1947* (New York: Farrar, Straus and Giroux, 1999), 204.

16. André Gerolymatos, *Red Acropolis, Black Terror: The Greek Civil War and the Origins of the Soviet-American Rivalry, 1943–1949* (New York: Basic Books, 2004), 236.

17. Richard Clogg, ed. and trans., *Greece, 1940–1949: Occupation, Resistance, Civil War: A Documentary History* (New York: Palgrave Macmillan, 2003), 171.

18. C. M. Woodhouse, *The Apple of Discord: A Survey of Recent Greek Politics in their International Setting* (London: Hutchinson, 1948), 306.

19. Ibid., 307.

20. Ibid.

21. L. S. Stavrianos, *Greece: American Dilemma and Opportunity* (Chicago: Henry Regnery, 1952), 123, 124.

22. Tsatsos, *The Sword's Fierce Edge*, 124.

23. Author's personal correspondence with Dimitri Augoustinos, June 2009.

# 9

# Civil War

The civil war was fought between Greek government troops and the Communist-controlled Democratic Army of Greece (DSE) from 1946 to 1949. Even though Michail Kerhoulas had to flee to the mountains when his village near Sparta was burned by the Nazi occupation troops, he felt that the civil war was worse. He said, "Brother fought against brother, father against son. In World War II, you knew who your enemy was. During the civil war you could not even trust your neighbor. He could kill you."[1]

Dr. Chrys Chrysanthou experienced the threat from fellow Greeks after the end of World War II. According to email correspondence with the author, in 1945, Chrysanthou had rejected repeated requests to enlist in Communist organizations. He writes,

> The Communists ruled Thessaloniki for a short period in 1945 after the German occupation forces withdrew from the city (not during the civil war). It was during that period of chaos, uncertainty, and apprehension that I escaped the communist threat.
>
> What I experienced was the terror when men of the "People's Police" with machine guns, came to my house to take me for interrogation, and the feeling that my life was threatened if I was not willing to enlist. I promised to think about enlisting and immediately started planning

This meeting, which took place on November 27, 1944, after liberation, includes two leaders of the resistance, General Stefanos Saraphis of ELAS (left) and General Napoleon Zervas of EDES (right), as well as Lieutenant General Ronald Scobie, commander of the British forces in Greece. Saraphis and Zervas agreed to be under the command of Scobie during the expulsion of Germans from Greece in 1944. (Photo by Dmitri Kessel; courtesy of Hellenic Literary and Historical Archive—National Bank of Greece Cultural Foundation [E.L.I.A-M.I.E.T.])

my escape. My apartment was on the second floor of a building in the center of the city. Being afraid that my building was watched, I tied a rope to the railing of a balcony in the rear of the apartment, and in the middle of a dark night, I climbed down two floors landing on the roof of a storage shack in the backyard of the building. From there I jumped to the roof of the shack of the neighboring building and so on until I was far enough from my block. Then I walked to a pre-arranged point of meeting with a few other people and someone who would drive us secretly to an Indian Unit of the British Army that was camping a few miles outside Thessaloniki.[2]

There is some disagreement as to when the civil war started. Some consider the six weeks of fighting from December 1944 until February 1945 in the streets of Athens between Communist forces and British and Greek government forces as part of the civil war. Others date the beginning from March 1946. The civil war, fought throughout Greece, ended in October 1949. A prelude to the civil war had started during the Axis occupation, when the two major resistance organizations, the Communist-dominated EAM-ELAS, fought the other major resistance organization, EDES.

## DEKEMVRIANA, 1944

On December 3, 1944, about 100,000 people gathered in the streets of Athens. The parade of people shouting slogans had been organized by EAM following the resignation of EAM ministers from the Greek government. The ministers resigned when Papandreou, under pressure from Scobie, reneged on the agreement that ELAS could retain their elite troops. They were also upset when they learned that Papandreou allowed the Greek militia, whom ELAS saw as former German collaborators, to keep their arms.

There are various accounts of who started the killing that occurred during the December 3 demonstration. The tragic outcome: at least 15 people killed, 148 injured. The next day, a general strike was called, and for nearly six weeks fierce fighting erupted in the streets of Athens between ELAS forces and the combined forces of the British army and the Greek government, as well as other anti-Communist groups. This tragic phase is referred to as the Dekemvriana (December events). The British forces had been bolstered by the Fourth Indian Infantry Division, as well as other forces that had come from Italy to Greece. The British and Greek government forces were victorious.

In the midst of the fighting, Winston Churchill left his family's Christmas celebration to fly to Athens. Anthony Eden accompanied him. For a couple of days, they met with Archbishop Damaskinos and British and Greek leaders, including ELAS leaders. Damaskinos, a former wrestler who was more than six feet tall, was a handsome, intelligent, and articulate man. He made a positive impression on Churchill.

Churchill's visit did not stop the fighting. However, it did convince Churchill that the king should be persuaded to stay in London until a plebiscite decided whether he should return as king. Churchill persuaded the king to appoint Damaskinos as regent until the plebiscite took place. He remained as head of the government (first as regent and then as self-appointed prime minister) until the return of the king in 1946.

The Dekemvriana devastated Athens. The fighting and the bombing by the Royal Air Force left part of the city in ruins. Around 11,000 lives were lost. Innocent citizens as well as combatants suffered. During their departure, ELAS forced 8,000 hostages to march out of Athens in the cold winter of February 1945. Many died.

These women are protesting the killings that occurred during December 3, 1944 in the streets of Athens. They kneel in front of the Parliament Building. The sign reads: "When the people are faced with the danger of tyranny, they must choose between the chains and the arms. EAM." (Photo by Dmitri Kessel; courtesy of Hellenic Literary and Historical Archive—National Bank of Greece Cultural Foundation [E.L.I.A-M.I.E.T.])

Following the Dekemvriana about 7,500 suspected Communists, many of whom had no affiliation at all with the Communists, were sent to remote prisons, such as the British concentration camp Al Dab'a in Egypt, where many were tortured. In 1947, the Greek government outlawed the Communist Party, and it remained outlawed until 1974.

## VARKIZA PEACE AGREEMENT

A short-lived peace came as a result of the Varkiza Peace Agreement, which was signed on February 12, 1945. Lieutenant General Ronald Scobie, commander of the British forces in Greece, met with the military leader of ELAS, General Stefanos Saraphis, and the military leader of EDES, General Napoleon Zervas. The general secretary of the KKE, Nikolaos Zahariadis, wanted to have a "people's democracy" through a general election, and not by fighting, and thus agreed to the peace agreement. The peace agreement included the reinstatement of civil liberties; the legalization of the Communist Party;

a plebiscite on the reinstatement of the king prior to a general election being called; disarmament of ELAS; and a general amnesty, with the exception of crimes against persons or property.

Aris Velouchiotis disagreed with the provisions of the Varkiza Peace Agreement. He felt ELAS should be mobilized for action, and he returned to the mountains. The KKE renounced him, and shortly afterward he died. He was reported to have been ambushed by Greek government forces. There is a debate about whether he was killed or committed suicide. His head and that of his second in command, Yannis Angeletos (known as Javellas), were hung from a lamppost in the town square in Trikala.

## PERCENTAGES AGREEMENT, OCTOBER 1944

Some surmise that Moscow advised the Greek Communists to accept the Varkiza agreement. Joseph Stalin did not help the Greek Communists by supplying either men or arms during the civil war. Stalin seemed to be honoring the "percentages agreement," which Stalin and Churchill first formulated in Moscow in October 1944. They came to the agreement that Stalin's government would take charge of Romania in exchange for Britain having influence in Greece. Churchill records his meeting with Stalin:

> The moment was apt for business, so I said, "Let us settle about our affairs in the Balkans. Your armies are in Rumania and Bulgaria. We have interests, missions and agents there. Don't let us get at cross-purposes in small ways. So far as Britain and Russia are concerned, how would it do for you to have ninety percent predominance in Rumania, for us to have ninety percent of the say in Greece, and go fifty-fifty about Yugoslavia?" While this was being translated I wrote out on a half a sheet of paper:

Rumania
    Russia    90%
    The others    10%

Greece
    Great Britain    90%
    (in accord with the U.S.A.)
    Russia    10%

Yugoslavia    50–50%

Hungary    50–50%

Bulgaria
    Russia    75%
    The others    25%

I pushed this across to Stalin, who had by then heard the translation. There was a slight pause. Then he took his blue pencil and made a large tick upon it, and passed it back to us. It was all settled in no more time than it takes to set down. After this there was a long silence. The pencilled paper lay in the centre of the table....

At length I said, "Might it not be thought rather cynical if it seemed we had disposed of these issues, so fateful to millions of people, in such an offhand manner? Let us burn the paper." "No, you keep it," said Stalin.[3]

## KING REINSTATED, 1946

In April 1946, the monarchist United Patriotic Party won the election, with Konstantinos Tsaldaris as prime minister. On September 1, 1946, the Greeks, in a plebiscite, decided that the king should be reinstated. On September 26, King George II returned to find the palace looted and the country in shambles. King George's reign did not last long. He died of arteriosclerosis on April 1, 1947. His brother, King Paul, succeeded him.

## EVENTS LEADING TO THE CIVIL WAR

The Varkiza peace agreement had specified that a plebiscite about the future of the king be conducted before any general elections. When elections were called prior to the plebiscite being held, the Communists became incensed. They were also upset that Nazi collaborators were not being identified and brought to trial. Some of the collaborators participated in what was called the "White Terror," the persecution of those they thought were Communists (i.e., members of EAM, EPON, or ELAS). Thus many young men and women who fought valiantly against the Germans as *andartes* (guerrilla soldiers) were sent to prisons to be "rehabilitated"; others were executed.

In protest against the government's actions, the KKE and ELAS leaders asked their supporters to refrain from voting in the 1946 election. Thus the Communists did not win any seats in the parliament.

About a year after the Varkiza peace agreement, the KKE came to the conclusion that control of the country could only be accomplished through armed resistance. By the spring of 1946, the renewal of civil conflict was tearing the country apart. In October, former ELAS troops were organized under the command of Markos Vafiadis. They were called the Democratic Army of Greece (DSE). The new rebel government, the Provisional Democratic Government of Free Greece, was announced on radio on December 24, 1947. An excerpt of the broadcast follows: "The first and overriding aim of the Provisional Government is to mobilize all the powers of the people for the rapid liberation of the country from the foreign imperialists and their local puppets, for the consolidation of national sovereignty, for the defense of its territorial integrity from foreign imperialist onslaught, and for the victory of Democracy."[4]

The Yugoslavian, Bulgarian, and Albanian Communists supported the DSE by giving them access to supplies and bases of operation, providing a means of escape across the borders. At first the DSE made important strides, taking over parts of the Peloponnese and making inroads near Athens.

## ASSISTANCE THROUGH THE TRUMAN DOCTRINE, MARSHALL PLAN, AND UNITED NATIONS

The Greek army got stronger, partly because of support from the British and then the United States. Britain had given more than 85 million pounds in aid. When Britain announced it would withdraw its support as of March 31, 1947, President Harry S. Truman asked the U.S. Congress to help. He requested $400 million for Greece and Turkey for the period ending June 30, 1948. An excerpt of his March 12 address to Congress follows:

> Greece is not a rich country. Lack of sufficient natural resources has always forced the Greek people to work hard to make both ends meet. Since 1940, this industrious and peace-loving country has suffered invasion, 4 years of cruel enemy occupation, and bitter internal strife.
>
> When forces of liberation entered Greece they found that the retreating Germans had destroyed virtually all the railways, roads, port facilities, communications, and merchant marine. More than a thousand villages had been burned. Eighty-five percent of the children were tubercular. Livestock, poultry, draft animals had almost disappeared. Inflation had wiped out practically all savings.
>
> As a result of these tragic conditions, a militant minority, exploiting human want and misery, was able to create political chaos which, until now, has made economic recovery impossible.

Later in his speech Truman said, "I believe that it must be the policy of the U.S. to support free peoples who are resisting attempted subjugations by armed minorities or by outside pressures. I believe that we must assist free peoples to work out their own destinies in their own way. I believe that our help should be primarily through economic and financial aid which is essential to economic stability and orderly political processes." He went on to say: "The free peoples of the world look to us for support in maintaining their freedoms. If we falter in our leadership, we may endanger the peace of the world—and we shall surely endanger the welfare of our own Nation."[5]

Between March 1947 and June 1949, the United States sent $400 million for military aid and over $300 million for economic aid to Greece. The money enabled the restoration of harbors in Piraeus, Thessaloniki, Volos, and Patras. The Corinth Canal was reopened. Highways that connected municipal cities with provincial towns were built. Farming was helped by importing farm machinery, seeds, and fertilizers. Education in farming was offered.

In 1949, the U.S. Marshall Plan (European Recovery Program) followed the Truman Doctrine. From 1949 to 1951, it gave assistance to 18 European countries. The purpose of this program was to create a strong economic foundation for the countries of Europe. During the Greek civil war, a substantial amount went toward military expenses. Also, about 300 military and civilian personnel served as advisors. The United States, through the Truman Doctrine and the Marshall Plan, helped Greece defeat the Communists and slowly rebuild its economy after the wars.

The United Nations also lent their assistance. After the war, the United Nations Relief and Rehabilitation Administration helped Greece wipe out malaria. One million out of a population of seven and a half million contracted the disease each year. That number rose to as many as one in three during epidemic years. In 1947, the cases dropped dramatically to less than 50,000, and that included cases contracted in previous years. This was 1/20th of what it had been before. Colonel Daniel E. Wright, who had experience with controlling yellow fever and malaria during the building of the Panama Canal, directed the campaign, using DDT in mosquito-infested swamps.

## ECONOMIC CONDITIONS DURING THE CIVIL WAR

The economic condition of the country was in dire straits in the spring of 1948, as reported by the Athens government's Information Office in London. Inflation was still on the rise, and no less than one-third of the population was destitute.[6]

Exports had dropped dramatically. Tobacco, which before the war consisted of 52 percent of the value of Greek exports, in 1947 fell off to 17,300 tons exported, which was 35 percent of prewar. In 1948, exports sank to 2,500 tons. Germany had been one of the chief importers of Greek tobacco. Afterward, it received most of its supply from the United States because it was less expensive. Other exports also fell, including olive oil and citrus.

Tax evasion, still a problem in 2011, was rampant in 1948, as evident in the striking of the Athens Merchants' Association after the government tried to control tax evasion by applying a law making mandatory the keeping of accounts for tax purposes.

After the civil war, there was continuing disunity and abuse of human rights. Suspected Communists were persecuted. Two years before the end of the war, in 1947, the Greek government adopted a tough anti-Communist policy, which continued for many years after the civil war. Successive governments made

Communism illegal, and the government imprisoned suspected Communists until the restoration of democracy in 1974, when the civilian government of Karamanlis legalized the KKE.

## DODECANESE ISLANDS OF AEGEAN ANNEXED IN 1948

Greece received some good news in the midst of all the chaos. The Dodecanese Islands were united with Greece in 1948. They had been occupied by the Italians from 1911 to 1943, by the Germans from 1943 to 1945, and by the British since 1945.

## TRANSPORT OF CHILDREN TO COMMUNIST-BLOC COUNTRIES, 1947–1949

From 1947 to 1949, the Communists gathered about 28,000 children from northern Greece and transported them to Communist-bloc countries. About 18,500 went to Bulgaria, Romania, Hungary, Czechoslovakia, Poland, East Germany, and Albania, and about 9,500 went to Yugoslavia.

There are two views about how the children fared. Some claim that many of the children were taken without the consent of their parents and suffered during the ordeal. The term they apply to the transporting of the children is *paidomazoma* (gathering of children). The same term had been used when referring to how Ottomans forcefully took Greek children from their parents.

Others feel that the transporting of the children saved them. They call it *paidofylagma* (protection of children). They say that the parents sent their children willingly to save them from the dangers of civil war, starvation, and disease and for the opportunity of education, since many of the schools had been closed during the wars.

How many of the children were taken without the consent of their parents has not been determined. Neither is there an answer as to whether this was a positive or negative experience for the children. This probably varied from country to country, from camp to camp, and from child to child in the same camp.

Nicholas Gage, author of the book *Eleni*, speaks out strongly against the *paidomazoma*. His village was under the control of the Communists, and children were being taken. His mother, Eleni, arranged for the escape of nine-year-old Nick and his sisters. The Communists executed her.

Niki Karavasilis in her book *Abducted Children* also relays a darker side of the paidomazoma, giving examples of bad treatment and children suffering because of the separation from their parents. She interviewed Dora, who spent 33 years behind the iron curtain and never got to see her widowed mother again.

On the other hand, many tell of the opportunities that were afforded in the Communist countries that received them and their parents' willingness for them to be evacuated. Thanasis Economou's father, along with village elders, agreed to their children being taken by the Communists. Economou in email correspondence wrote: "The places where we were living were a paradise compared to what we left behind in Greece of 1940s...I interacted with thousands of these children and not in a single case had anyone told me that he was abducted."[7]

This is an excerpt of the article written by George Chiagouris, based on his interview of Economou:

> After about three days of walking, they reached Albania, along with other children from nearby villages. The only items they carried were one change of underwear and some food, consisting mostly of bread and cheese. When they crossed the Albanian border, Communist organizers met them and divided the children into groups of 15 to 20. They stayed in homes for about a month. At the end of the month, the Communists took the children to Yugoslavia by buses and then to Czechoslovakia by trains. There they were placed in facilities that were operated like boarding schools. It was there that he [Economou] attended school for the first time in his life. After finishing elementary school, Economou was sent to a nearby resort town to attend high school and eventually to Charles University in Prague for studies in nuclear physics. Economou began first grade when he was 11 years old and obtained his Ph.D. degree in physics at the age of 24.[8]

In 1964, Economou immigrated to the United States, where he joined his two brothers, who had immigrated earlier. He is a senior scientist at the Laboratory for Astrophysics and Space Research, Enrico Fermi Institute, University of Chicago. Since the mid-1960s, he has worked on developing innovative and sophisticated instruments for use in space.

Partly in response to what she claimed was the "abduction" of Greek children by the Communists, Queen Fredericka set up 53 of her own camps to take care of orphaned and poor children from the war-torn areas of Greece. Critics say that some of the children that were housed in the camps were themselves forcefully abducted. The camps also took care of children who were left orphaned by the earthquake on the islands of Zakynthos and Kefalonia in 1953. Nearly 34,000 children passed through these camps from 1947 until 1964.

## AMERICAN JOURNALIST MURDERED, 1948

While covering the civil war, CBS journalist George Polk was shot in the back of the head, with his hands and feet bound. Gregorios Staktopoulos, a

Greek journalist, was accused of the murder but said that his confession was obtained under torture. No one else has ever been accused. In 1949, Long Island University established a yearly award in Polk's memory.

## END OF THE CIVIL WAR, 1949

The National Army, under the command of General Alexander Papagos, defeated the DSE in a counteroffensive at the end of August 1949, which took place in the Grammos and Vitsi Mountains in northern Greece. On October 16, 1949, DSE surrendered. Several things may have contributed to the defeat of the Communist forces. One was the closing of the borders of Yugoslavia by Josip Broz Tito and the disbanding of DSE camps there. Thus the DSE could no longer get supplies and armaments, nor could they escape the government troops by crossing the border. When Tito and Stalin broke off relations in June 1949, Tito, who wanted to remain independent of Stalin, was disappointed when many of the leadership of the KKE decided to support Stalin. Tito may have closed the borders in retaliation.

The rift between supporters of Tito and Stalin also led to disintegration within the KKE. Those supporting Stalin went on a witch hunt to rout the supporters of Tito.

A few days after the DSE loss at the Battle of Grammos, Vafiadis was relieved of his military position, and then his political position. Nikos Zahariadis, who had replaced Vafiadis as head of the army, reorganized it so that DSE could fight conventional warfare, rather than the guerrilla warfare in which they had gained expertise. Some believe that change to conventional warfare was a poor move on his part.

Many of the Communists and their supporters fled to Communist countries. They had no choice. If they stayed, they faced the possibility of prison or death at the hands of government forces. Not until 1982 did the Greek government welcome back those Greeks who had gone into forced exile after the civil war.

Many of those who had joined DSE had been Slavic-speaking Greek citizens. As of 2010, Slavic-speaking Greek citizens who had left for Soviet-bloc countries had not been welcomed back to Greece.

The defeat of the DSE did not lead to a unified nation. Deep schisms continued. By 1947, the government adopted a tough anti-Communist policy, which made Communism illegal. Suspected Communists were rounded up and imprisoned.

From 1950 to 1974, the government administered a system of surveillance that included paid informants. Information on citizens was compiled in files. Based on the information collected, the government issued certificates of loyalty. Those without certificates could not vote; get peddlers' licenses; obtain passports, public aid, or scholarships; or work in the public sector or for the merchant marine. Those suspected of being Communists had difficulty obtaining these certificates.

Researcher Minas Samatas said:

> Any candidate for public services who was him/herself (or any of his/her relatives) politically stigmatized as non-nationally-minded had to go through an official process of "destigmatization" or "decolorization" (*apochromatismos*). This procedure involved having officials cross-out all of the accusations of disloyalty written in red pen on the file of all 're-converted' ex-communists, as well as of those who had been recorded as cryptocommunists or as communist sympathizers. Even those neutral individuals who had never publicly declared themselves either *ethnikofrones* [nationally minded] or leftists were forced to publicize their loyalty (*ethnikofrosyni*) when applying for passports, driver's licenses, and professional licenses. This entailed signing official loyalty statements and being forced to renounce past politics, beliefs and any relatives or friends who had subversive records.[9]

## NOTES

1. Elaine Thomopoulos, *Greeks of Berrien County* (Berrien Springs, MI: Berrien County Historical Association, 2007), 3.

2. Email correspondence with author.

3. Winston Churchill, *Triumph and Tragedy* (Cambridge, MA: Houghton Mifflin, 1953), 227.

4. Richard Clogg, *Greece 1940–1949* (New York: Palgrave Macmillan, 2002), 205, 206.

5. "Recommendation for Assistance to Greece and Turkey: Address of the President of the United States Delivered before a Joint Session of the Senate and House of Representatives, 80th Congress, 1st session, March 12, 1947, Document 171," http://www.trumanlibrary.org/whistlestop/study_collections/doctrine/large/index.php.

6. L. S. Stavrianos, *Greece: American Dilemma and Opportunity* (Chicago: Henry Regnery, 1952), 193.

7. Email correspondence with author.

8. George Chiagouris, "Economou Explores the Solar System," Greek American Scientists, *The National Herald,* January 27, 2007, 8.

9. Minas Samatas, "Studying Surveillance in Greece: Methodological and Other Problems Related to an Authoritarian Surveillance Culture," in "Doing Surveillance Studies," *Surveillance and Society* 3, no. 2/3: 183, http://www.statewatch.org/news/2006/mar/samatas-greece-s-and-soc.pdf.

# 10

# Recovery after the Wars

When the civil war ended in 1949, with the government troops victorious, the country was in shambles. During the wars, hundreds of thousands had died, and over 10 percent of the Greek population had been displaced from their homes. Villages had been destroyed. Forests had been burned down. Crops were ruined. Those who made their living by farming had a hard time. In 1950, according to a special agricultural census, rural families comprised 4,770,783 persons, or 63 percent of the estimated total population of the country in that year. The farms were small, barely enough for subsistence. The average farm contained between 8 and 12.5 acres. Amenities were few. Much of the rural countryside did not have indoor plumbing or electricity. Some villages had only one phone and some had none. Radios were in short supply, even though after 1949, to strengthen the communication system, a push was made by the U.S. Information Service in Greece to put a radio in each village.

Families, for economical survival, migrated to the cities, which started a construction boom. Houses lost during the war were rebuilt, and in the cities rows of concrete flats, without aesthetic consideration or much greenery, were constructed.

The women of the rural villages had a hard life, taking care the household and children as well as farming. One of the tasks was to draw water from the village well, as these women were doing in Agios Basileos near Tripoli in 1965. Electricity and indoor plumbing were not available until the 1970s in many of the villages and islands of Greece. (Photo by Elaine Thomopoulos)

## ECONOMY GROWS

From the mid-1950s to the mid-1970s, Greece grew at an unprecedented rate. Several things contributed to that growth. The devaluation of the drachma helped curb inflation. The construction boom helped, as did the Marshall Plan. In addition, Greece also started to attract foreign investment. The tourist industry started to increase during the 1950s and escalated in the 1960s, 1970s, and 1980s. Besides tourists coming from nearby Europe, thousands of immigrants and their children from America reunited with Greek relatives. Young backpacking students from America as well as Europe discovered Greece's hedonistic pleasures. Easy access via jet planes made it easier to travel to Greece. By the 1980s, planes directly from Europe to islands such as Zakynthos or Rhodes bolstered tourism from Europe.

People of Greece also found employment in the government, which kept getting bigger and bigger. Another employment opportunity that opened up was in shipping, since the merchant marine was growing by leaps and bounds. Even the immigration of Greeks to other countries helped the economy, since they sent millions of dollars back to Greece.

## MERCHANT MARINE REBUILT

After the war, many young men joined the merchant marine. It was a chance for them to see the world and get a paycheck, and it gave some of those who could not get passage to America through legal means the opportunity to "jump ship" to better their way of life. New York was a popular destination.

During World War II, the merchant marine had lost more than half of its approximately 600 oceangoing vessels and more than 2,000 men had died at sea. They recovered after the war. The sale in 1947 of 100 Liberty Ships and seven T2 tankers to Greek shipowners by the U.S. government helped spur the recovery of the shipping industry after the war. The Liberty Ships, which were sold at a fraction of their real value, had served as U.S. cargo ships during World War II. By the 1960s, more than 800 of the 1,200 Liberty Ships sold had passed through Greek hands. By the early 1970s, the Greek merchant marine industry prospered so much that it became number one in the world in terms of total tonnage, a position it still held in 2010.

The history of many of the prominent shipping families goes back to the 19th and early 20th centuries, when Aegean and Ionian island shippers established offices in Russia, Britain, Italy, and the United States. Their power emanated from their ties to family and countrymen. Even though many lived and were educated in countries other than Greece, the shippers remained close to Greece.

From the 1910s to the 1960s, there were about 100 families from the Aegean and Ionian Islands who dominated the industry. A large proportion of them traced their heritage back to the shipowners of the 19th century.

After World War II nontraditional shipowners, Greeks who did not come from shipowner families and did not trace their roots to the islands of the Aegean or Ionian Seas, entered the shipping industry. These newcomers, as well as the traditional shipowners, built or purchased offices in Piraeus, making it an important European port. The nontraditional shipowners such as Aristotle Onassis, Stavros Niarchos, and John Latsis excelled in transporting bulk cargo around the globe. Their purchase of supertankers to transport oil served them well. Each of them became billionaires. Not all of the shippers have been tycoons, however. Smaller shipowners, with only a few ships, have also been an important part of the industry.

## LITERACY RATE IMPROVES

Schooling had been disrupted during the war, especially in the rural areas. In some cases there were no schools, or schoolteachers. Nikos Fiorentinos of Zakynthos, Greece, said, "I did not go to school. Not even one day."[1] He worked on the family farm to help support his five sisters and one brother.

While he was in the army, he received a letter from his girlfriend. Too embarrassed to have one of his fellow soldiers read it, he decided he had better learn to read and write. He became a successful small-business owner in Zakynthos.

In 1951, total illiteracy was 25.9 percent; for males it was 11.9 percent and for females 38.6 percent. The strides in education since the war can be noted in the literacy statistics of the census of 2001, where literacy for both sexes is 96 percent—97.8 percent for males and 94.2 percent for females.

## EMIGRATION FROM GREECE AFTER WAR

Despite the beginning of recovery that the Marshall Plan jump-started, things were still very difficult economically in the 1950s, 1960s, and 1970s. Greece could not sustain its citizens, and as in the years before the war, they started to emigrate. In 1964, the United States reopened the immigration gates. However, unlike in the past when the main immigration was to the United States, in the postwar years, the Greeks went to Germany (as guest workers) and Australia, as well as to the United States and Canada. Between 1950 and 1974, more than a million Greeks left their homeland. This includes about one

This abandoned building in Tegea in the Peloponnese was available for sale in 2009. After World War II, the emigration of Greeks overseas, to Western Europe and to cities such as Athens and Thessaloniki, left many homes abandoned. Many rural villages lost their young people and their vitality. (Photo by Elaine Thomopoulos)

## Table 10.1. Major receiving countries for Greek immigrants from 1955 to 1973

| | |
|---|---|
| Germany | 603,300 |
| Australia | 170,700 |
| U.S. | 124,000 |
| Canada | 80,200 |

*Source:* Charalambos Kasimis and Chryssa Kassimi, "Greece: A History of Migration," Migration Policy Institute, June 2004, http://www.migrationinformation.org/Feature/display.cfm? ID = 228.

in four of the labor force and about 12 percent of the total population. The majority of immigrants came from rural areas.

The major receiving countries from 1955 to 1973, with the number of immigrants, are listed in Table 10.1.

## RELATIONSHIP WITH TURKEY DURING THE 1950s AND 1960s

Just before the pogrom of 1955, around 100,000 Greeks lived in Turkey. Turkish citizens of Greek ethnicity living in Constantinople had been exempt from the 1923 exchange of population. They, as well as Greek citizens who had become permanent residents, had established a thriving and cohesive Greek community, with businesses, churches, and schools. All that changed after the pogrom that took place from 5:30 P.M. on September 6, 1955, to 2:30 A.M. on September 7, 1955. Scattered mobs of about 100,000 Turks instituted a night of terror in several locations within the city. Just prior to the pogrom, the headline in the newspaper *Istanbul Express* screamed that Greeks had destroyed Atatürk's childhood home in Thessaloniki. The home was not damaged, other than the shattering of some windowpanes. The Greeks were not responsible. A Turkish agent brought the dynamite to Greece, and it was detonated by the doorman.

The reporter Frederic Sondern Jr., whose article was published in *Reader's Digest,* described what had happened after the news vendors started hawking the papers:

Five main streets converge on Taksim Square, and mobs in solid phalanxes were already pouring down each one, jamming into the place: "Kill the Greeks!" the staccato shouts filled the square. In one corner stood a shanty used to store the tools of a street-car gang. The door was torn off and then some fifty angry men armed themselves with crowbars, pickaxes, sledge hammers, sections of rail.[2]

The violence against the Greeks was not just a spontaneous outbreak but a pogrom (a government-instituted and organized violence against an ethnic minority). As detailed in Spyros Vyronis's book *Mechanisms of Catastrophe*, Prime Minister Adnan Menderes secretly planned for the pogrom and even brought in people from Asia Minor and Thrace so that they could participate in the violence. They carried steel bars, pickaxes, wooden clubs, acetylene torches, and gasoline. The police and armed forces did not step in to control the destruction. The damage was as follows, 20–30 killed, 200 Greek women raped; 1,000 homes destroyed and 2,500 partially destroyed and looted; 4,000–4,500 stores looted, destroyed, or damaged; 59 out of the 83 Greek Orthodox churches burned with others suffering damage; tombs of the Patriarchs destroyed; and Orthodox Christian cemeteries defiled. Photos by Demetrios Kaloumenos document the damage.

Menderes was deposed in a coup in 1960 and arrested. Evidence presented at the trial indicated that the Menderes government was behind the 1955 events. He and two other former government officials were hanged after being convicted of corruption and abuse of power.

Within 10 years of the pogrom, the Greek community in Turkey was again dealt a hard blow. Reacting to the escalation of violence between the Greek and Turks of Cyprus, in March 1964 the Turkish government canceled about 17,000 residency permits of Greeks living in Turkey. They also confiscated their property. Around 40,000 Greeks who had Turkish citizenship also left.

The number of Greek nationals living in Turkey has steadily decreased. From about 300,000 Greeks in Istanbul in 1922, by 1955, before the pogrom, it had fallen to about 100,000. By 1978, the number of Greeks had been reduced to 7,000. A report prepared in 2008 by the Turkish foreign ministry estimated that between 3,000 and 4,000 lived in Turkey, with a majority living in Istanbul.

The Greeks who have emigrated from Turkey to Greece in the latter half of the 20th century, like those who immigrated earlier, have often had a hard time adjusting to life in Greece. The movie *Taste of Spice* shows a Greek family torn apart by their forced departure from Istanbul in the 1960s. Ten-year-old Fanis faces a difficult integration into the strange world of Greece, where he is not really welcomed. He longs for those he has left behind. They include his best friend, a little Turkish girl who captivated him with her dancing and gentle nature, and his beloved wise grandfather, a neighborhood spice merchant. This touching story, which bridges the ethnic divide, was popular when it was released in 2003 and continues to have a following today. This is not surprising since at least one in four Greeks living in Greece today can trace their heritage to Asia Minor. Many Greeks, even those several generations removed, have lingering memories of their original homeland in Turkey. They can relate to the food and culture shown in the film, as well as the trauma of immigration. Both Greek and Turkish audiences embraced the humanity shown in the film.

## EXODUS OF GREEKS FROM EGYPT FROM 1952 TO 1957

The Greek community in Alexandria, established in the 1840s, had prospered. After Gamal Abdel Nasser came to power in Egypt in 1952, he began a series of regulations that made it impossible for the Greek community to continue to thrive. These regulations included land redistribution, which affected the Greek cotton producers, as well as nationalization of foreign-owned banks, insurance companies, and manufacturing companies. Even community organizations and schools were placed under government jurisdiction. The once vibrant community, which in the 1920s numbered 100,000, now numbers a few hundred. Many repatriated to Greece, where they were treated as outsiders. Others left for other countries, such as Australia, Canada, and the United States.

## GOVERNANCE FROM 1949 TO 1967

From 1949 to 1952, none of the Greek prime ministers lasted much more than a year. It was like the game of musical chairs. From the end of the civil war in 1949 to the rule of the Junta in 1967, there were more than 20 changes of government (including caretaker governments). In 1951, Greece was admitted to the North Atlantic Treaty Organization (NATO).

General Alexander Papagos of the royalist Greek Rally Party, which he founded, won 49 percent of the popular vote in the 1952 election, which gave him control of 257 out of 300 seats in parliament. He was in office until 1955, lending some stability to governance.

Konstantinos Karamanlis, also of the Greek Rally Party (later reformulated as the National Radical Union) served from 1955 to 1963, winning three successive elections. His five-year plan, which he announced in 1959, included a heavy investment in infrastructure, improvement of agricultural and industrial production, and the promotion of tourism.

After a disagreement with King Paul in 1963, he resigned his office and left for Paris. He came back a few months later for the elections, but when he was defeated, he again left for Paris, where he remained in self-imposed exile until 1974.

Georgios Papandreou had served as prime minister briefly in 1944 during and after World War II, for nearly two months in 1963, and then for about a year and a half in 1964/1965. In 1965, he had a disagreement with King Constantine II, the 25-year-old king who had assumed the throne after the death of his father, King Paul, of cancer in March 1964. The king would not consent to Papandreou being in charge of the military. At the time, Papandreou's son Andreas was under investigation for his alleged participation in the Aspida affair, the conspiracy against the king that involved the army (he was not convicted). The period immediately following the resignation of Papandreou is referred to as the Apostasy, because defectors from Georgios Papandreou's Center Union Party supported the king and his appointment of the subsequent prime minister. One of the apostates (renegades) was Konstantinos Mitsotakis, who became Andreas Papandreou's political rival. Some of the so-called apostates were successively appointed as prime ministers by King Constantine II. None stayed very long in the job.

Taking advantage of the leadership chasm that followed Papandreou's resignation, a group of military men staged a bloodless coup and gained control of the government.

## RULE OF THE JUNTA, 1967–1974

On April 21, 1967, tanks rolled down the streets of Athens. Colonels George Papadopoulos and Nikolaos Makarezos and Brigadier General Stylianos Pattakos, referred to as the Junta or the Colonels, took control of the government in a coup. They said they took over to prevent a Communist takeover, although this threat did not exist. After King Constantine II unsuccessfully tried to overthrow the Junta in December, he escaped to Italy. The Junta governed the country until 1974.

There were those who hated the Junta, headed by Papadopoulos, but others welcomed the stability and continuing improvement of the economy. Roads were built, electricity was brought to islands and remote villages, and farmers' debt was forgiven. Also, the Junta took advantage of Greece's beautiful landscape and friendly people to bolster the tourist industry.

However, by 1973, inflation had risen to 30 percent. Also, many of the citizens of Greece became alarmed by the Junta's abuse of human rights. People were scared to speak out against the government, fearing that they would be labeled Communists and subsequently jailed and tortured.

The Junta censored the press and suppressed civil liberties. Political opponents were incarcerated in prisons or exiled to remote islands such as Yaros. Torture elicited their confessions.

The son of Prime Minister Georgios Papandreou, American-educated Andreas Papandreou, was arrested and imprisoned for his supposed participation in the alleged Aspida conspiracy. His friends in America, where he had earned his PhD and taught in universities, helped secure his release. President Lyndon Johnson spoke out on his behalf. During the rule of the Junta, Papandreou lived in exile in America and Europe.

Until 1973, the Junta forbade playing of certain music, such as the compositions of Mikis Theodorakis, a Communist. Films such as Costa-Gavras's Oscar-winning *Z* also were not allowed. Costas-Gavras based his film on the assassination of peace activist Dr. Grigoris Lambrakis by two right-wing thugs on May 22, 1963. Even certain books were banned.

## PROTESTS AGAINST THE JUNTA AND OVERTHROW OF THE JUNTA BY BLOODLESS COUP

On August 13, 1968, Alexandros Panagoulis had planted a bomb on a road outside of Athens so that it would blow up Papadopoulos's car when he passed. The plan failed. Panagoulis was captured and sentenced to death, but his death sentence was commuted. While imprisoned, he wrote poems with his blood. About three months later, former prime minister Georgios Papandreou's funeral became a massive demonstration against the Junta.

In 1970, geology student Kostas Georgakis set himself ablaze in Genoa, Italy, and brought world attention to the repression of the Junta. Nikiforos Vrettakos writes about Georgakis in his poem "The View of the World": "You were the bright summary of our drama...in one and the same torch, the light of the resurrection and our mourning by the gravestone."[3]

In his final letter to his father, Georgakis wrote:

My dear father. Forgive me for this act, without crying. Your son is not a hero. He is a human, like all the others, maybe a little more fearful. Kiss our land for me. After three years of violence I cannot suffer any longer. I don't want you to put yourselves in any danger because of my own actions. But I cannot do otherwise but think and act as a free individual. I write to you in Italian so that I can raise the interest of everyone for our problem. Long Live Democracy. Down with the tyrants. Our land which gave birth to Freedom will annihilate tyranny! If you are able to, forgive me. Your Kostas.[4]

In 1971, tens of thousands came out for the funeral of the Nobel Prize–winning poet, George Seferis, a vocal opponent of the Junta. They followed his coffin as it made its way through the streets of Athens to the First Cemetery of Athens. In an act of resistance to the Junta, they sang the banned composer Mikis Theodorakis's musical rendition of Seferis's poem "Denial."

On the hidden seashore
White as a pigeon
We thirsted at midday.
But the water was brackish.
On the blond sand
We wrote her name.

The breeze blew
Erasing the letters.
With our heart, with our breath,
With our longing and pathos,
We spent our life—a mistake!
And we changed it.[5]

On June 1, 1973, the Junta abolished the monarchy and declared a republic. In September 1973, Spyros Markezinis, a veteran politician, was appointed prime minister by Papadopoulos. Markezinis's task was to lead Greece to parliamentary rule. During this liberalization attempt many restrictions were lifted, such as the prohibition of broadcasts of Theodorakis's music.

During 1973, college students initiated a series of demonstrations against the Junta. They included a sit-in at the Athens law school in March and a demonstration at the Athens Polytechnic University in mid-November. When the students at the Polytechnic University began broadcasting for a student-worker alliance to overthrow the Junta, forces were sent to quell the disturbance. On November 17, they opened fire and sent a tank crashing into the gates of the university. The clash resulted in at least 24 dead. The public was appalled at the brutality, and public opinion mounted against the Junta.

On November 25, 1973, after six years of rule, the triumvirate of Papadopoulos, Makarezos, and Pattakos was ousted by a bloodless coup organized by the army and supported by the air force and navy. They were against the attempt at liberalization. The regime that followed became even more rigid, controlled by the so-called "invisible dictator," Brigadier General Dimitrios Ioannidis, chief of the Greek military police.

## TROUBLE IN CYPRUS

In 1974, Ioannidis overstepped his boundaries and hauled Greece into the messy internal affairs of Cyprus, overthrowing the president of Cyprus, Archbishop Makarios. The only good that came from this was that in April 1974 Ioannidis was deposed and democratic rule returned to Greece.

The eastern Mediterranean island of Cyprus achieved independence from Britain in 1960, after having been under her control since 1878. Two ethnic groups, a Greek majority and a Turkish minority, occupied the island. Rather than the island celebrating its independence, the Greek and Turkish Cypriots were at each other's throats. They did not agree about how the nation should be governed. In 1964, U.S. president Lyndon Johnson had to step in to prevent a Turkish invasion of Cyprus, and the United Nations sent a peacekeeping force. The commander of the peace effort, after stationing troops in different areas of Nicosia, drew a cease-fire line on a map of Cyprus with a green pencil. Thus the line is called the Green Line. As of 2011, the United Nations peacekeeping force still remained in Cyprus.

## Turkey Invades Cyprus, 1974

Ten years later, in 1974, the conflict between Greek and Turkish Cypriots continued. But there was also a struggle between two factions of the Greek Cypriots. One faction believed in union with Greece, while the other faction, which included President Archbishop Makarios of Cyprus, believed Cyprus should remain independent.

In Greece, Ioannidis, who believed in union with Greece, took things into his own hands by supporting the July 1974 plot to overthrow the duly elected president of Cyprus, Archbishop Makarios. Makarios heard of the plot and escaped. Five days after Makarios fled for his life, Turkish troops landed at Kyrenia, Cyprus. Greece, under the de facto government of Ioannidis, had made a grave error in supporting the coup against Makarios. In response, Turkey invaded Cyprus. Neither Greece nor the Greek Cypriots could stop this invasion, code named by the Turks as "Operation Atilla." After the debacle in Cyprus, senior military officials in Greece withdrew their support of the Ioannidis dictatorship, and it toppled on July 23, three days after the invasion.

## Turks Occupy 37 Percent of Cyprus

The Turkish nation said that the intervention of Greece in the affairs of Cyprus (the attempted overthrow of Makarios) justified their invasion. They continued their assault on the northern part of Cyprus. By August 16, 1974, the Turks occupied the northern part of the island, 37 percent of Cyprus.

In the wake of the invasion, nearly 200,000 Greek Cypriots had to flee their homes in northern Cyprus. Most of them settled in southern Cyprus. About 3,000 Greek Cypriots were killed or missing in action. They lost property and possessions that they have not been able to recover. To add insult to injury, Turkey settled Turkish nationals in northern Cyprus.

## The Greek American Community Speaks
## Out against the Turkish Invasion

In August 1974, two national organizations, the American Hellenic Institute, based in Washington, D.C., and the United Hellenic American Congress, based in Chicago, were organized in response to the Turkish invasion and occupation of Cyprus. The Greek American community objected that the United States had done nothing to deter the Turkish invasion. Secretary of State Henry Kissinger, in particular, was blamed. Turkey had illegally used American-supplied arms in violation of U.S. laws and agreements. A lobbying effort by the Greek American community helped bring about an arms embargo of Turkey, which started in February 1975 and lasted until October 1978.

## Cyprus Remains a Divided Island

The Turkish Republic of Northern Cyprus was established in 1983 but has not been recognized by anyone except Turkey and the Nakhchivan Autonomous Republic, an enclave of Azerbaijan. As of 2011, the situation in Cyprus had not been resolved. The Green Line goes through the capital of Cyprus, Nicosia, and separates northern and southern Cyprus. Until 2004, the line could not be crossed. Now there are places where it can be crossed. The island nation continues to be divided. The United Nation's Annan Plan, which attempted a reunification of the island, was defeated by a referendum held in 2004. The Greek Cypriots voted against it; the Turkish Cypriots for it.

## NOTES

1. Nick Thomopoulos, *100 Years: From Greece to Chicago and Back* (Bloomington, IN: Xlibris, 2011), 145.

2. Speros Vryonis Jr., *The Mechanisms of Catastrophe* (New York: Greekworks. com, 2005), 118, 119.

3. "Kostas Georgakis 1948–1979," http://www.sansimera.gr/biographies/194.

4. "*Kostas Georgakis: Ee tragikee thisia pou klonise tee junta*" [Kostas Georgakis: The tragic sacrifice which shook the junta], InOut Website, http://www.inout. gr/showthread.php?t=31628.

5. This poem in Greek appears in "Mikis Theodorakis in East Berlin 1987: 22 Sto Perigiali (Arnisi)," YouTube, http://www.youtube.com/watch?v=B9IqV5SazpU. Translation by Elaine Thomopoulos.

# 11

# Democracy Returns to Greece

Democracy finally took hold in Greece with the election of Konstantinos Karamanlis in 1974. The first section of this chapter briefly covers the prime ministers who governed during this period. The second part of the chapter discusses the recurring issues that arose from 1974 through 2010.

## KONSTANTINOS KARAMANLIS RETURNS
## AS PRIME MINISTER, 1974–1980

After the toppling of the Greek dictatorship under Ioannidis on July 23, 1974, President Phaedon Gizikis convened a meeting of politicians and heads of the armed forces. They decided to invite conservative politician Karamanlis to come back from his self-imposed exile in France to assume the office of prime minister. Celebrations broke out throughout Greece, with his supporters shouting *"Erhetai. Erhetai"* ("He is coming. He is coming"). When he first returned, there was the fear of a new coup and that Karamanlis might be assassinated. For three weeks, he slept aboard a yacht watched over by a naval destroyer.

In the elections held in November 1974, Karamanlis's newly formed New Democracy (ND) Party emerged as the winner. Karamanlis retained his role as prime minister. After a referendum resulted in the abolition of the monarchy, the parliament established a republic and adopted a new constitution, which instituted reforms regarding civil liberties and the role of women. The new 1975 constitution stated: "Greek men and women have equal rights and equal obligations." In 1974, in the aftermath of the Turkish invasion in Cyprus, the Karamanlis government withdrew from the military wing of NATO.

In 1977, ND won the majority of the seats in the parliament and Karamanlis went on to serve another term as prime minister, until 1980. Under the governance of the Junta, Greece's application to become a member of the European Economic Community had become a dead issue. In 1975, the new government reapplied, and on January 1, 1981, Greece became the 10th member of the European Economic Community (precursor of the European Union). During the Karamanlis administration, the Greek Communist Party (KKE) was legalized.

George Rallis, the new leader of the ND Party, succeeded Karamanlis as prime minister but served only 1 1/2 years. In 1980, while Rallis was prime minister, Greece rejoined the military wing of NATO.

## ANDREAS PAPANDREOU OF PASOK SERVES AS PRIME MINISTER, 1981–1989 AND 1993–1996

The Panhellenic Socialist Movement (PASOK) won in the parliamentary elections held in October 1981. Andreas Papandreou took over as prime minister. He served nearly eight years, until 1989. The economy continued to progress during Papandreou's governance.

In 1982, the Papandreou administration tried to heal the rift that had occurred as a result of the civil war by welcoming back thousands of civil war refugees who had lost their citizenship and had been living in Eastern-bloc countries for more than 30 years.

The following laws, passed in the early and mid-1980s, strengthened the rights of women and dealt with marriage and family issues:

- Civil marriage was made legal, despite opposition from the church;
- the dowry system was abolished;
- a woman could choose to maintain her family name after marriage;
- married couples could choose the surname of their children—it did not have to automatically be the surname of the husband;
- no-fault and mutual-consent divorce was established;
- a husband and wife could jointly claim property acquired during the marriage;
- illegitimate children were granted rights equal to those held by legitimate children; and
- abortion was legalized, despite opposition from the church.

Papandreou also introduced educational reforms. In the universities, students could participate in the election process for their professors, deans, and rectors.

Papandreou's wife, Margaret Papandreou, originally from Elmhurst, Illinois, had worked for decades in programs to better the condition of women in Greece. She earned respect for her work in women's rights. In 1986, Papandreou created a scandal by divorcing his wife of 40 years to marry a former Olympic Airlines flight attendant, Dimitra Liani, who was half his age. Papandreou's party lost the 1989 election. He became prime minister again in 1993. He resigned in 1996 because of poor health and died six months later.

## KONSTANTINOS MITSOTAKIS OF ND SERVES AS PRIME MINISTER, 1990–1993

After three short-term governments that together lasted about a year, in April 1990, the New Democracy Party took over and remained in office until 1993. Mitsotakis worked to have a good relationship with the United States when he assumed office. He made the first official visit to Washington, DC, in decades. To show Greece's support, a frigate was dispatched to the Persian Gulf War in 1991. Greece allowed the continuing use of facilities at Souda Bay in Crete. However, the U.S. Hellinikon Air Base at Athens's main airport was closed, and the naval communication station near Athens was phased out. In the 1990s, three of the four U.S. bases were phased out. In 2011, only Souda Bay remains.

## KOSTAS SIMITIS OF PASOK SERVES AS PRIME MINISTER, 1997–2004

Kostas Simitis of PASOK took over for Papandreou in 1997. He continued in that office until March 2004 and while in office focused on modernizing the country. The following projects were initiated during his tenure:

- "Eleftherios Venizelos," Athens International Airport, which was completed in 2001.
- "Charilaos Trikoupis," Rio-Antirio Bridge, the world's longest multi-span cable-stayed bridge, which was completed in 2004.
- Athens Metro, which was partially completed in 2000.
- Egnatia Odos, a road linking northwestern Greece with northeastern Greece, which was completed in 2009.

Simitis succeeded in getting Greece admitted to the Eurozone in 2001 and worked hard to achieve the strict criteria needed to be accepted. According to data released during his administration, the country's inflation rate decreased, and the public deficit was reduced. However, the deficit was later discovered to be larger than his administration claimed.

An important change the government instituted under Simitis was removing religion as a category from the national identity card. An embarrassment was the Öcalan affair. In 1999, Öcalan, the leader of the Kurdistan Workers Party (PKK), was allowed to enter Greece and flown to Kenya, where he was housed at the Greek embassy in Nairobi, Kenya.

## KOSTAS KARAMANLIS OF ND SERVES AS PRIME MINSTER, 2004–2009

The ND Party again took the reins when Kostas Karamanlis, nephew of Konstantinos Karamanlis, was elected in 2004. He served until 2009, when PASOK, under Andreas Papandreou, took over. As did the administrations before him, he sought to bring unity to the Greek people. He was the first in his party to attend National Resistance Day, which was celebrated prior to his taking office as prime minister. He spoke on November 26, 2000, at the Gorgopotamos Bridge, where the two major Greek resistance organizations, ELAS and EDES, along with British forces, had blown it up in 1942. As reported by the *American News Agency Athens* on November 27, 2000, Karamanlis said: "The era of partition and discord is past history, without prospects of repetition, because this is the conscious choice of all of us." Karamanlis called on everyone to "overcome the prejudices of the past."[1]

## THE TRIUMPHANT RETURN OF THE OLYMPICS TO GREECE, 2004

'Welcome home" was the motto at the Olympic games held in Athens from August 13 to August 29, 2004. The Olympics had come home to Athens, the city where the first modern Olympic games were played in 1896. The games, under the direction of the president of the Olympic Organizing Committee, Gianna Angelopoulos-Daskalaki, hosted 10,625 competitors in 28 different sports. The opening ceremony by avant-garde choreographer Dimitris Papaioannou exceeded expectations. A spectacular pageant told the story of Greek culture and history from its mythological beginnings to modern times.

The years 2004 and 2005 emerged as years of triumph. Greece's soccer team, the underdog, won the 2004 UEFA European Football Championship. In 2005, Greece became the EuroBasket Winner and also won the Eurovision song contest, with Helena Paparizou singing "My Number One."

## GEORGIOS PAPANDREOU BECOMES PRIME MINISTER, 2009

In 2009, Karamanlis's party, ND, held only a narrow majority. Because of the need for a stable party to handle the economic crisis Greece was facing, Karamanlis asked for a general election before the end of his term.

## Table 11.1 Hellenic Republic, Legislative Elections of October 4, 2009

| Name of party | Percentage of popular vote | Number of ministers |
|---|---|---|
| Panhellenic Socialist Movement (PASOK) | 43.9 | 160 |
| New Democracy (ND) | 33.5 | 91 |
| Communist Party (KKE) | 7.5 | 21 |
| Popular Orthodox Rally (LAOS) | 5.6 | 15 |
| Coalition of the Radical Left (SYRIZA) | 4.5 | 13 |

Source: http://psephos.adam-carr.net/countries/g/greece/greece2009.txt

As a result of the general election, in October 2009 Georgios Papandreou of the socialist-oriented PASOK Party became prime minister. He is the grandson of former prime minister Georgios Papandreou and the son of former prime minister Andreas Papandreou and his wife, Margaret Chant Papandreou.

Georgios was born and raised in the United States and was educated in universities in the United States, Canada, and England. He came to Greece with his parents after the restoration of democracy in 1974, at age 22.

Table 11.1 lists the results of the election (only the top five parties are shown).

## IMMIGRATION TO GREECE

Since the 1980s, growing numbers of immigrants have come to Greece. Immigrants include Greeks from the former Soviet Union as well as non-Greeks from Europe, Asia, and Africa. According to 2001 census data, they numbered 761,813, although their real number was believed to be much larger. In 2010, it is estimated that up to 10 percent of the immigrants residing in Greece were foreigners, with 40 to 50 percent of these Albanian.

### Greeks from Former Soviet Union

During the 1980s and 1990s, most of the thousands of Greeks who emigrated from the countries of the former Soviet Union were Pontian Greeks. By the end of the 1980s, they were arriving at about 20,000 per year. It is estimated that by 2000, about 200,000 had immigrated to Greece. They included those from Georgia, Kazakhstan, Russia, and Armenia.

During the 1920s through the 1990s, the quality of life of Greeks residing in the former Soviet Union varied according to the policies of the administration. Life during the beginning of the Soviet regime was good. The Greeks taught

The smiling face of this young man from Bangladesh, selling toys in the Plaka area of Athens, belies the hardship faced by thousands of foreigners who have come to Greece seeking a better way of life. (Photo by Elaine Thomopoulos)

the Greek language to their children, and they enjoyed a rich cultural life that included Greek newspapers, music, and dance.

The scene drastically changed after Joseph Stalin came to power. During the collectivization of farms, in 1928, the Greek farmers in southern Russia and the Ukraine resisted and were persecuted. In the purges of the 1930s, Greek leaders were charged with treachery or Trotskyism and murdered. Greek schools were closed, and Greek literature and culture went underground. During and shortly after World War II, conditions became even worse. In the Crimea, 70,000 Greeks, mostly Pontians, were forced to leave their homes. The same fate awaited the Greeks of Kuban and southern Russia. Finally on the night of June 14 and 15, 1949, the entire Greek population of the Caucasus, more than 100,000 people, was expelled to Central Asia: the Urals, Siberia, Kazakhstan, and Uzbekistan. These included not only those who held foreign passports, but also Greeks who had become Soviet citizens. They lost their citizenship and their rights. Some perished on the crowded, suffocating train trips to their destinations. Those who survived the trips were not permitted to have schools in which to teach their children the Greek language and culture. Greek newspapers, once numerous, ceased publication.

Many of the Greeks struggled to retain their Greek culture and identity, teaching Greek to their children in secret. However, knowledge of the Greek language suffered, not only because of discrimination, but in some cases because of intermarriage. Although they faced severe discrimination, the Greeks of the Soviet Union could not escape to Greece or other countries because for 50 years the Soviet bloc's gates remained shut. Mikhail Gorbachev opened the gates in the mid-1980s. Thousands fled to Greece to escape the civil strife that followed the breakup of the Soviet Union.

Besides the Greeks who had lived in the former Soviet Union for centuries, thousands of Greek citizens were forced to flee from Greece to Communist states after the Communists lost the civil war in Greece in 1949. In 1982, the Greek government allowed them to return.

Thus tens of thousands of Greeks from the former Soviet Union returned to their "homeland," a homeland most of them did not know. Neil Ascherson in his book *Black Sea* described the exodus of Pontian Greeks from Central Asia to Athens or Thessaloniki in the 1980s and 1990s:

> Travelling westwards from central Asia by train and then by ship, they brought with them enormous wooden packing-cases, crammed not only with their own possessions but with every kind of cheap Soviet household goods they could buy before they set off. Arriving at a Greek port, the new immigrants levered open the cases and sold their contents on the stalls of suburban flea-markets. Finally, when the trade goods had gone, the packing-cases were recycled as shacks for Pontian families to live in. They had come 'home' to a poor country, which had forgotten that they existed.[2]

Ascherson described the discrimination the Pontians received from both sides of the political spectrum. The right mistrusted them as Communists since they came from Russia. On the other hand Communists could not believe their stories of their suffering under the Soviet regime. Both left and right thought of them as "outsiders" because of their peculiar way of talking and their unique customs. They spoke a type of Greek that fewer than one-third of their neighbors could understand. Most of them were very poor.

During the 20th century, it is estimated that more than one million Pontians had immigrated to Greece from Turkey and the Soviet Union.

In Greece and throughout the diaspora, including the United States and Australia, Pontians have lived in what has been described as a "village within a village." They have continued to retain their own unique language, music, dance, and customs. More than 200,000 Greeks speak the Pontic Greek language, although most know modern Greek as well.

## Albanians

Emigration from Albania started after the collapse of Communism in 1991 and continued in the late 1990s, following the caving in of the Albanian economy. Many Albanians had invested in financial institutions that promised huge returns but lacked the assets to back them up. The investors lost money, and the whole economy suffered. Desperate Albanians crossed the border to Greece to get work in industry, construction, and agriculture. The Greeks welcomed the small minority of Albanians who were of Greek descent, but the others were not as welcome. In the 1990s, the Greek government deported tens of thousands of Albanians. This occurred in December 1991, June 1993, autumn 1994, August 1996, and July 1999. Many of them were undocumented. However, some claimed that they were deported even though they had paperwork indicating that they had entered Greece legally. The deportations caused tension in Greek-Albanian relations.

## Dealing with the Immigrants

The debate about the "foreigners" in Greece is similar to the debate about undocumented workers in the United States. Immigrant advocates point out that the immigrants to Greece fill jobs that would otherwise go unfilled. They take menial and low-paying jobs as laborers, domestic workers, and farm workers. Those on the opposite side of the debate say they compete for jobs with the native-born Greeks and blame them for the rise in crime. They also are concerned that they are not true Greeks, that they speak a foreign language and practice the Muslim or Catholic religion, not the Eastern Orthodox religion. They worry about intermarriage and about how Greece will retain its ethnic character.

Since the 1990s, the Greeks have grappled with the problem of immigration. Schoolchildren have been swept up in the national debate about what to do about the foreigners. Each year, children participate in the celebrations of Greek Independence Day and "Ohi" Day, which is commemorated each October 28, 1940, the day that Greece said "No" to Italy and resisted its invasion. The best students are awarded the honor of carrying the Greek flag in the parades celebrating these events.

Since 2000, several Albanian students excelled in their grades and were awarded that honor. They were not Greek citizens. Many of the communities welcomed the Albanian students as flag bearers. However, parents and children in several communities objected to an Albanian child carrying the flag.

One of these communities was New Michaniona, a small coastal town near Thessaloniki. In the fall of 2000, community members as well as politicians objected to 15-year-old Odysseus Cenai, an Albanian, carrying the flag and leading the parade in honor of "Ohi" Day.

On October 30, 2000, Dina Kyriakidou from Reuters News Agency reported:

> Cenai's parents told Greek media their son decided to stay home to avoid creating more tension in the community. "He cried all night. He's not doing well," his mother told *Ta Nea* daily.
> On Monday, Macedonia and Thrace Minister George Paschalidis invited Cenai to his ministry, gave him an award, promised him a scholarship and praised his academic achievements and maturity.

Unfortunately, the same situation presented itself again to Cenai three years later. He again was selected the best student, thus earning the honor of carrying the flag. Since the earlier incident, he had been baptized Greek Orthodox, but the family had still not received Greek citizenship. Although government officials supported him, there was protest from parents and students. He again gave up his right to carry the flag. Cenai's family has since moved to the United States, where he enrolled in a university with the objective of becoming a doctor.

Some of the Greeks, such as those who demonstrated against Cenai, continue to be prejudiced against the foreigners, but others believe that Greece will become stronger by integrating those of various ethnicities into their nation.

In March 2010, the parliament passed a bill in principle (Law #3838/2010) that will allow children born in Greece to parents who are legal immigrants the right to obtain Greek citizenship and to vote in elections. As of February 13, 2011, the law was in limbo. A council of judges recommended that the law be scrapped, but the Council of State's plenary could reject the judges' recommendations.

## GREEK-TURKISH RELATIONS IN THE 1970s, 1980s, AND 1990s

Another concern for Greece during this period was the worsening of relations with its neighbor Turkey. From the 1970s through 2010, relations with Turkey have been stormy, with just a few periods of calm. Several incidents illustrate their tempestuous relationship.

### Disputed Continental Shelf Rights

In 1973, in the midst of the Arab oil embargo, Greece discovered oil off the coast of Thasos. In November 1973, Turkey claimed continental shelf rights to this oil and awarded exploration rights to the Turkish State Petroleum Company. Greece disputed Turkey's claim. Despite Greece's protest, a survey ship entered the water space accompanied by 32 warships. Then Turkey, a month later, extended its claims even further south, to include water around the Do-decanese Islands.

Another altercation occurred during the summer of 1976 when a Turkish ship attempted to engage in seismic research in disputed waters.

The dispute regarding continental shelf rights came up again in 1987 when another Turkish ship, the *Sismik-I*, came into the area to explore for oil. When *Sismik-I* was about to enter the contested area once again, Prime Minister Andreas Papandreou put the armed forces on a high alert. Because of pressure put upon him by the United States and the United Nations, Turkey's prime minister, Turgut Özal, ordered the boats to avoid the water around Lesbos, Lemnos, and Samothrace.

## Invasion of Cyprus, 1974

The invasion of Cyprus by Turkish troops in the summer of 1974 escalated the tensions between Greece and Turkey, and as of 2010 the situation had not been resolved. The United Nation–brokered Annan Plan was rejected by the Greek Cypriots in 2004, although it was approved by the Turkish Cypriots.

## Davos Agreement, 1988

In 1988, the two countries met at Davos, Switzerland, and signed an agreement to avoid future war. They created a hotline between the two countries' leaders. As a result of the agreement, restrictions against Greek property owners in Turkey were lifted, and there was an increase in tourism in Greece.

## Imbros (Gökçeada) and Tenedos (Bozcaada)

The islands of Imbros (Gökçeada in Turkey today) and Tenedos (Bozcaada in Turkey today) became part of Turkey as a result of the Lausanne Treaty of 1923. The Greeks made up 97.5 percent of the population of Imbros in 1927 and a majority of the population of Tenedos. The treaty guaranteed the Greek inhabitants their right to a self-governing status, which was to be exercised by the local authorities. The police force was to be recruited from the local Greek population.

However, the islands have not been self-governed. On the contrary, with the exception of an interval between 1951 and 1963, the teaching of Greek was forbidden. In 1964, about 90 percent of the arable land on the island of Imbros was confiscated; thus the Greeks were not able to pursue their livelihood of farming. Shepherds were not allowed to graze on the land they had previously used; the government of Turkey declared those lands out-of-bounds because they were forested or to be reforested.

The people of Imbros also objected to an open prison being built on the island in 1965. The residents lived in fear of the prisoners until it was closed in 1992. Without any means of livelihood and without a sense of security, the Greeks left the island. Thus the population in Imbros dropped from 8,000 in 1922 to about 300 in 1990. In Tenedos, the reduction was from 5,320 people in 1922 to not more than 100 in 2010. Today, with fewer restrictions on traveling there, about 2,500 Greeks come to Imbros each summer.

## Dispute over Two Tiny Uninhabited Islands Bring Greece and Turkey to the Brink of War, 1995

On December 25, 1995, a Turkish vessel ran aground on the coast of Imia/ Kardak. Imia is the Greek name and Kardak the Turkish name for the two uninhabited isles in the Aegean used only for grazing goats. The grounding of the vessel set off a dispute over who had jurisdiction over the islands. Greece claimed that the islands, as a part of the Dodecanese Islands, were ceded to Italy by Turkey and in turn by Italy to Greece in 1947. Turkey says they were hers and never officially transferred to Italy.

When news of the dispute hits the Greek papers about a month later, things turned tough. On January 26, 1996, the mayor and priest of the nearby island of Kalymnos raised a Greek flag on the island. A Greek TV station covered this event. In response, the Turkish newspaper *Hürriyet* flew a team of journalists and photographers and hoisted a Turkish flag on the island. The story ran in the next day's edition and was aired on TV.

Both Greece and Turkey sent battle-ready naval ships. Both Greek and Turkish commandos landed on the rocky isles, with the Greek contingent on the larger of the islands and the Turkish contingent on the smaller island. On January 29 and 30, the two countries positioned themselves, ready for war. To add to the crisis, a Greek helicopter crashed. Throughout the world, newscasters broadcast, "Greece and Turkey are on the brink of war." Fortunately, President Bill Clinton's intervention diffused the tension.

In 2008, the focus was again on Imia/Kardak, this time regarding fishing rights; fishing there became very attractive because of the remarkable price of the gilt-head sea bream.

The tensions about the ownership of isles like Imia/Kardak and rights to oil, fish, and other resources in the waters of the Aegean have created a stir for decades. The territorial claims have never been settled.

## Violation of Greek Airspace

In 2011, Greece reported continuing violations of Greek air space. It pointed out that Turkey stages mock dogfights over Greek territory while giving no advance warning of such exercises. In February 10, 2010, Greece complained when fighter jets penetrated Greek airspace near the island of Samos and the islet of Famakonisi. Turkey says that Greece's national air space in the Aegean extends only six kilometers (approximately 3.7 miles), whereas Greece claims its airspace extends 16 kilometers (approximately 9.9 miles).

## The Öcalan Affair, 1999

The Öcalan affair created a huge rift in Greek-Turkish relations. Abdullah Öcalan, a Kurdish separatist and leader of the Kurdistan Workers Party (PKK), entered Greece on January 29, 1999. A few days later he was flown to the Greek embassy in Nairobi, Kenya. The plan was that he would stay there temporarily, until another country could be found to give him refuge. When the Kenyans discovered that he was at the embassy, they pressed for his departure. Öcalan believed that he would be transported to a safe haven. Instead, Turkish commandos seized him and put him on an airplane not to a safe haven, but to Turkey, where he was tried and jailed. He was sentenced to death, but his sentence was commuted to life in prison in 2002. As of June 2011, he remained in solitary confinement in an island jail off Istanbul.

The Turkish public felt enraged when they learned that Greece had harbored Öcalan. In a February 23, 1999, *New York Times* article, "Turkey and Greece Trade Words over Kurd," Stephen Kinzer reported that Turkish president Süleyman Demirel asked Greek leaders to explain to the international community how they came to support a "terrorist murderer who has killed thousands of people." Demirel warned, "If Greece continues its illegal behavior, we reserve the right given to us by international law to take the necessary measures for legitimate self-defense."

The Greek public questioned the Simitis government when they found out about Öcalan. They asked, "Why was he allowed to come into Greece in the first place? Who was in charge of the plans to take him to Kenya? Why did they allow him to be kidnapped by the Turkish commandos?"

Some Greeks felt sympathetic toward Öcalan. Ill regard toward the Turks had been harbored in the Greek psyche because of 400 years of Ottoman occupation. They saw the struggle of the Kurdish separatists, who were fighting for a separate Kurdish state, as similar to their own struggle for independence from the Ottomans in 1821. Greeks had also experienced the oppression of the Turks toward the Greeks in Smyrna in 1922, in the Istanbul pogrom in 1955, and the repressive measures taken against the Greek community in Turkey during the 1960s. A wound that continued to fester was the Turkish occupation of the northern part of Cyprus (37 percent) in 1974. More recently there had been territorial disputes about rights in the Aegean Sea as well as rights regarding air space.

Both factions of Greeks, those who felt sympathetic toward Öcalan and those who did not, criticized the Simitis government for this surreptitious botched affair. Heads rolled. Prime Minister Simitis forced out three of his cabinet officials for their role in the Öcalan affair.

## Turkish Relations with the Ecumenical Patriarchate

Turkish relations with the Ecumenical Patriarchate, which is in Istanbul, have been shaky. Greece expressed its concern to the government of Turkey following several attempts by criminals to damage buildings of the Patriarchate by hand grenades, bombing, or arson. These attempts, which took place from 1994 to 2005, on one occasion resulted in a serious injury to a deacon and on another, to the death of a custodian.

The government of Turkey has not been supportive of the Patriarchate. They object to the Patriarchate calling itself Ecumenical, as it has done since the Byzantine era, and prefer to see it as in charge of just the Greek Orthodox community in Turkey.

In 2010, the Turkish government allowed the celebration of the liturgy at the historic Pontian-Greek Soumela Monastery in Trabzon Province. This had last happened in 1923. Also, in 2010, the Turkish government returned the deed to the building that once housed the Prinkipo Orphanage on the Marmara Sea isle of Büyükada (Prinkipo). It had been seized from the Patriarchate in 1997. Since 1936, the Turkish government had seized about 7,000 properties belonging to Greek trusts. They included churches, schools, and orphanages. In 2011, the Turkish government published a decree regarding properties seized from Greek, Armenian, or Jewish trusts since 1936. They will return Greek properties from Istanbul, Tenedos, and Imbros or pay compensation for those sold.

The Turkish government closed the Patriarchate's Halki Theological School to new students in 1971. The school was founded in 1844 on Halki (in Turkish, Heybeliada), one of the Princes' Islands in the Sea of Marmara. From 1951 to 1971, it had three years of high school classes and four years of theological school. The Turkish government says it was closed because of a Turkish law that forbids private universities that are not under state supervision. The Patriarchate argues that Article 24 of the Turkish Constitution guarantees religious freedom and education. In October 1998, both houses of the U.S. Congress passed resolutions that supported the reopening of Halki. During his visit to Turkey in 2008, U.S. president Barack Obama also urged the Turks to open the school. However, as of 2011 it has not reopened.

## Earthquake Diplomacy, 1999

A major breakthrough in Greek-Turkish relations came as a result of earthquakes in Greece and Turkey. First Turkey experienced a major earthquake on August 17, 1999. Greece was the first foreign country to pledge aid and support to Turkey. A few weeks later, on September 7, Athens experienced a major earthquake, with its epicenter in a suburb 12 miles north of Athens. It resulted in the death of 145 people and 2,000 injured, with 70,000 homeless. Turkish aid was the first to arrive. These two events resulted in what is called earthquake diplomacy, a lessening of the rift between Turkey and Greece. An article written by Stephen Kinzer of the New York Times Service for the September 14, 1999, edition of the *International Herald Tribune* captured the sentiment felt by the people:

> The day after Athens was struck by its most serious earthquake in decades, millions of television viewers watched in awe as Turkish rescue workers pulled a Greek child from under a pile of rubble. Announcers struggled to control their emotion.
>
> "It's the Turks!" one of them shouted as his voice began to crack. "They've got the little boy. They saved him. And now the Turkish guy is drinking from a bottle of water. It's the same bottle the Greek rescuers just drank from. This is love. It's so beautiful."

An excerpt of the article "Whereas the Pain of the Enemy Made Us Cry," written by Anna Stergiou for the Greek newspaper *Eleftherotypia,* follows:

> Family, school, and military service....We Greeks who pass through all these institutions have been persuaded through some historical and political examples that the Turks were our enemies, and we nourished hatred. Then how is it that this feeling of hatred and enmity, which lasted for centuries, vanished in one day and the foe becomes a friend overnight? ...
>
> Those feelings of hatred and enmity literally disappeared. It was as if we did not know that we possessed these humane feelings, and we discovered them suddenly. We caught ourselves in tears when watching how the Turks were being rescued from the demolished buildings. Those same mothers who would shed tears in a probable Turkish-Greek war for their sons cried for the Turks. However, the god of the earthquake does not recognize difference of culture or nation.
>
> When we heard the screams and moans of those who were struck by the earthquake, we felt as if we had been punched on our stomach. There is no god of poverty and pain. For this reason we joined the lament of the Turks, and we lamented as if they were our own people. Those billions that had been spent on armament all these years did not suffice nor serve to bring happiness nor did they prevent catastrophes from befalling. On the contrary, this lavish and futile expenditure leaves a queer, bitter aftertaste in our mouth when such natural disasters hit us.[3]

## Greece and Turkey Work Together

Since the Greece Helsinki EU Summit in 1999, Greece has been in support of Turkey's becoming a member of the European Union. Although they still have their differences, there are ways the two countries have attempted to work together.

As Othon Anastasakis, director of Oxford University's South East European Studies, points out in an April 16, 2007, article about Greek-Turkish relations in the *Harvard International Review:* "The two governments have stipulated a number of high-level agreements regarding the promotion of tourism, transport, environmental protection, cultural cooperation, trade, double taxation, shipping, refugee smuggling, drug trafficking, and fighting terrorism." There is now a joint rail link between Thessaloniki and Istanbul and tourist exchanges in the island regions, as well as academic exchanges and joint popular culture projects. There have also been bilateral investments, including Greek banks investing in Turkish banks. In July 2007, Greece and Turkey as well as Italy signed a regional agreement to create a natural gas pipeline that would transport natural gas from the Caspian Sea area to Italy. The pipeline spans the border of Greece and Turkey and is expected to be operational in 2012.

In 2006, Greece made an effort to revise the sixth-grade textbook. One of the aims of the revision was to present a less-biased account of the Turks. However, to achieve political correctness, the author of the book neglected to include some historical events, such as the burning of Smyrna/Izmir. Besides this and other omissions, the text had errors of facts. It was withdrawn.

## WHAT'S IN A NAME? MACEDONIA

Greece has been involved in an ongoing dispute with its neighbor to the north, which the United Nations refers to as the Former Yugoslav Republic of Macedonia (FYROM). In 1993, FYROM, because of the objection of Greece to the name Republic of Macedonia, was accepted to the United Nations under the name FYROM. The country of FYROM shares borders with the Greek province of Macedonia. The dispute about the name dates to the breakup of the former Yugoslavia. In 1991, out of the breakup came a new nation that called itself the Republic of Macedonia. The Greek government became upset with the use of the name. Greece feared that FYROM might next lay claim to the Greek province of Macedonia, which borders FYROM to the south. It wasn't only the name that disturbed Greece, but the new nation also claimed one of Greece's heroes, Alexander the Great, and used the 12-pointed Star of Vergina on its flag. Greece considers the Star of Vergina its own national symbol. After complaints from the Greek government, the FYROM government adopted a different flag, but it still claims Alexander the Great and continues to refer to itself as the Republic of Macedonia. On November 3, 2004, when U.S. president George W. Bush recognized FYROM as the Republic of Macedonia instead of FYROM, Greece strongly objected. As of 2010, Greece and FYROM have not resolved the name issue.

## NOVEMBER 17 TERRORIST GROUP, 1975–2002

On July 19, 2002, in Lipsi, an island in the eastern Aegean, a force of 700 police and soldiers, navy divers, navy gunboats, and commandos in helicopters appeared, like a scene from a blockbuster action movie. They captured 59-year-old Alexandros Yiotopoulos, who was accused of being the leader of November 17. For 27 years, from 1975 to 2002, Greece had been plagued by November 17.

Yiotopoulos and other members of this Greek Marxist urban guerrilla group were convicted of assassinating 19 people. In 1975, they started their reign of terror by killing CIA station head Richard Welch and three others. Victims included Greek tycoons and politicians as well as foreign British, Turkish, and U.S. military personnel serving in Greece. In 2003, suspected members of the November 17 group were brought to trial; 15 members of the group were convicted, but two of the 15 were acquitted during the appeal.

## RELATIONS WITH THE UNITED STATES

Greek citizens have had a love-hate affair with the United States. The connection with the United States goes back to the beginning of the Greek nation's struggle for independence in the 19th century. Although the U.S. government did not give any financial support, organizations and individuals did. A few were so moved by the struggle that they volunteered as soldiers.

Since the turn of the 20th century, Greeks have immigrated to the United States in large numbers. At present there are more than a million U.S. citizens of Greek descent living in the United States. For many decades, the Greeks of the United States have been an important economic resource to Greece. They have sent money back to Greece to support relatives left behind, contributed toward sisters' and/or daughters' dowries, paid off debts on property or bought property, built hospitals, and planted trees. Many Greeks have either worked or been educated in the United States before returning to their place of birth. Prime Minister Georgios Papandreou was born and raised in the United States.

The U.S. State Department Report of April 2010 reported that there were 90,000 American citizens in Greece. A great number of them are U.S. citizens of Greek descent. Many hold dual citizenship and go back and forth between Greece and the United States.

Greeks, depending on whether they are to the left or right side of the political spectrum, either praise or condemn the U.S. government. The anti-Communists praise the United States for rescuing the country from the Communists during the civil war and for the aid they gave through the Marshall Plan that helped rebuild the country. Others deride the United States for interference in Greece's affairs.

Many Greeks continue to believe that the CIA was behind the Junta's coup in 1967, a coup that toppled the government's democratic system. There has

The policeman stands ready at a demonstration of truckers and railroad workers that took place in front of the Parliament Building in September 2010. A soldier is to the right. The stoic kilt-wearing evzone guards the Tomb of the Unknown Soldier. (Photo by Elaine Thomopoulos)

been no evidence found to back up this accusation. Greeks also objected to the United States supporting the Junta while it was in power from 1967 to 1974.

On November 17, 1999, a violent demonstration, including the setting of fires and smashing of stores and banks, took place in Athens during President Clinton's visit to Greece. The 10,000 or so demonstrators objected to U.S. policy in Kosovo and Bosnia and the bombing of Yugoslavia, which hurt their long-standing allies, the Serbians. Did Clinton choose the wrong day to visit? November 17 is the date that commemorates the student demonstration against the Junta in 1973.

As reported by Terence Hunt, AP, in the *Topeka Capital Journal* on November 21, 1999, Clinton said, "When the Junta took over in 1967 here, the U.S. allowed its interests in prosecuting the Cold War to prevail over its interest, I should say its obligation, to support democracy, which was, after all, the cause for which we fought the Cold War. It is important that we acknowledge that."

Greek leftists have expressed their lingering hate against the United States by the periodic defacing and toppling of the 12-foot tall, three-ton statue of Harry S. Truman, which was given to Greece by the fraternal organization American Hellenic Educational Progressive Association (AHEPA) in 1963. It was a token of their appreciation for all that Truman, through the Truman Doctrine and the Marshall Plan, did for Greece. In 2006, it was toppled once again.

In 2007 a terrorist group took even more violent action. They fired a rocket-propelled grenade through a front window of the U.S. Embassy.

## STRIKES AND DEMONSTRATIONS

Strikes and demonstrations are not unusual in present-day Greece. If there is dissatisfaction with government services or a proposed change in government policy, the people flock to the streets, shouting their objections. Police show up in riot gear, shields in front of them, with tear gas ready for deployment.

In February 2008, two unions, the General Confederation of Greek Workers and the Civil Service Union, went on strike. They displayed their dissatisfaction regarding proposed changes to the cuts to the pension system. The strike shut down air service as well as public services. The strikers included journalists, doctors, lawyers, and teachers.

On December 6, 2008, a policeman fired his gun to disperse a group of young people congregating late at night in the streets of the Athens neighborhood of Exarchia. The policeman's shot killed 15-year-old Alexandros

On December 6, 2008, a policeman fired his gun to disperse a group of young people who had been congregating in the streets of Exarchia in Athens. His shot killed 15-year-old Alexandros Grigoropoulos. The death of Grigoropoulos sparked demonstrations in Athens and other cities that lasted until mid-January. The photo of his memorial in Exarchia was taken in September 2010. (Photo by Elaine Thomopoulos)

Grigoropoulos. Protests rocked the streets until mid-January 2009. Young people, some of them hooded, threw rocks and Molotov cocktails and burned cars and buildings in downtown Athens. The riots and demonstrations reflected outrage not only about the death of Grigoropoulos but also about the inefficiency and corruption of the government and frustration about not being able to find employment. More than 20 percent of those between the ages of 15 and 24 were unemployed. The protests lasted more than a month and involved cities throughout Greece as well as Europe. On October 11, 2010, the Greek policeman who was accused of shooting Alexandros was sentenced to life in prison. His colleague was found guilty of being an accomplice to murder and sentenced to a 10-year jail term.

Unrest continued in 2009 and 2010. Farmers participated in a 10-day strike in the winter of 2009, blocking major highways and border crossings. They protested falling commodity prices and demanded an increase in farm subsidies and pensions. Once again, in February 2010, farmers blocked the highways. After more than a week, they called off the strike. Additional protests in late 2009 and 2010 followed the government's announcement of the lowering of wages for government workers and changes in benefits. Protests continued throughout Greece in 2011. More than 25,000 converged on Syntagma Square in Athens on June 15 to demonstrate against the additional cuts proposed by the Papandreou cabinet, cuts required so that Greece could receive the next installment of international aid. Protesters hurled water bottles, rocks, and firebombs, with police responding with tear gas.

## FIRES

In the past 10 years, especially in 2007 and 2009, Greece has been plagued by fires. During the summer of 2007, 3,000 forest fires broke out in several areas across Greece, but they mainly affected the Peloponnese and southern Euboea. In 2009, a fire raged for four days, mostly affecting an area northeast of Athens.

Greece's fires have destroyed tens of thousands of acres and ruined crops. Olive trees, some more than 1,000 years old, were burned. A newly planted olive tree takes at least 10 years to produce olives, so the loss is grave. Even worse, 84 people lost their lives in 2007.

On August 28, 2007, in the *New York Times* article entitled "In Greece, Wine Saves Life; a Mother's Arms Do Not," reporters Jan Fisher and Anthee Carassava wrote about the fire:

When the water ran out, with pine cones popping and the flames still high around his house, George Dimopoulos switched to wine. He made it himself two years ago, and, nearly alone in his village as it all but burned down on Friday night, he poured liter after liter, 200 in all, into his little copper hand-pumped crop sprayer, and sprayed and sprayed.

"I had nothing else," said Mr. Dimopoulos, 63.

His wine helped save his life, his house and possibly his neighborhood.

A photo in the article shows a woman looking upon the graves of her cousins, lamenting, "Why didn't you come?" She got a ride out of the inferno, but her cousins, a brother and sister, declined the ride since they did not want to leave their donkey behind.

Another heartbreaking story reported in the article was that of a mother on vacation who "shielded her four children, Angeliki, 15; Maria, 12; Anastassia, about 10; and Constantinos, 5, but was unable to protect them from the flames."

Some blame the government, not only for its inability to control the fires and for not apprehending suspected arsonists, but because they believe that the government has encouraged developers to take much of the land. When an area is burned, the government determines whether or not it had been a forest and if they should proceed with reforestation. Younger trees do not count, and sometimes the previously forested area has already been cut down prior to the fires. If it is not determined to be a forest, developers then can start building soon after the area is cleared.

## TROUBLE WITH THE ECONOMY

The economic crisis that Prime Minister Georgios Papandreou faced in late 2009 started about 10 years earlier. The records that Greece presented prior to admission to the Eurozone in 2001 as well as afterward did not present the true picture of her economic condition. The Eurozone requires that countries fulfill certain membership criteria, including a budget deficit that does not exceed 3 percent of the gross domestic product and a public debt limited to 60 percent of the GDP. Greece met these criteria but did so by leaving out certain military expenses at one time and hospital debt at another. A derivatives deal that Goldman-Sachs first put in place in 2001 masked the true nature of Greece's deficit.

When Papandreou was elected in the fall of 2009, he discovered the extent of the deficit and debt and announced it to the public. Several debt-ratings agencies then downgraded Greece's rating to the lowest level in the Eurozone. In May 2010, Papandreou dropped another bomb. He reported that the Greek deficit was 13.6 percent of GDP for 2009, higher than the 12.9 percent originally reported. Beginning in the fall of 2009, stock markets around the world fell with each bit of news of Greece's economic woes.

The members of the Eurozone became very concerned that Greece's economic situation would explode, and they would suffer the fallout. Thus, in May 2010, the EU countries and the International Monetary Fund (IMF) decided to get things under control by giving Greece a $146.2 billion loan, but under the condition that Greece would institute structural reforms in the economy. The reforms instituted by the Papandreou government, which included cutting the wages and benefits of government workers and retirees, raising taxes, and increasing the tax-collection ability of the state but also liberalizing certain professions and labor market reform, resulted in recurrent demonstrations and strikes. The Papandreou government had already started making some of these changes, but after May 2010 they became particularly harsh. In July 2011, another loan package of $153.5 billion was approved.

Financial experts point out that the worldwide recession, as well as graft and nonpayment of taxes, has contributed to Greece's deficit. Partly because of bad press, in 2010 the income generated by tourism had also fallen.

The unemployment rate continues to go up. Greece's unemployment rate in May 2010 was 12 percent compared to 8.5 percent in May 2009. In the first quarter of 2011, the unemployment rate was 15.9 percent compared with 14.2 percent in the previous quarter, and 11.7 percent in the corresponding quarter of 2010.

Some of the measures mandated by the IMF/Eurozone deal, such as market liberalization and more efficient tax collection, had been recognized by previous Greek governments as necessary and could have helped Greece avoid the crisis in the first place. However, the measures had been very difficult to implement because of vested interests and popular reaction against them.

## CORRUPTION AND TAX EVASION

Papandreou ran on the slogan "Change," which included changing a corrupt political system. Politics in Greece runs the same way it does in many other parts of the world: on bribes, favors, and patronage. Each political party blames the other for corruption and economic malfeasance.

On May 11, 2012, the radio station WBEZ broadcast an interview with a vegetable vendor. Grabbing a potato, she said, "See this potato. If I stole it I would end up in jail. Yet our politicians steal millions and nothing happens to them." She continued, "The two main political parties here robbed us blind, but its our fault. We voted for them."[4]

Some economists blame part of Greece's bleak economic picture on the underground economy—the use of bribes and patronage. *Fakelakia* (little envelopes) are part of doing business in Greece. Money is stuffed in a fakelaki and slipped to officials to help gain access to medical services, to avoid taxes, for building permits or driver's licenses. For years, Greeks have complained about this system. A telephone survey done by Transparency International between November 17, 2008, and December 3, 2009, showed how widespread the practice is. Greek residents were asked: "In the past 12 months have you or anyone living in your household paid a bribe in any form?" A whopping 18 percent of the respondents reported that they had. This compares to a response rate of 2 percent in the United States. Even though bribery is widespread, the survey found that 80 percent of Greeks condemn corruption in public.[5]

In recent years, government officials have been accused and sometimes even arrested for taking bribes. Few have been convicted. The German electronics and engineering firm Siemens allegedly paid bribes during the 1990s and the last decade for contracts with the Greek government. The big payoff was the contract for the security system of the 2004 Olympics. As of 2010, the Greek government was investigating the bribery scandal.

Another scandal involved the Vatopedi Monastery on Mount Athos in northern Greece. No money changed hands, but the media reported that the government had lost 100 million euros ($123 million) in land swaps. In 2010, the suspected land swaps between the state and the wealthy monastery came under investigation. Because of the statute of limitations, charges were dropped against three ministers who were thought to have been involved.

Widespread tax evasion has also contributed to the deficit. In September 2011, the government used a new tactic in its approach to this problem. The finance minister named 6,000 firms that owed a total of 59 billion dollars.

Anastasia Stefanidou, in an email to the author, summed up her feelings:

> We feel very disappointed by the lies and the corruption, we feel trapped by years and years of bad governing and we feel stupid because we voted for them! Also, in the last couple of years there has been a tremendous change in our social life. I say this both from personal experience and from what others say. There is a huge number of small businesses closed, more people unemployed than ever before (including educated ones) and the bad economy has affected our innate tendency to be extroverted and have fun. You can see it if you go out on weeknights. Very few people, compared to recent past years, are out at cafes or bars. Also you can hear it in people's words, always complaining and worrying. We have become miserable, pessimistic, and insecure.[6]

## CHALLENGES: 2011 AND BEYOND

The Greek people glowed with pride after the successful 2004 Olympics. This highlighted their emergence as a respected modern nation.

However, the first decade of the 21st century also illustrated their vulnerabilities. This included allegations of corruption in the government as well as the economic crisis of 2009 and 2010. In 2011, they are striving to deal with these issues, as well as the changing multiethnic character of the nation.

Greece's economic growth has been stymied, but Greece is a survivor. The Greek people have stamina, grit, and endurance. The small, impoverished nation that emerged wounded from World War II and the civil war healed itself. Greece has another opportunity to emerge from the current economic crisis as a stronger and healthier nation.

## NOTES

1. "Gorgopotamos Anniversary Celebrated," *American News Agency Athens,* November 27, 2000, http://www.hri.org/news/greek/ana/2000/00–11–27. ana.html#05.

2. Neil Ascherson, *The Black Sea* (New York: Hill and Wang, 1995), 194.

3. As quoted in Fuat Aksu, "Turkish–Greek Relations: From Conflict to Détente the Last Decade," *Turkish Review of Balkan Studies,* Annual 2001, http://www.turkishgreek.org/makaleler/trgrdetente.htm.

4. Gerry Hadden, "How Did Greece Get Here?", Public Radio International's *The World* broadcast in Chicago on May 11, 2010, at 7 P.M. Central Standard Time, http://www.theworld.org/page/2/?s=potato.

5. "Global Corruption Barometer 2009," Transparency International, http://www.transparency.org/policy_research/surveys_indices/gcb/2009.

6. Email correspondence with author.

# Notable People in the History of Greece

**Alexander the Great** (356–323 BC) became king at the age of 20 upon the death of his father, Philip of Macedon. He took control of the Persian Empire and extended his domain all the way to India. Alexander, while tolerating local religious and cultural practices, also introduced his empire to Hellenic ideals and language. He died of a fever.

**Archimedes** (c. 287–212 BC), who was born in the Greek colony of Syracuse, Italy, used mathematical concepts to investigate the world. He developed formulas for finding areas and volumes of spheres and cylinders. Farmers continue to use his irrigation method. Shaped like a large screw, it draws water from rivers. His experiments with the lever resulted in his statement of the law of simple machines. When the king of Syracuse challenged him to single-handedly drag a barge out of the water, he did so with a compound pulley. He also determined whether the king's new crown was made of pure gold. He used the law of buoyancy, which he discovered while taking a bath. While leaping from the bath he shouted, "Eureka!" ("I have found it!").

**Aristotle** (c. 384–322 BC), Plato's student, was born in Stagira in northern Greece. He tutored Alexander the Great and founded the Lyceum in Athens. He made careful observations, collected various specimens, and summarized and classified the specimens—the basis for the scientific method. His treatises on logic, metaphysics, physics, ethics, and natural sciences provided a foundation for modern science. Aristotle also had a tremendous influence in the shaping of Muslim science and philosophy.

**Maria Callas** (1923–1977), a world-renowned opera singer, was admired for her wide-ranging voice and dramatic presentation. Born of immigrant parents in New York, she moved to Greece when she was 13. There she continued her music education. She had a long-standing love affair with the wealthy shipowner Aristotle Onassis.

**Odysseus Elytis (given name: Alepoudelis)** (1911–1996) won the Nobel Prize in Literature in 1979 "for his poetry, which, against the background of Greek tradition, depicts with sensuous strength and intellectual clear-sightedness modern man's struggle for freedom and creativeness." He spent 11 years working on "To Axion Esti" ("Worthy It Is"), first published in 1959.

**Hippocrates** (c. 460–377 BC), at a time when doctors thought that vengeful gods caused diseases, believed that each disease had a natural cause and by finding the cause, you could cure the disease. He advised his patients to eat healthy, get plenty of rest, and have clean surroundings. Upon graduation, many of today's medical students take a modern version of the Hippocratic Oath, based on his guidelines for honorable conduct.

**Ioannis Kapodistrias** (1776–1831), who served as the first president of Greece from 1828 to 1831, came to Greece at the invitation of the insurgent nation's national assembly. He had previously served Russia as a foreign minister. He was assassinated in 1831 by Georgios and Konstantinos Mavromichalis of Mani, Greece.

**Konstantinos Karamanlis** (1907–1998) spent almost 50 years of his life in public service. He governed the country as prime minister for 14 years (1955–1963; 1974–1980). After his party failed to win the elections of 1963, he lived in France. He was called back in 1974 to establish a government of national unity. His administration applied for membership in the European Economic Community, an objective that was achieved in 1981.

**Theodoros Kolokotronis** (1770–1843) showed his mettle as a leader of soldiers in the first year of the War of Independence when the insurgents under his command took control of Tripoli from the Ottomans and then went on to victory in the Dervenakia Pass. In 1825, he was jailed by enemies in Greece's provisional government under Petrobey Mavromichalis. However, a few months later he was released to rejoin the war effort. In 1834, because of his opposition of the king, he was tried for treason and given the death sentence. He was pardoned by King Otto.

**Adamantios Korais** (1748–1833), born in Smyrna (present day Izmir, Turkey), lived in Paris for 45 years. Through publishing books on the Greek classics, he raised the Greeks' consciousness of their Hellenic heritage and paved the way for the revolution against their Ottoman oppressors. He introduced a revised Greek, which was later called *katharevousa*. Scrubbed *katharos* (clean) of foreign influences, it was a compromise between ancient Greek and modern spoken demotic Greek.

**Ioannis Metaxas** (1871–1941) served as dictator of Greece from 1936 to his death in 1941. He is best known for standing up to Italy on October 28, 1941, by responding, "Ohi" ("No"), to the Italian demand that Greece allow Italian troops to enter Greece. Within hours of Metaxas's saying "No," the Italians invaded Greece. Although greatly outnumbered, Greek troops repelled the Italians and advanced into Albania. Metaxas died of an infection just before the German troops invaded mainland Greece.

**King Otto** (Othon in Greek) (1815–1867) served from 1833 to 1862. He was 17 years old when he was crowned king of Greece. Three Bavarian regents ruled until he turned 20. The neoclassical government buildings that were constructed in Athens during his reign complement the ancient edifices of the Acropolis. He organized a public education system that included a university in Athens. Under his watch, Greece established a legal code and judicial system. King Otto's land reform in 1835 helped thousands of farmers buy small plots of land with a low-cost loan program. In 1862, after a revolt, he was forced out. He spent his remaining years in Bavaria.

**Georgios Papadopoulos** (1919–1999), a colonel, along with other midlevel military men, grabbed control of the Greek government in a bloodless coup in 1967. He emerged as the leader of what is referred to as the Junta. The Junta suppressed the press and freedom of speech and imprisoned suspected Communists. In 1974, a demonstration by students at the Athens Polytechnic National University resulted in brutal tactics by government forces in which at least 23 were killed. Shortly afterward, Papadopoulos was overthrown by another bloodless coup organized by Major General Dimitrios Ioannidis, the chief of the military police. After the fall of the Ioannides dictatorship, Papadopoulos was found guilty of treason. His death sentence was commuted to life in prison.

**Andreas Papandreou** (1919–1996) served a total of eight years as prime minister. He first became prime minister after his party, PASOK, won the 1981 elections. During his administration, the parliament passed a law allowing civil marriage. Other laws passed served as an impetus to strengthen the rights of women. Not only was the dowry system abolished, but a woman could choose to maintain her family name after marriage; a married couple could choose the surname of their children—it did not have to automatically be the surname of the husband; there was the establishment of no-fault and mutual consent divorce; a husband and wife could jointly claim property acquired during the marriage; and illegitimate children were granted rights equal to those held by legitimate children.

**Georgios Papanicolaou** (1883–1962) invented the Papanicolaou test, commonly known as the Pap smear, a screening test for cervical cancer. He received his medical degree at the University of Athens and his PhD from the University of Munich. In 1913, he immigrated to the United States, where he had a better opportunity to pursue his research.

**Pericles** (495–429 BC) furthered the development of democracy. Under his rule, the assembly of citizens met 40 times each year to decide how the city should be governed. However, only a minority of the population of Athens could actually vote—only males who were free and whose fathers had been born in Athens. The buildings on the Acropolis of Athens, including the Parthenon, were built under his administration. He died of the plague that devastated Athens.

**Rigas Pheraios (Velestinlis)** (1757–1798) hailed from Thessaly, near ancient Pherae, but took up residence in Vienna. He envisioned a state built upon a revived Byzantine Empire, consisting not only of Greeks but of other Balkan peoples of various ethnicities and religions, and put forth his view in a publication. He was betrayed by a Greek and arrested by the Austrian authorities. They delivered him and his co-conspirators to the Ottomans and in May 1798, he was executed. The last line of Velestinlis's poem "War Song," "Better one hour of free life, than 40 years of slavery and prison!" became the Greek revolutionaries' rallying cry.

**Phidias** (c. 480–430 BC) sculpted a magnificent gold and ivory-covered statue of Zeus at Olympia, Greece. Archaeologists discovered what they believe was Phidias's workshop at Olympia. They found shards of ivory, moulds, casting equipment, and a drinking cup with the engraving, "I belong to Phidias." Pericles appointed Phidias to supervise the decoration of the buildings of the Acropolis of Athens and to sculpt the statue of Athena. Phidias was accused of stealing some of the gold meant for the statue but was acquitted of this charge. However, he was jailed because of sacrilege—accused of inserting portraits of himself and Pericles onto the statue Athena's gold shield.

**George Seferis (Seferiadis)** (1900–1971) was born in Anatolia, near Smyrna. With his family, he moved to Athens in 1914. He studied law at the Sorbonne in Paris. He was a poet as well as a career diplomat. In 1963, Seferis was awarded the Nobel Prize for Literature. Anders Österling, in his presentation speech at the awards ceremony, said, "Seferis's poetic production is not large, but because of the uniqueness of its thought and style and the beauty of its language, it has become a lasting symbol of all that is indestructible in the Hellenic affirmation of life." Seferis became a vocal critic of the dictatorial Junta. As an act of defiance, thousands attended his funeral.

**Socrates** (469–399 BC), an Athenian philosopher and teacher, is known through the writings of his pupil Plato, since he did not commit his teachings to writing. He taught his students by asking a series of questions that encouraged them to think critically. Among his words of wisdom are the following: "I know one thing, and that is that I know nothing"; "It is not living that matters, but living rightly"; "Let him that would move the world first move himself"; and "The greatest way to live with honor in this world is to be what we pretend to be." Socrates was condemned to death for "corrupting youth" and "impiety."

**Solon** (c. 638–559 BC), as the chief magistrate of Athens, worked to bring order to the chaos that gripped the city-state. When he took office, small farmers who went into debt and borrowed on the security of their person could be forced into slavery. He cancelled debts. Under Solon's rule, the class system of Athens continued. However, to the three upper classes, he added a fourth class, those without property. He gave them the privilege of taking part in the public assembly and acting as judges, although they could not hold office. This led to government by all free men, not just the owners of property. Solon is thought to have instituted a rule of law that applied to marriage, adoption, farming, and the calendar.

**Charilaos Trikoupis** (1832–1896) served as prime minister of Greece intermittently between 1875 and 1895. He spent the first 15 years of his life in London, where his father served as a minister for the Greek government. In 1874, he wrote an article blaming the instability of Greece's government on the king exercising his prerogative to appoint and dismiss prime ministers and thus entrusting the formation of government to minority leaders. As a result, the king put into effect the principle of *dedilomeni,* which obliged the king to appoint the leader of the party with a plurality of parliamentary votes as prime minister. Under Trikoupis's administration, a railway line, still in use, was built. His crowning achievement was the Corinth Canal, which linked the Aegean and Ionian Seas. Trikoupis worked to curb the brigands (thieves) who harassed the countryside and bring order and stability to Greece.

**Aris Velouchiotis (Athanasios Klaras)** (1905–1945), whose nom de guerre was derived from the god of war (Aris) and Mount Velouchi, was a leader in ELAS, a resistance organization during World War II. Some worship him for his role in the resistance. Others despise him for alleged atrocities he committed against innocent citizens during the Greek civil war. As a youth, Velouchiotis became a member of the Greek Communist Party (KKE). He was jailed twice because of his political activities. After his release, he fought the Italians at the Albanian front and then joined ELAS. After liberation, he commanded rebel Communist troops who fought against Greek government forces. In June 1945, Greek government forces ambushed him. There is a debate about whether he was killed by them or committed suicide.

**Eleftherios Venizelos** (1864 to 1936) served as prime minister several times from 1909 to 1920 and then again from 1928 to 1933. His government instituted labor reforms such as prohibition of child labor and the six-day workweek. Venizelos basked in glory after victories in the First and Second Balkan Wars, when a major portion of Epirus, Macedonia, Crete, and some of the other Aegean islands became part of Greece's territory. A disagreement between Venizelos and King Constantine over Greece's entry into World War I began a long-term struggle between those who supported Venizelos and those who supported the monarchy. In 1916, a rival Greek government was established under Venizelos. It governed northern Greece and Crete. Venizelos became prime minister of a united Greece in 1917, after the British and French officially recognized Venizelos's government and forced the king to leave. Greece's entry in World War I helped the Entente gain victory over the Central Powers. As a result, Greece added Western Thrace to its territory. Venizelos sought to strengthen Greece by building her infrastructure and introducing a modern economy. Instead, because of an excessive debt and the Great Depression, the nation had to declare bankruptcy in 1932.

**Alexandros Ypsilantis** (1792–1828) was the leader of Philiki Etairia, a secret society that aimed to overthrow the Ottomans and establish a Greek state. He was born in Constantinople but received his higher education in Imperial Russia. He became the czar's aide-de-camp. While he served in the czar's army, he lost his right arm, which was torn off by a shell in the Battle of Dresden. Ypsilantis left the czar's service to lead the first battle of the War of Independence, which took place in present-day Romania. Ypsilantis and his troops lost the battle, and he was captured by the Austrians, who held him until 1827. He was released in poor health and died the next year.

# Bibliography

Aksu, Fuat. "Turkish–Greek Relations: From Conflict to Détente the Last Decade." *Turkish Review of Balkan Studies, Annual 2001:* 167–201. http://www.turkishgreek. org/makaleler/trgrdetente.htm.

Anastasakis, Othon. "Power and Interdependence: Uncertainties of Greek-Turkish Rapprochement." *Issue: Ethnic Conflict, Harvard International Review,* April 16, 2007. http://hir.harvard.edu/ethnic-conflict/power-and-interdependence?page=0,0.

Antonopoulos, Tasos. *Calvary of Meligalas.* Chicago: Tom Anton, 2006.

Apostolakou, Lito. "The Greek War of Independence of 1821: Greek Revolution—Origins and Outbreak." http://greekhistory.suite101.com/article.cfm/origins_ of_the_greek_war_for_independence#ixzz0ZXQenRHV.

Apostolakou, Lito. "Trikoupis and the Dedilomeni Principle: Greek Political Parties in the Reign of King George." http://www.suite101.com/content/ trikoupis-and-the-dedilomeni-principle-a111698#ixzz0Shs5A4ia.

Apostolakou, Lito."Trikoupis and the Modernization of Greece: The Greek Railways in the 19th Century." http://greekhistory.suite101.com/article.cfm/ trikoupis_and_the_modernization_of_greece#ixzz0s9bShbuH.

Arapoglou, Stergios. "Dispute in the Aegean Sea: The Imia/Kardak Crisis." Research report, Air Command and Staff College, Air University, Maxwell Air Force Base, Alabama, 2001. http://www.dtic.mil/cgi-bin/GetTRDoc?AD=ADA420639 &Location=U2&doc=GetTRDoc.pdf.

Arvanides, Seraphim, investigator. "Population Change Project Funded by a British Academy Award: Information Related to the Project 'Geographical Analysis of Population Changes of Communities in Greece: 1940 to 2001.'" http://www. staff.ncl.ac.uk/s.alvanides/grpopchange/.

Ascherson, Neil. *The Black Sea.* New York: Hill and Wang, 1995.

Badikian-Gartler, Beatriz. *Old Gloves: A 20th Century Saga.* Chicago: Fractal Edge Press, 2006.

Bailey, Ronald H. "Greece's Mountain Warriors." In *Partisans and Guerrillas.* Morristown, NJ: Time Life Books, 1978.

"Balkan Human Rights Web Pages: Greece 2004." http://www.greekhelsinki.gr/bhr/english/countries/greece/index.html.

Barbour, Stephen, and Cathie Carmichael (eds.). *Language and Nationalism in Europe.* New York: Oxford University Press, 2001.

Black, Joshua. "Greek Diplomacy and the Hunt for Abdullah Ocalan." http://wws.princeton.edu/research/cases/greekdiplomacy.pdf.

Bowman, Steven. "The Jews in Greece." University of Cincinnati Judaic Anniversary Volume. http://www.umass.edu/judaic/anniversaryvolume/articles/30-F3-Bowman.pdf.

Bowra, C. M. *Classical Greece.* New York: Time Life, 1970.

Brecher, Michael, and Jonathan Wilkenfeld. *A Study of Crisis: A Comprehensive Study of the Causes and Consequences of War in the Twentieth Century.* Ann Arbor: University of Michigan, 1997.

Brewer, David. *The Greek War of Independence.* Woodstock, NY: Overlook Press, 2003.

Burn, A. R. *The Warring States of Greece: From their Rise to the Roman Conquest.* New York: McGraw-Hill, 1968.

Butler, Chris. "The Flow of History: The Ancient Greeks." http://www.flowofhistory.com/units/birth/3.

Bzinkowski, Michal. *"Eleuthería E Thánatos!* The Idea of Freedom in Modern Greek Poetry during the War of Independence in 19th Century. Dionysios Solomos' 'Hymn to Liberty.'" Paper given at the conference "To Be Free: Freedom and Its Limits in the Ancient World" in Krakow, September 21–23, 2003. http://www.scribd.com/doc/21531010/The-Idea-of-Freedom-in-Modern-Greek-Poetry.

Carey, Jane Perry Clark, and Andrew Galbraith Carey. *The Web of Modern Greek Politics.* New York: Columbia University Press, 1968.

Casson, Lionel. *The Greek Conquerors.* Chicago: Stonehedge Press,1981.

Chesser, Preston. "The Battle of Actium." http://ehistory.osu.edu/world/articles/ArticleView.cfm?AID = 16.

Chrysanthou, Chrys. *Cries and Whispers.* Bloomington, IN: Xlibris, 2006.

Chryssis, George C. "American Philhellenes and the Greek War for Independence." Hellenic Communication Service L.L.C. http://www.helleniccomserve.com/greek_war_for_independence.html.

Churchill, Winston. *Closing the Ring.* Vol. 5 of *The Second World War.* Boston: Houghton Mifflin, 1951.

Churchill, Winston. *The Grand Alliance.* Vol. 3 of *The Second World War.* Boston: Houghton Mifflin, 1950.

CIA. "World Factbook: Greece." https://www.cia.gov/library/publications/the-world-factbook/geos/gr.html.

Clark, Bruce. *Twice a Stranger: Greece, Turkey and the Minorities They Expelled.* London: Granta, 2005.

Clogg, Richard. *A Concise History of Greece.* 2nd ed. Cambridge, England: Cambridge University Press, 2002.

Clogg, Richard. *A Short History of Modern Greece.* 2nd ed. Cambridge, England: Cambridge University Press, 1986.

Clogg, Richard, ed. and trans. *Greece, 1940–1949: Occupation, Resistance, Civil War: A Documentary History.* New York: Palgrave Macmillan, 2003.

Colovas, Anthone C. *A Quick History of Modern Greece.* Baltimore: PublishAmerica, 2007.

Constantinou, Stavros T., and Nicholas D. Diamantides. "Modeling International Migration: Emigration from Greece to the United States, 1820–1980." *Annals of the Association of American Geographers* 75 (September 1985): 352–69.

Crawley, C. W. *The Question of Greek Independence: A Study of British Policy in the Near East, 1821–1830.* Cambridge: Cambridge University Press, 1930. Questia Media America, Inc. http://www.questia.com/PM.qst?a=o&d = 4911867.

Curtis, Glenn E. (ed.). *Greece: A Country Study.* 4th ed. Federal Research Division, Library of Congress. Lanham, Maryland: Berman, 1994.

Dakin, Douglas. *The Greek Struggle for Independence, 1821–1833.* Berkeley: University of California Press, 1973.

Daley, Frank (ed.). *Greece—Gallant—Glorious. Greek War of 1940–41.* Haverhill, MA: Record, 1941.

Davis, William Stearns, and Willis Mason West. *Greece and the East.* Vol. 1 of *Readings in Ancient History: Illustrative Extracts from the Sources.* Boston: Allyn and Bacon, 1912. http://books.google.com/books?id=Hh4NAAAAIAAJ&pg=PR1& dq=.+Readings+in+Ancient+History:+Illustrative+Extracts+from+the+Sources, +Volume+I:+Greece+and+the+East.+Boston:+Allyn+and+Bacon,+1912&hl=en &ei=dsP_TZLrJpOFtgfN1PC8Dg&sa=X&oi=book_result&ct=result&resnum=2 &ved=0CDQQ6AEwAQ#v=onepage&q&f=false.

Department of State, United States of America. "International Boundary Study, No. 41— November 23, 1964 Greece—Turkey." The Geographer, Office of the Geographer, Bureau of Intelligence and Research. http://www.law.fsu.edu/library/ collection/LimitsinSeas/IBS041.pdf.

Dobkin, Marjorie Housepian. *Smyrna 1922: The Destruction of a City.* New York: Newmark Press, 1998.

Ekinci, Mehmet Ugur. "The Origins of the 1897 Ottoman-Greek War: A Diplomatic History." The Institute of Economics and Social Sciences of Bilkent University, master's thesis, Bilkent University, Ankara, 2006. http://www.Thesis.Bilkent. Edu.tr/0003114.pdf.

Finlay, George. *History of Greece under Othoman and Venetian Domination.* Edinburgh: William Blackwood and Sons: 1856. http://www.archive.org/stream/ historyofgreeceu00finluoft/historyofgreeceu00finluoft_djvu.txt.

Finlay, George. *History of the Greek Revolution.* Edinburgh: William Blackwood and Sons, 1861. http://ia700302.us.archive.org/BookReader/BookReaderImages. php?zip=/26/items/historygreekrev00finlgoog/historygreekrev00finlgoog_tif. zip&file=historygreekrev00finlgoog_tif/historygreekrev00finlgoog_0009.tif& scale=8.740213523131672&rotate = 0.

"Formation of the Greek State 1821–1897." http://www.fhw.gr/chronos/12/en/ index.html 2000.

Frommer, Rebecca Camhi. *The House by the Sea: A Portrait of the Holocaust in Greece.* San Francisco: Mercury House, 1998.

Fulton, C. C. "Greece, Ancient and Modern." Lectures Delivered before the Lowell Institute. Boston: Houghton, Mifflin and the Riverside Press, Cambridge, 1893. http://www.archive.org/stream/greeceancientmod00feltiala#page/n7/ mode/2up.

Gage, Nicholas. *Eleni.* New York: Ballantine Books, 1983.

Gallant, Thomas W. *History of Greece.* New York: Oxford University Press, 2001.

Gerolymatos, André. *Red Acropolis, Black Terror: The Greek Civil War and the Origins of the Soviet-American Rivalry, 1943–1949.* New York: Basic Books, 2004.

Gerolymatos, André. *The Balkan Wars: Conquest, Revolution, and Retribution from the Ottoman Era to the 20th Century.* New York: Basic Books, 2002.

Gordon, Thomas. *History of the Greek Revolution and of the Wars and Campaigns Arising from the Struggles of the Greek Patriots in Emancipating their Country from the Turkish Yoke.* Vol. 2, 2nd ed. Edinburgh: William Blackwood and T. Cadell, 1844. http://books.google.com/books?id=31AbNr81wS4C&printsec=frontcover&d

q=History+of+the+Greek+Revolution:+And+of+the+Wars+and+Campaigns+
Arising+from+the+Struggles+of+the+Greek+Patriots+in+Emancipating+Their
+Country+from+the+Turkish+Yoke&hl=en&ei=urE7TfCmCoS8lQecmMDqBQ
&sa=X&oi=book_result&ct=book-preview-link&resnum=1&ved=0CCoQuwU
wAA#v=onepage&q&f=false.

Greek Helsinki Monitor. "Minority Rights Group—Greece." http://www.Greekhel-
sinki.Gr.

Halo, Thea. *Not Even My Name.* New York: Picador USA, 2001.

Hart, Janet. *New Voices in the Nation: Women and the Greek Resistance, 1941–1964.* Ithaca,
NY: Cornell University Press. 1996.

Hellenic Parliament. *Greeks in the Diaspora 15th–21st C. Exhibition Guide.* Athens: Hellenic Parliament, 2007.

Hellenic Statistical Authority. http://www.statistics.gr/portal/page/portal/ESYE.

Hellenic Statistical Authority. News Release: "Publication of Provisional Results of the
2011 Population Census." http://www.statistics.gr/portal/page/portal/ESYE/
BUCKET/General/A1602_SAM01_DT_DC_00_2011_01_F_EN.pdf.

Hellier, Chris. *Monasteries of Greece.* London: Tauris Parke Books, 1996.

Hemingway, Colette, and Seán Hemingway. "Mycenaean Civilization." In Heilbrunn
Timeline of Art History. New York: Metropolitan Museum of Art, 2000. http://
www.metmuseum.org/toah/hd/myce/hd_myce.htm.

Hionidou, Violetta. *Famine and Death in Occupied Greece, 1941–1944.* Cambridge, England: Cambridge University Press, 2006.

Hirschon, Renée. *Heirs of the Greek Catastrophe: The Social Life of Asia Minor Refugees in
Piraeus.* Oxford: Berghahn Books, 1998.

Hirschon, Renée (ed.). *Crossing the Aegean: An Appraisal of the 1923 Compulsory Population Exchange between Greece and Turkey.* Oxford: Berghahn Books 2003.

Hoffman, Susanna. *Adventures in Greek Cooking: The Olive and the Caper.* New York:
Workman, 2004.

Hondros, John Louis. *Occupation and Resistance: The Greek Agony 1941 to 1944.* New
York: Pella, 1983.

Hooker, Richard. "Athens." http://www.wsu.edu:8080/~dee/GREECE/GREECE.HTM.

Hooker, Richard. "Sparta." http://www.wsu.edu:8080/~dee/GREECE/SPARTA.HTM.

Horton, George. *The Blight of Asia.* Indianapolis: Bobbs-Merrill Company, 1926. http://
www.hri.org/docs/Horton/HortonBook.htm8.

Jenkins, Romilly. *The Dilessi Murders: Greek Brigands and English Hostages.* London:
Longmans, Green, 1961.

Jennings, Robert. "One Man Changed Greek and Turkey Forever." AmericanDiplo-
macy.org. http://www.unc.edu/depts/diplomat/item/2010/0103/comm/
jennings_oneman.html.

Karakasidou, Anastasia. "Affections of a Greek Hero: Pavlos Melas and Heroic Rep-
resentation in Greece." In *Balkan Identities: Nation and Memory,* edited by Maria
Todorova. New York: New York University Press, 2004.

Kassimis, Charalambos, and Chryssa Kasimi. "Greece: A History of Migration." Migration Policy Institute. June 2004 (web report). http://www.migrationinformation.
org/Feature/display.cfm?ID = 228.

Katrougalos, George. "Greek Constitutional History, the Constitution of 1864." http://
www.servat.unibe.ch/verfassungsvergleich/gr00m____.html.

Keeley, Edmund. *Inventing Paradise: The Greek Journey 1937–1947.* New York: Farrar,
Straus and Giroux, 1999.

Koliopoulos, John S., and Thanos M. Veremis. *Modern Greece: A History Since 1821.*
Hoboken, NJ: Wiley-Blackwell, 2009.

Kolokotronis, Theodore. *Memoirs of the Greek War of Independence, 1921–1933.* Translated
by G. Tertzetis. Chicago: Argonauts, 1969.

Kontogeorgi, Elizabeth. *Population Exchange in Greek Macedonia: The Forced Settlement of Refugees 1922–1930.* Oxford, England: Clarendon Press, 2006.

Kotora, Jeffrey C. "The Greek Civil War, 1943–1949, April 26, 1985." War since 1945 Seminar and Symposium, Quantico, Virginia, Marine Corps Command and Staff College, Marine Corps Development and Education Command, http://www.globalsecurity.org/military/library/report/1985/KJC.htm.

Kourvetaris, George A., and Betty A. Dobratz. *A Profile of Modern Greece in Search of Identity.* Oxford: Clarendon Press, 1987.

Kousoulas, George. *Modern Greece: Profile of a Nation.* New York: Scribner's, 1974.

Kyrou, Alexandros K. "The Greek-American Community and the Famine in Axis-Occupied Greece." In *Bearing Gifts to Greeks,* edited by Richard Clogg. Hamsphire, England: Palgrave Macmillan, 2008.

Lambros, Sp. P., and N. G. Polites. *The Olympic Games B.C. 776.–A.D. 1896.* London: H. Grevel, 1896.

Leontis, Artemis. *Culture and Customs of Greece.* Westport, CT: Greenwood Press, 2009.

Lovejoy, Esther Pohl. *Certain Samaritans.* 1927. New York: Macmillan, 1933. http://www.ourstory.info/library/2-ww1/Lovejoy/awhTC.html, Chapter XVII.

Mackridge, Peter. "The Greek Language Controversy Focus on Language." Hellenic Communication Service, LLC, http://www.helleniccomserve.com/greeklanguage.html.

Macartney, C. A. "The Greek Settlement." *Refugees: The Work of the League.* London: League of Nations Union, 1931. http://www.promacedonia.org/en/cm/index.html.

Marder, Brenda L. *Stewards of the Land, The American Farm School and Greece in the Twentieth Century.* Macon, GA: Mercer University Press, 2004.

Martin, Thomas R. *An Overview of Classical Greek History from Mycenae to Alexander.* New Haven, CT: Yale University Press, 2000.

Mathews, Nikiforos. "Imbrians Inspired: Vindication and Hope Follow the Gross Report." *The National Herald,* January 10, 2009, 7.

Matsas, Michael. *The Illusion of Safety: The Story of the Greek Jews during World War II.* New York: Pella, 1997.

Mazower, Mark, ed. *After the War Was Over: Reconstructing the Family, Nation and State in Greece, 1943–1960.* Princeton, NJ: Princeton University Press, 2000.

Mazower, Mark. *Inside Hitler's Greece. The Experience of Occupation, 1941–1944.* New Haven: Yale University Press, 1993.

Mazower, Mark, ed. *Networks of Power in Modern Greece.* London: Hurst, 2008.

Mazower, Mark. *Salonica: City of Ghosts.* London: City Harper Collins, 2004.

McNeill, William Hardy. *Greece: American Aid in Action 1947–1956.* New York: Twentieth Century Fund, 1957.

Mediterranean Migration Observatory, UEHR, Panteion University. "Statistical Data on Immigrants in Greece: An Analytic Study of Available Data and Recommendations for Conformity with European Union Standards: A Study Conducted for ΙΜΕΠΟ [Migration Policy Institute], Greece." http://www.mmo.gr/pdf/general/IMEPO_Final_Report_English.pdf.

"Metaxas Project: Inside Fascist Greece (1936–1941)." http://www.metaxas-project.com/the-metaxas-era/.

Miller, David. *Official History of the Olympics and the IOC: From Athens to Beijing, 1894–2008.* Edinburgh, Scotland: Mainstream, 2008.

Miller, William. *Greek Lives in Town and Country.* London: Newnes, 1905. http://books.google.com/books?id=-nUKAAAAIAAJ&printsec=frontcover&source=gbs_atb#v=onepage&q&f=falsePublisher.

Milton, Giles. *Paradise Lost: Smyrna, 1922.* London: Sceptre; Hodder & Stoughton, 2008.

Morgenthau, Henry. *Ambassador Morgenthau's Story*. Garden City, NY: Doubleday, Page, 1919.

Moskos, Charles. *Greek Americans: Struggle and Success*. New Brunswick, NJ: Transaction, 2001.

Nashmani, Amikam. *International Intervention in the Greek Civil War: The United Nations Special Commission on the Balkans, 1947–1952*. New York: Praeger, 1990.

National Herald. *The Greeks: The Triumphant Journey, From the Ancient Greeks and the Greek Revolution of 1821, to Greek Americans*. New York: National Herald, 2002.

O'Balance, Edgar. *The Greek Civil War 1944–1949*. New York: Praeger, 1966.

Pallis, A. A. "The Greek Census of 1928" *Geographical Journal* 73, no. 6 (June 1929): 543–48. http://www.jstor.org/stable/1785338.

Panourgia, Neni. *Dangerous Citizens: The Greek Left and the Terror of the State*. New York: Fordham University Press, 2009.

Papacosma, Victor S. *The Military in Greek Politics: The 1909 Coup d'Etat*. Kent, OH: Kent State University Press, 1977.

Papandreou, Andreas. *Democracy at Gunpoint*. Harmondsworth, United Kingdom: Penguin, 1971.

Papavizas, George C. *Claiming Macedonia: The Struggle for the Heritage, Territory and Name of the Historic Hellenic Land, 1862–2004*. Jefferson, NC: McFarland, 2006.

Papoutsy, Christos. *Ships of Mercy: The True Story of the Rescue of the Greeks, Smyrna, September 1922*. Portsmouth, NH: Peter E. Randall, 2008.

Petmezas, S. "History of Modern Greece." http://video.minpress.gr/wwwminpress/aboutgreece/aboutgreece_history.pdf.

Petrakis, Marina. *The Metaxas Myth: Dictatorship and Propaganda in Greece*. New York: Tauris Academic Studies, 2006.

Petropulos, John A. *Politics and Statecraft in the Kingdom of Greece*. Princeton, NJ: Princeton University Press, 1968.

Phillips, W. Alison. *The War of Independence 1821 to 1833*. London: Smithe, Elder, 1897. http://www.archive.org/stream/warofgreekindepe00philiala#page/n3/mode/2up.

Plutarch. *Lycurgus*. Translated by John Dryden. Internet Classics Archive. http://classics.mit.edu/Plutarch/lycurgus.html.

Rivlin, Bracha (ed.). *Encyclopaedia of Jewish Communities from Their Foundation till after the Holocaust, Greece*. Jerusalem: Yad Vashem, The Holocaust Martyrs' and Heroes' Remembrance Authority, 1998. http://www.zchor.org/greece/jewry.htm.

Samatas, Minas. "Studying Surveillance in Greece: Methodological and Other Problems Related to an Authoritarian Surveillance Culture." In "Doing Surveillance Studies," *Surveillance and Society* 3, no. 2/3: 181–97. http://www.statewatch.org/news/2006/mar/samatas-greece-s-and-soc.pdf.

Saloutos, Theodore. *The Greeks in the United States*. Cambridge, MA: Harvard University Press, 1964.

Schoenberg, Shira. "Virtual Jewish History Tour: Greece." Jewish Virtual Library. http://www.jewishvirtuallibrary.org/jsource/vjw/Greece.html.

Scotes, Vasiliki, and Thomas J. Scotes. *A Weft of Memory: A Greek Mother's Recollection of Songs and Poems*. Scarsdale, NY: Caratzas/Melissa International, 2008.

Smith, Ole Langwitz. *Studies in the History of the Greek Civil War, 1945–1949*. Copenhagen: Tusculanum Press, 1987.

"Socrates." BrainyQuote.com. Xplore Inc., 2011, http://www.brainyquote.com/quotes/authors/s/socrates_2.html.

Sowards, Steven W. "Twenty-Five Lectures on Modern Balkan History: The Balkans in the Age of Nationalism." http://staff.lib.msu.edu/sowards/balkan/.

Spyropoulos, Evangelos. *The Greek Military and the Greek Mutinies in the Middle East, 1941–1944.* Boulder, CO: East European Monographs, 1993.

St. Clair, William. *That Greece Might Still Be Free: The Philhellenes in the War of Independence.* London: Oxford University Press, 1972.

Stavrianos, Leften S. *The Balkans since 1453.* New York: Holt, Rinehart, and Winston, 1965.

Stavrianos, Leften S. *Greece: American Dilemma and Opportunity.* Chicago: Henry Regnery, 1952.

Stavrolakis, Nikos. "A Short History of Greek Jews." http://www.greecetravel.com/jewishhistory/index.html.

Thomopoulos, Elaine. *The Greeks of Berrien County Michigan.* Berrien Springs, MI: Berrien County Historical Association, 2007.

Thomopoulos, Nick. *100 Years: From Greece to Chicago and Back.* Bloomington, IN: Xlibris, 2011.

Triandafyllidou, Anna, and Michaela Maroufof. "Immigration towards Greece at the Eve of the 21st Century. A Critical Assessment." Hellenic Foundation for European and Foreign Policy, Athens, June 2008. http://www.eliamep.gr/en/wp-content/uploads/2009/02/immigration-towards-greece-at-the-eve-of-the-21st-century-a-critical-assessment.pdf.

Tsatsos, Jeanne. *The Sword's Fierce Edge: A Journal of the Occupation of Greece, 1941–1944.* Translated by Jean Demos. Nashville, TN: Vanderbilt University Press, 1969.

Tsitselikis, Konstantinos. "Citizenship in Greece: Present Challenges for Future Changes." ANTIGONE: Information and Documentation Centre on Racism, Peace and NonViolence." 2004. antigone.gr/en/projects/files/project_deliverables/.

Tsoucalas, Constantine. *The Greek Tragedy.* Baltimore: Penguin, 1969.

Tzanelli, Rodanthi. "Haunted by the Enemy Within: Brigandage, Vlachian/Albanian Greekness, Turkish 'Contamination,' and Narratives of Greek Nationhood in the Dilessi/Marathon Affair (1870)." *Journal of Modern Greek Studies* 20, no. 1 (2002): 47–74.

United States Holocaust Memorial Museum. "The Holocaust in Greece." http://www.ushmm.org/museum/exhibit/online/greece/.

U.S. Congress. "Recommendation for Assistance to Greece and Turkey: Address of the President of the United States Delivered before a Joint Session of the Senate and House of Representatives." 80th Congress, 1st Session, March 12, 1947, Document 171. http://www.trumanlibrary.org/whistlestop/study_collections/doctrine/large/index.php.

U.S. Department of State. "Diplomacy in Action." November 23, 2010. Bureau of European and Eurasian Affairs. "Background Note: Greece." http://www.state.gov/r/pa/ei/bgn/3395.htm#econ.

U.S. Department of State. "International Religious Freedom Report 2008." http://www.state.gov/g/drl/rls/irf/2008/108449.htm.

Vallianatos, Evaggelos G. *The Passion of the Greeks: Christianity and the Rape of the Hellenes.* Harwich Port, Mass.: Clock and Rose, 2006.

Vasilief, Al. "A History of the Byzantine Empire." Translated by S. Ragozin. Madison: 1928. http://www.ellopos.net/elpenor/vasilief/default.asp.

Veremis, Thanos. *The Military in Greek Politics: From Independence to Democracy.* Montreal: Black Rose Books, 1997.

Vickers, Miranda. "The Cham Issue: Albanian National and Property Claims in Greece." Conflict Studies Research Centre, Royal Military Academy, Sandhurst, Surrey, 2002.

Vryonis, Speros Jr. *The Mechanisms of Catastrophe.* New York: Greekworks.com, 2005.

Waddington, George. *A Visit to Greece 1823–1824.* London: John Murray, 1825. http://books.google.com/books?id=SX82AAAAMAAJ&printsec=frontcover&dq=

Waddington+Visit+to+Greece&hl=en&ei=1LhpTfWPAcOBlAfn4JGCAg&sa=
X&oi=book_result&ct=result&resnum=1&ved=0CEMQ6AEwAA#v=onepage&
q&f=false.

Whitney, Elspeth. *Medieval Science and Technology.* Westport, CT: Greenwood, 2004.

Woodhouse, C. M. *The Apple of Discord: A Survey of Recent Greek Politics in their International Setting.* London: Hutchinson, 1948.

Woodhouse, C. M. *Capodistria: The Founder of Greek Independence.* Oxford: Oxford University Press, 1973.

Woodhouse, C. M. *Modern Greece: A Short History.* 6th ed. London: Faber, 1998.

Woodhouse, C. M. *The Philhellenes.* 6th ed. Cranbury, NY: Associated University Presses, 1964.

Zacharia, Katerina (ed.). *Hellenisms, Culture, Identity, and Ethnicity from Antiquity to Modernity.* Burlington, VT: Ashgate, 2008.

# Index

**About the Author**

ELAINE THOMOPOULOS, PhD, is an independent scholar who has authored local history books and is editor of *Greek-American Pioneer Women of Illinois*. She has published articles about Greece and Greek Americans and is curator of the Greek Museum of Berrien County, Michigan.